# Privatization and Development

Osama J. A. R. Abu Shair
*Visiting Research Fellow*
*University of Salford*

Foreword by Barbara Ingham

First published in Great Britain 1997 by
**MACMILLAN PRESS LTD**
Houndmills, Basingstoke, Hampshire RG21 6XS
and London
Companies and representatives
throughout the world

A catalogue record for this book is available
from the British Library.

ISBN 0–333–67852–4

---

 First published in the United States of America 1997 by
**ST. MARTIN'S PRESS, INC.,**
Scholarly and Reference Division,
175 Fifth Avenue,
New York, N.Y. 10010

ISBN 0–312–16581–1

Library of Congress Cataloging-in-Publication Data
Abu Shair, Osama J. A. R., 1961–
Privatization and development / Osama J. A. R. Abu Shair.
p. cm.
Includes bibliographical references and index.
ISBN 0–312–16581–1 (cloth)
1. Privatization—Jordan. 2. Jordan—Economic policy.
3. Privatization—Developing countries. 4. Economic development.
I. Title.
HD4279.A55 1996
338.95695—dc20                                            96–36191
                                                              CIP

© Osama J. A. R. Abu Shair 1997
Foreword © Barbara Ingham 1997

All rights reserved. No reproduction, copy or transmission of
this publication may be made without written permission.

No paragraph of this publication may be reproduced, copied or
transmitted save with written permission or in accordance with
the provisions of the Copyright, Designs and Patents Act 1988,
or under the terms of any licence permitting limited copying
issued by the Copyright Licensing Agency, 90 Tottenham Court
Road, London W1P 9HE.

Any person who does any unauthorised act in relation to this
publication may be liable to criminal prosecution and civil
claims for damages.

10  9  8  7  6  5  4  3  2  1
06  05  04  03  02  01  00  99  98  97

Printed in Great Britain by
The Ipswich Book Company Ltd
Ipswich, Suffolk

# PRIVATIZATION AND DEVELOPMENT

For my family

# Contents

| | |
|---|---|
| List of Tables | x |
| List of Figures and Map | xii |
| Foreword by Barbara Ingham | xiii |
| Preface | xv |
| Acknowledgements | xvi |

1 Introduction: Privatization and Development from a Holistic Perspective — 1

**Part I  Privatization and Development: Theory and Practice** — 11

2 The Role of the State in Development — 13
  2.1 Introduction — 13
  2.2 The High Development Theory: Interventionist State with Unlimited Capacity — 14
  2.3 The Neoclassical Counter-Revolution: Minimalist State with Limited Capacity — 17
  2.4 The Counter-Counterrevolution: Active State with Strategic Capacity — 25
  2.5 Concluding Remarks — 33

3 Public vs Private Ownership: The Economic Rationale for Privatization in Developing Countries — 35
  3.1 Introduction — 35
  3.2 'Market Failure' and the Allocative Role of the State — 36
  3.3 The Origins of Public Sector Growth — 38
  3.4 The Performance of SOEs — 44
  3.5 The Firm and the Theory of X-Efficiency — 50
  3.6 The Economic Theory of Property Rights — 53
  3.7 The Principal–Agent Theory — 56
  3.8 Concluding Comments — 62

## Contents

| | | |
|---|---|---|
| 4 | Review of the Empirical Evidence on Privatization in Developing Countries | 65 |
| | 4.1 Introduction | 65 |
| | 4.2 Efficiency Comparison | 72 |
| | 4.3 The Factors Determining Private Investment | 77 |
| | 4.4 The Relationship between Government Size and Economic Growth | 80 |
| | 4.5 The Relationship between Public Enterprises and Budgetary Deficit | 83 |
| | 4.6 The Relationship between Privatization and Development | 85 |
| | 4.7 The Reasons behind Privatization | 86 |
| | 4.8 The Relationship between Privatization and the Distribution of Gains and Losses | 88 |
| | 4.9 Summary and Conclusions | 90 |
| 5 | Privatization, Decentralization, Participation and Development | 92 |
| | 5.1 Introduction | 92 |
| | 5.2 The Meaning of Development: Growth vs Human Development | 93 |
| | 5.3 Privatization, Choice and Participation | 96 |
| | 5.4 Privatization: Exit or Voice | 100 |
| | 5.5 Decentralization and Participation | 102 |
| | 5.6 Privatization vs Territorial Decentralization | 104 |
| | 5.7 Paradigms of Decentralized Development | 106 |
| | 5.8 Decentralization in Practice | 115 |
| | 5.9 The Effect of Privatization on Technological Choice and the Informal Sector | 119 |
| | 5.10 Some Concluding Reflections | 123 |
| **Part II** | **The Case of Jordan** | 125 |
| 6 | Privatization in Jordan | 127 |
| | 6.1 Introduction | 127 |
| | 6.2 The Role of the State | 129 |
| | 6.3 Objectives and Reasons for Privatization of SOEs | 143 |
| | 6.4 Performance of SOEs | 150 |
| | 6.5 Privatization Progress to Date | 161 |

## Contents

|  |  |  |  |
|---|---|---|---|
| | 6.6 | Obstacles to Privatization | 168 |
| | 6.7 | Future Prospects | 176 |
| 7 | Privatization, Decentralization, Participation and Development in Jordan | | 179 |
| | 7.1 | Introduction | 179 |
| | 7.2 | The Objectives of Decentralization and Participation | 180 |
| | 7.3 | The Design of Decentralization and Participation | 183 |
| | 7.4 | Decentralization in Practice | 185 |
| | 7.5 | Measuring Decentralization and Participation | 187 |
| | 7.6 | Privatization and Small Farmers | 196 |
| | 7.7 | Dissatisfaction and the Institutional Role | 199 |
| | 7.8 | Democracy, Participation and Privatization | 203 |
| | 7.9 | The Shift from Decentralization and Participation | 207 |
| 8 | Policy Framework: Necessary Ingredients for Successful Reforms | | 211 |
| | 8.1 | Introduction | 211 |
| | 8.2 | Reforming SOEs | 211 |
| | 8.3 | Bureaucratic Reforms | 215 |
| | 8.4 | Supporting the Informal Sector | 216 |
| | 8.5 | Legal Decentralization | 218 |
| | 8.6 | Summary and Conclusions | 219 |
| *Notes* | | | 222 |
| *References* | | | 227 |
| *Index* | | | 249 |

# List of Tables

| | | |
|---|---|---|
| 3.1 | Public enterprises: share of GDP and investment in developing countries, 1976–82 | 41 |
| 3.2 | Public sector share in non-agricultural employment in comparative perspective, 1979–82 | 42 |
| 3.3 | The social opportunity cost of public enterprise losses, 1988–90 | 49 |
| 3.4 | The differences between X-efficiency theory and the neoclassical theory | 51 |
| 4.1 | The number of SOEs (1986) and cases of privatization (1980–87) in the low-income countries | 65 |
| 4.2 | The number of SOEs (1986) and cases of privatization (1980–87) in the lower-middle-income countries | 66 |
| 4.3 | The number of SOEs (1986) and cases of privatization (1980–87) in the upper-middle-income countries | 67 |
| 4.4 | Total major privatization proceedings in the world by income groups and geographical regions 1988–94 | 69 |
| 4.5 | Total privatization proceedings in developing countries by geographical regions, 1988–94 | 70 |
| 5.1 | Alternative approaches to rural development | 113 |
| 5.2 | Financial decentralization in local governments in selected countries | 117 |
| 5.3 | Shares of men and women workers in the informal sector to the total workforce | 122 |
| 6.1 | Jordanian government spending and its share of GDP, 1980–94 | 130 |
| 6.2 | Jordanian government spending by function, 1981–92 | 131 |
| 6.3 | The origins of tax revenues to the Jordanian central government and their relative importance, 1980–92 | 133 |

## List of Tables

| | | |
|---|---|---|
| 6.4 | Jordanian gross fixed capital formation (governmental and private) and its relative importance to the GDP, 1980–94 | 135 |
| 6.5 | Non-financial state-owned enterprises in Jordan | 141 |
| 6.6 | Overall deficit in the Jordanian central government budget, 1980–94 | 147 |
| 6.7 | Jordan's external debt, 1984–93 | 148 |
| 6.8 | Net private foreign investment in Jordan, 1979–89 (selected years) | 149 |
| 6.9 | Performance indicators of Jordan Electricity Authority, 1987–94 | 152 |
| 6.10 | The financial performance of Jordan Electricity Authority, 1987–94 | 155 |
| 6.11 | Jordanian non-financial SOEs' external debt, 1970–90 | 157 |
| 6.12 | The financial returns of government investment in shareholding companies, 1989–91 | 158 |
| 7.1 | Regional planning units in Jordan's development plan (1986–90) | 184 |
| 7.2 | Expenditure decentralization ratios in Jordan, 1980–84 | 189 |
| 7.3 | Revenue decentralization ratios in Jordan, 1980–84 | 190 |
| 7.4 | Estimated municipal councils' expenditure according to Jordan's governorates for 1988 | 192 |
| 7.5 | Estimated municipal councils' revenue in Jordan according to source of revenue in each governorate for 1988 | 193 |
| 7.6 | Allocation notion of the loans given by Cities and Villages Development Bank to Jordan's municipalities | 194 |
| 7.7 | Comparison between trends of human development in Jordan and those of developing countries | 209 |

# List of Figures and Map

| | | |
|---|---|---|
| 4.1 | Total privatization proceedings in the world according to income groups, 1988–94 | 68 |
| 4.2 | Total privatization proceedings in developing countries, 1988–94, by geographical regions | 71 |
| 6.1 | Real GDP growth rates in Jordan, 1981–94 | 145 |
| 6.2 | Real annual per capita income in Jordan, 1980–92 | 146 |

*Map* of Jordan   126

# Foreword

Dr Abu Shair's approach to privatization differs from that of most economists. For that reason it may be helpful to draw the reader's attention to the central thesis of the book.

Privatization and the free-market context within which it is customarily (though regrettably not invariably) set, have been widely claimed as offering a solution to many of the economic difficulties of developing countries. What Dr Abu Shair does is to distinguish between privatization in developing countries as a means of improving efficiency and raising real income (though the jury is 'still out' in terms of empirical evidence) and privatization as a way of tackling the fundamentals of good governance, democratization, public management, participation, and the general strengthening of civil society in poor and middle-income countries. In this respect, he argues, privatization in its current context offers no guarantees of success.

The strength of the book is not that it asks the relevant questions about privatization, important though they are, but that it also provides a striking analytical framework, grounded in institutional economics, for arriving at the appropriate answers, on a case-by-case basis.

A. K. Sen once remarked that the problem with development economics is not that we misunderstand the sources of economic growth, but rather that we fail to recognize that economic growth may be only a means to other objectives. The same is true of privatization. Economists have expended much effort on assessing the impact of privatization on income and efficiency. But what is its impact on what Goulet has termed the 'core values' of a society: sustenance, self-esteem and freedom? The warning of this book is that unless privatization and its attendant policies deliver in all three 'core' areas, nothing will change for the better. Popular capitalism may have little meaning where there are few private investors, and even fewer small shareholders. At its worst, privatization in developing countries may mean no more than selling state assets to local minority interests or to members of the ruling elite. But at its best, within an appropriate framework of institutional reform, decided on a country-by-country or even a case-by-case basis, privatization still has the *potential*, as the author shows, to deliver improvements not only in economic participation but also in social and cultural well-being in developing countries.

BARBARA INGHAM

# Preface

Most economists study privatization as a theoretical concept and consider its effects on efficiency and economic growth. There is therefore a gap in the literature on privatization as a way of enhancing human capabilities and choices.

In this book, which attempts to address this deficiency, privatization is considered as an economic, political and social phenomenon. Treating privatization in isolation, I argue, can lead to the neglect of many factors that affect the indispensable dynamic required for development. The book therefore represents a departure from the narrow approaches which characterize privatization offered by economists.

The case of Jordan highlights the difficulties decision-makers face in implementing western policies such as privatization. On the positive side however, where privatization is linked to participation, decentralization, and development, it is found that there are opportunities to increase people's choices and capabilities beyond those intended by the narrower policy of privatization. Decision-makers and the leaders in developing countries should consider alternative approaches to privatization. Past failures have often been the result of policies being crisis-driven rather than the outcome of strategic policy.

OSAMA ABU SHAIR

# Acknowledgements

My interest in privatization began as a World Bank Scholar researching for a PhD in economics in the United Kingdom. Therefore, I owe a special debt of recognition and thanks to the World Bank.

This book in addition to its reliance on the sources and documents referred to, benefits from a number of Jordanian institutions which offered their valuable information and research materials, particularly the Royal Jordanian Scientific Society, Jordan Electricity Authority, and the Ministry of Planning.

I owe a particular debt of gratitude to Dr Barbara Ingham who contributed through her discussion, comments, and unlimited support to the introduction of this work. My special appreciation also goes to Professor Robert Millward and Dr Colin Simmons for their valuable comments. To my colleagues at the University of Salford, I extend thanks for their support.

In addition, I would like to express special gratitude to my friend Mr David Kirwan for his assistance and support, and finally, I owe the biggest debt to my dearly beloved wife, Nada, and our daughter, Amna, without whose constant support and sacrifice this task could never have been completed.

# 1 Introduction: Privatization and Development from a Holistic Perspective

The expansion of the public sector in both size and scope has been a feature of post-Second World War economic development, most markedly in Europe although, during the 1960s and 1970s, this sector also dominated economic activity in developing countries.

However, after three decades of state intervention the world has seen a marked reversal in the 1980s and 1990s. Instead of government control and centralized planning there has been a renewed emphasis on market-oriented strategy. Privatization constitutes one of the cornerstones.

Privatization has different meanings and different definitions. As a concept it covers a wide range of possibilities, from a change in the geometry of ownership and control at one end of the spectrum and the introduction of market discipline within the context of liberalization and deregulation at the other.

Ramanadham (1989, Figure 1.1, p. 5), for example, traces three groups of privatization measures. The first relates to ownership and includes total denationalization (management buy-out, cooperatives, and special shares), joint venture and liquidation. The second concerns organizational changes to holding company structures and changes within monolithic structures such as leasing competition and restructuring. The third and final group of measures is operational and comprises contracting-out, incentive rewards, investment criteria, pricing principles, targets, resorting to the capital market and the rationalization of government control.

Other scholars define privatization as the concept which 'covers the transfer from the public to the private sector of the ownership and/or control of productive assets, their allocation and pricing, and the entitlement to the residual profit flows generated by them' (Adam *et al.*, 1992, p. 6). This definition implies the complete or partial sale of state assets, leasing, and management contracting arrangements.

Researchers in the field, such as Prager (1992), identify five definitions of privatization; the partial sale of state assets, which does not imply attenuation of state control; change in ownership and control; private ownership without any constraints on entry into the industry; changes only in patterns of control rather than ownership (e.g. leasing state-owned enterprises [SOEs]), and finally both ownership and key decision-making remain with the state while production, in contrast with service provision, lies in private hands (e.g. management contracts and contracting).

Theoreticians, on the other hand, like Bös (1991) define privatization narrowly as the sale of public sector assets and exclude issues such as contracting out, debureaucratization and the promotion of competition by market forces. Others, like Boycko, Shleifer and Vishny (1996, p. 310), see privatization as 'a combination of the reallocation of control rights over employment from politicians to managers and the increase in cash flow ownership of managers and private investors'. Also, privatization may mean 'policies designed to improve the operating efficiency of public sector enterprises through increased exposure to competitive market forces' (Domberger and Piggott, 1986, p. 146).

It is important to realize that the impact and implementation of liberalization (exposure to market forces) and privatization are quite different. De Walle, therefore, interprets the term privatization as the 'transfer of ownership and control from the public to the private sector, with particular reference to asset sales' (De Walle, 1989, p. 601). This definition is similar to that of Hemming and Mansoor (1988) and also Rees (1986). Other researchers believe that privatization is the goal of SOE reform and the concept of reforming public enterprises has been used as a synonym for privatization (Galal, 1991) (Shirly, 1990; Shirly and Nellis, 1991).

This book, however, looks at two different meanings of privatization which both serve the objectives of the study. The first is privatization as the transfer of ownership and/or control (whole or partial) from the state to the private sector. This definition does not include SOE reform programmes, deregulation or liberalization policies because these necessitate neither a change in control and ownership nor a change in the source of supply for goods and services. Thus, this definition employs the term privatization as a means of divestiture and is employed exclusively in Chapter 3 as a way of analysing the economic rationale for privatization, particularly that of economic efficiency, which is the first aim of the book. The second objective is to analyse the effect of privatization on economic development within the context of decentralization. In this domain, privatization equates with functional decentralization, as opposed to territorial decentralization, and this definition is employed in Chapter 5.[1]

Both definitions of privatization will be argued to be complementary to a wider effort by scholars [particularly those who subscribe to Neoclassical Political Economy (NPE) or what is called the New Institutional Economics (NIE)] as well as such international organizations as the World Bank and the IMF to reduce the extent of 'government failure'.

Privatization is introduced as a means of reducing the size of the governmental apparatus and rolling back the boundaries of state responsibility. Privatization, in shifting responsibility from the state to the market, transforms the institutional framework through which people usually expound, negotiate and promote their individual and group interests.

Chief among the objectives of this study is an assessment of the success of privatization policies in tackling the main economic problems of developing countries during the 1990s. Among the important priorities are the alleviation of poverty as well as balanced and sustainable development. There is no easy solution to the challenge of achieving economic development. Instead it requires discussion and interaction with the people in order to bring about new ideas and potential for economic development.

In theory, privatization should assist in the task of overcoming the problems of poverty and sustainable development. It should benefit the poor through the 'trickle-down' effect as private ownership and/or control brings greater economic efficiency, more innovation, improved responsiveness to consumer demands, and wider choice for individuals. The argument of maximizing profits also implies increased savings and greater investment, which in their turn produce rapid growth and higher incomes, both symbols of development according to the advocates of privatization.

Against such theoretical background, it will be argued that, in practice, privatization rarely lives up to its theoretical ideal; the experience of developing countries, which is derived from the empirical work conducted on the issue of privatization by many scholars, does not exclusively lead, on the grounds of efficiency, to a successful cure for their economic ills.

The book also seeks to develop an analysis of privatization which departs from the mainstream view. The alternative approach, which is the outcome of an effort to interpret commonalities in the privatization movements of developing countries, will depend on linking privatization as an economic, social and political phenomenon with decentralization, participation, and development. Development according to this approach means human development, and the enhancement of capabilities as the ultimate objective of development rather than growth in GNP.

As a specific case study of privatization, the book looks at the experience of Jordan. The specific objectives are:

1   to examine the effect of privatization on the role of the state in development and question whether it will necessarily imply a minimalist state.
2   to discover whether a change in the geometry of ownership would crucially affect enterprise performance, in the context of developing countries generally and of Jordan in particular. If not, what are the reasons for privatization?
3   to explore the impediments to the implementation of the privatization programme in Jordan.
4   to investigate privatization and its impact on participation, decentralization and development, particularly within the context of establishing participatory development.

To achieve the specific objectives a large number of empirical studies are reviewed in the various chapters.[2] In particular, two empirical studies have been carried out on the case of Jordan. The studies are set in the general context of the theory and practice of privatization and decentralization, and the broader experience of Jordan. The first attempts to evaluate the economic performance of an SOE, the Jordan

## Introduction: A Holistic Perspective

Electricity Authority (JEA), and the second to estimate the degree of fiscal decentralization in Jordan.

In addition, the author provides for the first time a complete record of the Jordanian authorities' announcements and comments on the privatization plans drawn up between 1986 and 1995.

The book employs an innovative methodology: namely, an institutional approach to studying the case of privatization in developing countries. The main value in utilizing such an approach is its *holism*. It considers privatization as one part of a whole system and can be understood within the context of development only in terms of the whole system. Consequently, the inquiry has been constructed in a way that accommodates the historical, social, political and economic factors which comprise the whole system. In this way the book represents a departure point from the universal laws which stamp the analysis of privatization in many studies. Studying privatization in isolation can lead to the neglect of many major economic and non-economic factors that affect the indispensable dynamic required in a development study. In other words, studying privatization without considering the whole system could lead to judgements without having specified all the relevant factors. The main purpose of employing this methodology is its ability to explain rather than to predict specific results. This requires a continuous reference to observations and events. The holistic methodology forms an integral part of the work of this book.

The book is presented in two parts. Part I, which investigates the relationship between privatization and development in theory and practice, consists of four chapters. Chapter 2 is devoted to a review of the development literature on the role of the state in development. This is necessary when viewing privatization as an integral part of the shift in development thinking during the 1970s and 1980s.

Chapter 3 looks at the economic rationale for privatization in developing countries within the context of ownership change. A useful starting point is to consider the relationship between the theoretical justification for an allocative role of the state, and the real reasons behind the expansion of the public sector in developing countries. The question is; were the reasons for the growth of the public sector identical in all cases? The next point to underline is the performance of state-owned enterprises (SOEs), with the aim of establishing whether the record of SOEs' performance world-wide provides solid and conclusive evidence for the superiority of private ownership. The chapter also reviews the economics of privatization within the context of ownership change.

Chapter 4 assesses a large body of empirical evidence for privatization in developing countries. This is rarely brought together in the literature. This review has been constructed so as to provide readers with different aspects of privatization in developing countries. Section 4.2 provides an efficiency comparison between public and private enterprises, corresponding to the arguments in Chapter 3. The remaining sections cover the wider dimension of privatization. These are the factors determining private investment, the relationship between government size and economic growth, the relationship between public enterprises and budgetary deficit, the relationship between privatization and development, the reasons behind privatization, and finally the relationship between privatization and the distribution of gains and losses.

The last chapter of this part is Chapter 5. This chapter is devoted to an investigation of privatization within the context of decentralization, participation and development. Thus, an alternative approach has been developed to imply the use of concepts such as 'choice', 'participation', 'voice', 'appropriate technology', 'linkages', and 'territorial decentralization or devolution'.

Part II looks at the broader experience of privatization in Jordan within the general context of part I of the book. This part comprises three chapters.

Chapter 6 investigates the issues surrounding the initiation of and the failure to implement, privatization in Jordan. The following question will therefore be raised: why has privatization been included within the agenda of economic reforms? It will be asked whether this implies a change in ideology or is the result of other factors related to the worsening state of the economy.

Chapter 7 examines the issues of privatization, decentralization, participation, and development within the context of Jordan. The chapter explores government objectives in decentralization and participation, the design of decentralization and participation; and the relationship between democracy, participation and privatization.

The conclusions of the book are provided in Chapter 8, which accommodates a policy framework that discusses the necessary ingredients for successful reforms. These ingredients are indispensable to the relationship between privatization and development. However, a number of other conclusions can be traced in this work.

First, given the economic challenges facing decision-makers in developing countries and Jordan in particular it is unlikely that privatization will lead to a minimalist role for the state in economic development. What is required is a new role with an improved quality of action. Decision-makers should look for long-term objectives rather than depend on policies geared to short-term goals. The role of the state then becomes strategic rather than crisis-driven.

Second, the institutional factors which characterize the markets of developing countries and those of Jordan (e.g. the domination of large monopolies, the lack of efficient capital markets, inefficient property rights) mean that privatization through ownership change will not necessarily mean enhanced efficiency. Alternatively, the search for SOE problems in the context of each country may provide a better understanding of the reasons behind the difficulties of SOEs, taking into account the fact that profitability does not necessarily mean economical efficiency. The conclusion, therefore, is that it is not ownership but market structure and institutions which determine the success or failure of privatization. The case study of the Jordan Electricity Authority shows that the economic efficiency parameters suggested positive trends even though there were losses in this SOE. Consequently the problem of financial performance lies behind factors which are sometimes outside the direct control of the enterprise.

Third, from the review of the empirical evidence on the issue of privatization in developing countries it is concluded that the reasons behind privatization are not based on clear-cut evidence of the superiority of private ownership, the crowding-out hypothesis, an over-extended public sector, a positive relationship between privatization and development, or large gains for the consumers. Rather privatization is a reaction to financial crisis based on the budgetary deficits resulting from the operation of such enterprises and the subsequent pressure exerted by international aid agencies such as the World Bank and the IMF. Within Jordan, however, the reasons behind the initiation of the privatization plan in 1986 were the deep economic recession after 1985, the growing budgetary deficit, the debt crisis, a desire to attract foreign investment, and a series of imitation factors.

Fourth, while the factors behind the initiation of the privatization plan in Jordan were strong, they were not sufficient to induce the government to start the implementation phase. Obstacles to the privatization of SOEs in Jordan rest on economic factors (the time needed for the valuation of the enterprises, the need for restructuring the enterprises, the lack of a regulatory capacity, and an inefficient capital market) and the non-economic factors, particularly those derived from the special characteristics of the state–society relationship.

Fifth, given the experience of the top-down approach towards development in developing countries, empowering people at the local level might be the only viable alternative for human development during the 1990s. Such development cannot be achieved by a single decision, as is the case in privatization, but requires commitment to an institutional building process beyond the scope and objectives of privatization. This also means that within privatization as functional decentralization there is a need for the interests of underprivileged groups to be articulated at all stages of the privatization process. Through the promotion of a more open and interactive process an environment can be created which is more conducive to improving public confidence in the state privatization programme and more favourable to its implementation. Employing the 'exit' and 'voice' options simultaneously will lead to far better outcomes than when privatization is employed as a symbol of 'exit' alone. The latter approach may not increase territorial decentralization nor even fiscal decentralization, as the measurement of decentralization ratios in developing countries, including Jordan, reveals.

In summary, development may mean decentralization, which certainly means participation, but privatization will not necessarily secure participation. It depends on how it is designed and implemented. If privatization is to be sustainable and people-centred, it has to be gradual, relatively crisis-free, untroubled and unenforced, marked by the fusion of collective participation from below (e.g. grass roots) and individual participation in the marketplace. This will depend exclusively on the commitment of the decision-makers and their vision of empowering the people.

# Part I
# Privatization and Development: Theory and Practice

# 2 The Role of the State in Development

## 2.1 INTRODUCTION

The process of economic development in the developing countries has been underway for 40 years. Different groups of economists have given advice on the useful functions of the state varying from recommendations on maintaining law and order, justice and defence to greater state responsibility in bringing about development.

During the 1980s, however, the policies of privatizing state-owned enterprises (SOEs) became part of a general effort to reduce the role of the state in development. Within this context, how far has the change in development thinking affected the role of the state in development?

In the development theories of the 1940s and 1950s industrialization, modernizing agriculture and providing the infrastructural base for urbanization were all tied to the goal of achieving development. The pivotal difference between the present emphasis, getting prices or the basics right, and the previous emphasis (industrialization), mainly reflects a change in the image of the state: from an active agent for change to a set of interest groups concerned with maximizing their own benefit rather than that of the public. This has led to the emergence of the so-called neoclassical counter-revolution in development. Other titles such as the neoclassical political economy (NPE), the New Institutional Economics (NIE), the neo-utilitarianism, and neoliberalism have also been used to describe the relationship between the state and the market where the state is represented as a group of rent-seekers who should be restricted in their actions and responsibilities to protecting property rights.

In the mid-1980s a new literature started to emerge which has served as a counter-literature to that of the neoclassical counter-revolution. Both require review when considering whether the state can resign from its responsibilities and transfer the task of development to the private sector, or still have scope to accomplish the socio-economic goals of the nation. Within this period, however, policy-makers in developing countries have been advised, and even obliged, to follow conflicting views of their role in development.

This chapter serves three purposes. Firstly it shows the dynamism with which development thinking has been changing during the last three decades so that there is now no one simple prescribed role for the state in development. Secondly, it emphasizes that the single most important actor in generating sustained and robust development has been the existence of a particular type of state, particularly in the case of the East Asian Miracle (ESA), a developmental rather than a minimal or a protective state. Thirdly, this chapter provides a basis for the discussion in the following chapter on the role of the public sector in developing countries. This will enable an assessment of privatization policies to be attempted.

## 2.2 THE HIGH DEVELOPMENT THEORY: INTERVENTIONIST STATE WITH UNLIMITED CAPACITY

Throughout the 1950s and 1960s development economists such as Rosenstein-Rodan, Nurkse and Kuznets shared the view that there was a significant role for the state in lifting an economy out of its backwardness. This consensus stemmed from the dominance of Keynesian ideas during the 1950s.

Development during this period was seen primarily as a matter of economic growth, particularly in providing capital and investment in social overheads. The transitional stage for the latecomers, as Rostow (1960) emphasized, required increasing food production, expanding export earnings (through agriculture and/or extractive industries), and increasing investment in infrastructure. Development economists mainly concerned themselves with the lack of capital accumulation. Therefore, they neglected in practice the two dimensions of food production and exports. The Harrod–Domar formula emphasized capital accumulation as the source of growth, with the capital–output ratio in the denominator of the formula being taken more or less as constant.

Gerschenkron (1962) criticized Rostow's theory for its linearity and argued that depending on a given country's degree of economic 'backwardness' (although the latter is a relative term), new private institutions may emerge to speed up the pace of industrialization or development. However, in the absence of institutions that spread large risks across a wide network of capital holders, the state must serve as surrogate entrepreneur.

Historically, the state in the field of development not only acted as a surrogate entrepreneur but also provided other prerequisites to secure the functioning of the market. Even in England, according to Karl Polanyi (1957, p. 138), the birth of economic liberalism was attributable to three specific legislative acts: the reform of the Poor Law (1834), which allowed a free market for labour; the Bank Act (1844), which meant money was supplied by a self-adjusting mechanism; and the reform of the land laws and repeal of the Corn Law (1846), which both created a world market of grain and foodstuffs. He argued that the transformation from liberalism to an interventionist economic system originated from the necessity to protect society from the threat of the market.

> For if market economy was a threat to the human and natural components of the social fabric, as we insisted, what else would one expect than an urge on the part of a great variety of people to press for some sort of protection? This was what we found (Polanyi, 1957, p. 150).

The critical problem in development, as the structuralists argued, was the lack of Schumpeterian entrepreneurs in developing countries; therefore, planned industrialization through investment in large units would provide training for labour and introduce complementarities, both unprofitable investments for private entrepreneurs.

The role of the state, accordingly, was closely linked with promoting industrialization, the key factor in achieving development. Planning was necessary in order to ensure the appropriate levels of saving and capital required to achieve the targeted rate of growth. The role of the state as investment planner means that the state should 'get the price right' in the sense of reflecting the correct opportunity costs and benefits. The essence of this literature, particularly on the key shadow prices of investment, foreign exchange and labour, has become the cornerstone for planning, particularly in the evaluation of state investment in developing countries. The two-gap model of domestic savings and foreign exchange that Chenery and Bruno (1962) developed emphasized the limitations on policy choice in developing countries. The effect of such constraints led international aid agencies such as the World Bank to initiate a new policy in aiding developing countries requiring planned investment by their governments as a justification for aid programmes.[1] Scitovsky (1954) noticed that market prices are only useful for coordinating current production decisions. Investment allocation, on the other hand, requires state intervention.

Hirschman's strategy of 'unbalanced growth' (1958) gave policy-makers in LDCs a justification to channel investments towards projects and industries with strong linkage effects, creating a large number of big public enterprises. Two other economists, Singer (1950) and Prebish (1959), provided further justification for a more interventionist state role in development, particularly through import substitution industrialization (ISI) and a preference for generalized protection.

The inward development strategy was further supported by the neo-Marxist school (Baran, Sweezy, Magdoff) and the dependency school (Frank, Cardoso and Amin), which emphasized that the international economic relations between the centre and periphery nations were the major factor in the 'development of underdevelopment'. In continuing the path of dependency, developing countries will lose their endogenous technology because of the technological package imposed from the centre resulting in a widening of the technological gap as well as increased dependency (Street and James, 1982, p. 680).

These views were developing in the era of political independence in LDCs. As the number of newly independent developing countries rose during the 1950s and 1960s, economic independence called for the rejection of the international division of labour as instituted under the colonial administrations. Industrialization, the major objective of development, found popular support among the developing countries, which were in the era of building their national identities through 'self-reliance'.

# The Role of the State in Development

The Soviet model of development had a major influence with increased state intervention through direct investment in SOEs, planning, regulation, protectionism and credit policies through special development banks. Such activities ran contrary to the theories of the mainstream classical and neoclassical economists who had dominated economic philosophy before the 1930s. However, it clearly reflected acceptance of the 'developmentalism' ideology of the time. These theories implied that the state with unlimited capacity and autonomy could intervene to correct the march toward development without incurring any problems:

> In this literature the state was often left floating in some behavioral and organizational vacuum, making it easy to be used for a blanket endorsement of indiscriminate state intervention, the adverse effects of which for both economic growth and income distribution are now painfully obvious in many countries (Bardhan, 1990, pp. 3–4).

A major role for the state was announced in the previous literature, but the political and institutional conditions for its effective functioning were never identified. In other words, the central weakness of this literature was its rather naive conception of the state as well as the political mechanisms underlying effective state intervention. As a result, during the 1970s and 1980s, the role of the state came under attack from the neoclassical political economy or what was called the New Institutional Economics (NIE) school.

## 2.3 THE NEOCLASSICAL COUNTER-REVOLUTION: MINIMALIST STATE WITH LIMITED CAPACITY

At the end of the 1960s and the beginning of the 1970s the emphasis of the neoclassical counter-revolution in development policy was on the solution of three main problems claimed to impede development. Firstly, the problem of an over-extended public sector; secondly, the problem of an overemphasis on physical capital formation, and finally the proliferation of distorting economic controls (Toye, 1987, pp. 48–9).

Two objectives constitute the essence of the neoclassical counter-revolution. The first is *pricism* (getting the price right) through *laissez-faire* policies and the second is *statism* (reducing the scope of state intervention to a minimal requirement). The current literature merges the two, that is, free market with minimum state intervention.

Among the first studies to focus on getting prices right, was the comparative study by Little, Scitovsky and Scott (1970) of industry and trade in some developing countries. The study attributed the poor economic performance of developing countries to the protectionist policies of ISI. The distortions in prices (overvalued exchange rates, wages, import prices) created by highly protectionist policies needed to be relaxed. A central weakness of the ISI strategy was that it did not positively substitute for imports. Due to the lack of strong sectoral linkages and vertical integration, it shifted imports from final products to inputs of intermediate and capital goods, saving very little foreign exchange in the process. Therefore, the study concluded that outward-oriented policies directed towards exports may prove more beneficial to achieving sustainable development.

So, the emphasis on the role of the state in development has shifted towards attacking the development theories of the 1940s, 1950s and 1960s as well as introducing, in a new style, the argument of 'government failure' and the need for a minimalist role for the state.[2] Development policies have swung towards *laissez-faire* policies as the solution to the problems of developing countries. This argument implies in itself a minimal role for the state. There are four major schools of thought which constitute the backbone of the Neoclassical Political Economy (NPE) or what may be called the New Institutional Economics (NIE).[3]

### 2.3.1 Interest Groups and the Collective Action Theory

The first school of thought in the NIE concerns collective action and the elimination of 'the free-rider problem'. Even when groups of individuals have some common interest and as a result expect to organize a lobby for that interest, rational individuals will not act in their group interest. The reason is that the cost of lobbying for one individual will exceed the benefits he may obtain. As a result each individual will try to be a free-rider, in the sense of benefiting without any contribution to the group (Olson, 1965).

In practice governments exist because they possess a monopoly over taxation. The existence of large associations or organizations will depend on their ability to provide 'selective incentives' rather than on the collective goods they provide.[4] But small groups can engage in collective action without selective incentives because their small size enables them to provide feasible benefits for the group members even when the fruits of individual efforts are shared by the entire group.

A major implication of the theory is the emergence of '*distributional coalitions*' which 'are oriented to struggles over the distribution of income and wealth rather than to the production of additional output' (Olson, 1982, p. 44).[5] These distributional coalitions or special interest groups, while attempting to promote their self-interest through lobbying or rent-seeking, will tend to reduce efficiency and growth wherever they operate, leading to special legislation and regulations to the benefit of such groups rather than the benefit of society. Thus, the role of the state and the complexity of its regulations will increase.

Despite many criticisms of the government, the theory does not lead to the conclusion that the *laissez-faire* option is a solution to the problem of 'government failure' because markets will not solve the interest group problems, particularly in LDCs where such groups dominate the market.

Therefore, scholars like Bates believe that the current policies of substantial liberalization and privatization, and market orientation advised by international agencies such as the IMF and the World Bank, have given African politicians more influence over public policy and this is more consistent with the government objective of retaining power rather than removing the incentives that exist for lobbying and rent-seeking (Bates, 1988, pp. 351–8). Likewise, Nafziger in a review of three studies concerning the role of the state in the development of African countries found that 'regime survival in a politically fragile system requires marshalling elite support at the expense of economic growth' (Nafziger, 1990, p. 150).[6]

The theory of collective action is also essential in the analysis of other NPE theories. One of its main links is with the international trade theory of rent-seeking.

### 2.3.2 The International Trade Theory of Rent-Seeking Activities

The concept of rent-seeking is defined as the expenditure of scarce resources to establish, acquire or maintain a government-granted monopoly or government-granted monopoly power (Buchanan, 1980; Posner, 1980; Tollison, 1982). Therefore, the government in this context is seen as an arena of competing interest groups which work to implement protectionist policies in favour of their own interests, and whose power base is further strengthened by protectionist policy measures.

According to this theory import regimes with quantitative restrictions enhance lobbying activities, which generate rents through the allocation of import licences. Krueger (1974) observed that rent-seeking activities took the form of bribery, corruption, smuggling and black markets and therefore the social costs of tariffs are less than the costs resulting from quantitative restrictions.[7]

Bhagwati and Srinivasan (1980) presented another model, in which revenue-seekers compete to secure a share in the disbursement and/or transfer of revenue, resulting in the imposition of tariffs following collective lobbying. However, it was only with the works of Bhagwati (1982), Bhagwati, Brecher and Srinivasan (1984) and Srinivasan (1985) that the concept of '*directly unproductive, profit-seeking activities*' (DUP) made its formal appearance in the literature. DUP means activities which

> yield pecuniary returns but do not produce goods and services that enter the utility function directly or indirectly via increased production or availability to the economy of goods that enter a utility function (Bhagwati, 1982, p. 989).

Therefore, DUP activities will include monopoly-seeking, tariff-seeking, and revenue-seeking, all of which result from the institutional imperfections caused by government policies which impeded the functioning of the free market.

The first conclusions of this theory are that the role of the state should be minimized and that competition in the market will ensure the dissipation of rents. A further conclusion is that inward-oriented development strategies are likely to lead to more resource wastage through DUP activities; an outward-oriented strategy, therefore, will be the best alternative for developing countries to follow (Srinivasan, 1985, pp. 53–8).

The main evidence this literature relies on to support its validity is the success story of the dynamic export-oriented policies of the East Asian countries (World Bank, 1987; Balassa, 1988).

In sum, extensive micro-level state intervention in the form of heavy protectionism, subsidized credits, subsidies for industries, overvalued exchange rates, and so on, designed to encourage growth and industrialization, led to the emergence of powerful interest groups which spend valuable resources in order to secure favours from the state instead of investing to increase production and growth. To overcome these problems, considerable liberalization and privatization measures are required, to minimize the role of the state, and open the economy for domestic and external competition through outward oriented strategy of development.

### 2.3.3 The Public Choice Theory

Another theory which is closely connected to the trade school above is the public choice theory which lies at the heart of the neoclassical counter-revolution.

This theory has applied the tools and methods of neoclassical mainstream economics to the study of politics and rests on the assumption that rational individuals act in their own self-interest both in the market and the non-marketplace.

As welfare economics does not make any behavioural assumptions about the behaviour of bureaucrats and politicians, Buchanan (1972) extended the assumption of rationality and utility maximizing individuals to the non-market or political scene. Thus, he argued that 'government failure' should be taken more into account than the traditional emphasis on 'market failure'. On the basis of the rationality assumption there is no reason to assume that government or state intervention would generate improvements in the efficiency of the market. But rather they generate rent-seeking activities. This statement is derived from Buchanan's (1987) definition of politics and politicians:

> Politics is a structure of complex exchange among individuals, a structure within which persons seek to secure collectively their own privately defined objectives that cannot be efficiently secured through simple market exchanges. (Buchanan, 1987, p. 1434).

The question is what is the social cost of government intervention in the voluntary exchange of the market? Buchanan confined the social loss associated with a distorted government policy to rent-seeking activities on three levels. Faced with the prospect of differentially favourable or unfavourable government action (i.e. tax treatment), groups and individuals may waste resources through first engaging in lobbying efforts; second, engaging directly in politics to secure access to decision-making power; and/or third, making plans to shift into or out of the affected activity (Buchanan, 1980, p. 14). Consequently, political intervention will create disorder and depress efficiency below the social optimum. In other words, both the state and politics need to be taken out of the market because free market transactions are the only way to produce maximum efficiency and equal the social optimum. That is to say, free market competition leads to the dissipation of rents.

The role of the state in the economy, therefore, should be minimized to the protection of individual rights, persons and property, and the enforcement of voluntarily-entered private contracts because 'predation or invasion of rights, whether actual or potential, give rise to appeals to the protective capacity of the state, or, with uncertainty in rights definition, to potential litigation' (Buchanan, 1986, p. 92).

Public choice theory does *not believe* in the three oft-quoted functions of the state: 'social objectives', 'national goals', and the 'social welfare function', and therefore there is no role for the state in achieving 'distributional justice'. The state can only provide equal opportunity through its protective role. The question unanswered is whether such protection can be provided for by a passive or minimalist state, particularly in the context of developing countries.

## 2.3.4 Transaction Cost Theory and Institutional Change

Transaction costs had no place in the previous two theories (trade and public choice). This theory thus differs from the previous two through its questioning of causes and origins of state intervention in the economy. The main assumption is that institutions are transaction-cost minimizing arrangements which may evolve over time as a result of changes in the nature and sources of transaction costs (North, 1989).

There are three different dimensions of transaction costs.[8] In the context of institutional change transaction costs are described as the cost of 'defining, protecting and enforcing the property rights to goods (the right to use, the right to derive income from the use of, the right to exclude, and the right to exchange' (North, 1991, p. 28).

In contrast to the assumption of the utility-maximizing individuals adopted by the international trade and the public choice theories, institutions in this approach are the main factors which shape the repeated interaction of individuals in the political, social and economic structure.[9] As a result institutions tend to create order and reduce the uncertainty derived from cheating, shirking and opportunism, which constrains the choices of individuals as well, as they will determine the degree of transaction and production costs in a society.

In traditional societies with dense social networks exchanges tend to be personal. Although there is a lack of specific property rights, transaction costs tend to be low while production costs are high because of limited specialization and division of labour. As a traditional society develops, the cost of transacting will rise because information is costly and asymmetrically held by the parties to exchange. The incentives to cheat and indulge in free-riding will also increase without specified property rights and this will lead to imperfect markets.

The question is: who determines the specification and enforcement of property rights? According to North, the development of the state as a third, unbiased party is the most important factor in the establishment and enforcement of an efficient structure of property rights. The second factor is the development of norms to constrain the parties in interaction where high measurement costs, even with the existence of the government, pose problems (i.e. opportunistic behaviour) (North, 1989, p. 1320).

Effective government is, therefore, an essential factor in economic performance, but the problem with the state is that the rise of state power leads to the production of an inefficient structure of property rights and with it an unequal distribution of coercive power to the advantage of special interest groups. There are two reasons for such behaviour. The first is that an efficient property rights system will require higher transaction costs which go against the rulers' objective of maximizing revenues. The second reason is that rulers can barely afford efficient property rights because they may offend their constituents and risk their security. As a result such a structure of property rights does not produce economic growth (North, 1991, p. 7).

Unless, therefore, government establishes, specifies and monitors an efficient system of property rights, similar to those existing in the western world, free markets will not equate with efficiency. Efficient markets require unbiased governments which build in incentives to create and enforce efficient property rights while minimizing transaction costs in order to achieve growth and development.

However, North's approach criticized public choice theory for its assumption of individual rationality because the latter can only be understood within the context of institutional factors which determine such behaviour (North, 1991, p. 108). The central weakness of the public choice theory is that it has started from a given structure of property rights which characterized the sphere of the western countries and consequently led to the minimization of transaction costs, the key factor determining economic performance. So North's theory does not disregard the role of the state and can explain the existence of inefficient markets in developing countries as well as the role of the state in maintaining such inefficiency.

In summary, the neoclassical counter-revolution or the NIE has emphasized that 'government failure' in development is greater than the presumed 'market failure'. Thus, the ideal state envisaged by the NIE scholars is a state that establishes, specifies and monitors an efficient system of property rights; yet it is a minimalist state in terms of both its share in productive activities and the extent of its indirect intervention over market transactions.

To support their claim the neoclassical theorists have emphasized the story of success in the East Asian countries (the East Asian Miracle) as evidence for their theoretical justification of less state and more market. Such views on the role of the state in East Asian countries have come under attack from a number of scholars who believe that the governments of those countries had in fact played a major role in development. Another dimension of this literature has recommended a new role for the state in development which is more than minimalist. This literature underlines a counter-counter-revolution in development economics.

## 2.4 THE COUNTER-COUNTERREVOLUTION: ACTIVE STATE WITH STRATEGIC CAPACITY[10]

Development success in the East Asian countries was one of the main factors in support of liberalization. Other economists, however, realized the importance of government intervention in guiding the success of those economies.

The high economic performance of East Asian countries, as Wade (1990) thought, was the result of a level and composition of investment different from that which free market policies *per se*, and interventionist policies *per se*, would have produced. The role of the state was a combination of direct investment in certain key industries in the initial phase of development and a package of policies which employed certain incentives, controls and mechanisms to spread risk. This enabled the government to guide or govern the market processes of resource allocation in order to achieve efficient investment and production results. Contrary to what neoclassical counter-revolution economists argued, Wade said that

> Government policies deliberately got some prices 'wrong', so as to change the signals to which decentralized market agents responded, and also used non price means to alter the behaviour of market agents. The resulting high level of investment generated fast turnover of machinery, and

hence fast transfer of newer technology into actual production (Wade, 1990, p. 29).

Thus, it was not simply 'get the price right' and a minimalist state that brought about the exceptional achievements of those countries; it was the 'directive' as opposed to 'promotional' forms of state intervention that led to the success (Luedde-Neurath, 1988, p. 102).

Perhaps the most important form of state intervention was the 'land reform' programme to redistribute agricultural land in the initial phase of development (Wade, 1990; Koo and Kim, 1992). This led to the elimination of the landlord class and to the creation of a relatively egalitarian class structure. Sachs (1989, as cited in James, 1992) argued that the broad distribution of land in East Asian countries has contributed to the adoption of an outward-oriented industrialization while in the case of Latin American countries the unequal distribution of land led to resistance against the devaluation of exchange rates which would have resulted in the transfer of income from workers and capitalists to a small elite of landlords.

Contrary to the expectation of the public choice literature, Morris and Adelman (1989) observed that development is more dependent on effective initial institutions and human resources than on other major sources of growth (i.e. market systems, export policies and capital inflows). Therefore, a shift in development strategy towards free markets and export orientation can impose losses on the majority of the population 'if pursued in countries where institutions cause a very narrow distribution of the proceeds from economic change' (Morris and Adelman, 1989, p. 1428). Thus, high growth rates through the factors of accumulation, allocation, and productivity growth has to be understood through the study of the institutional designs and the historical institutional changes which have provided the basis for the East Asian Miracle (Page, 1994, p. 624; Kwon, 1994, p. 642; Perkins, 1994, p. 660).

In a recent study for the World Bank (1993), entitled *The East Asian Miracle: Economic Growth and Public Policy*, World Bank economists concluded that the main reasons behind the miracle in the high performing Asian economies were the employment of the 'market-friendly approach' and 'getting the basics right'. The basics are private domestic investment and rapidly growing human capital. The lesson for other developing countries, the Bank argues, is to forget successful intervention and focus only on the fundamentals. The superior record is 'largely due to superior accumulation of physical and human capital' (World Bank, 1993, p. 5).

Scholars from the NIE school, such as Krueger (1990), argued that 'government failure' in developing countries was due to two reasons, the first being 'commission' (widespread state intervention in productive activities) and the second 'omission' (deterioration of the infrastructure). The solution, according to Krueger, is to understand the comparative advantages of state intervention. In large-scale activities such as infrastructure and the provision of information the state is in a good position to intervene successfully. While Krueger is a strong advocate of a minimalist state, comparative advantage activities of the state need more of a developmental rather than a minimalist state (Leftwich, 1995).

The evidence shows that the market cannot by itself create appropriate industries, or strategic investment. There is, therefore, a need for selective government intervention (Amsden, 1994, p. 631). However, government intervention in the production process has to be decided pragmatically. In the Korean case the government intervenes through its public enterprises for three reasons. It intervenes firstly if there are no private parties willing to take the risk; secondly, through a desire to exercise control over an industry with multiple linkages; and thirdly, where there is a belief that the state has a better negotiating position than private investors with foreign parties, particularly in the supply of capital and technology (Westphal, 1990). One of the major advantages from such intervention was the apparent success in the process of learning and acquiring technological capabilities which 'belong to the core of the development process' (Bardhan, 1990, p. 4). Others such as protection in the context of outward-oriented policies, selective education and training, and the creation of an efficient civil service were also effective in guiding success (Lall, 1994, p. 652).

Another important dimension in this literature is the importance of understanding the main focus to be organizational structure and institutions rather than getting the price right. The role of the state in establishing non-market institutions is fundamental in solving the problems of information, coordination and externalities, particularly in LDCs. In developed countries many of the externalities are internalized by non-market institutions (Stiglitz, 1989; Bardhan, 1990). This was the case in South Korea where government and large private enterprises constituted a quasi-internal organization. The same applied to Korea's financial system, an internal capital market which allocated resources more efficiently than would have been possible in a free-market financial system (Lee, 1992). The central point is that scholars should consider the state as a component of the institutional arrangement rather than as an exogenous actor (Doner, 1992).

The role of the state in development is both to reduce the wastage of resources and to initiate the institutional building process. This requires the cooperation of rather than the domination of the state. To achieve broader institutionalism a framework is needed which combines private and public sector arrangements, appreciates the coalitional bases of such arrangements, and observes the importance of providing political support for local firms as well as pressurizing them to use market forces (Doner, 1992, p. 401). Economic agents 'do not always correctly perceive the various trade or technological possibilities open to them' (Datta-Chaudhuri, 1990, p. 33). However, successful state intervention is not a possibility in all cases. It depends on the composition of interest groups and their effect on the allocation of resources.

Following the public choice perspective has led to a serious questioning of the link between free markets and the strength of the state. In economic terms, 'strong' states would be expected to take correct economic decisions with little regard for their political and social consequences. 'Soft states', on the other hand, would employ ineffective regulatory policies to protect incomes and avoid social conflict. Thus, in Singapore, South Korea and Taiwan the states have been authoritarian and strong, high economic records have been achieved. In India and Mexico on the other hand, soft states have led to ineffective intervention and increased corruption. It follows that free-market oriented policies have more need for a strong state than for a soft one and consequently the state has to move beyond the limits of the minimalist state advocated by the neoclassical political economists. This inconsistency is apparent in this quotation from Lal (1983) who said that in order to achieve efficiency 'a courageous, ruthless and perhaps undemocratic government is required to ride roughshod over the newly-created special interest groups' (Lal, 1983, p. 33). Such characteristics of government have to be viewed in the context of North's analysis of the state. The result is an authoritarian government with an inefficient property rights structure.

Another attack on the neoclassical counter-revolution stems from its failure to assess the conditions under which the state can play a positive role:

> Beyond creating (minimalist) rules to enhance the market, there is no policy advice. Nor, except for resort to authoritarian tutelage, is there guidance about creating and sustaining political support, even for liberalization (Banuri, 1991, p. 12).

Unlike the public choice theorists, Shapiro and Taylor (1990) explained the conditions which delimit appropriate strategic choices for the state. These conditions are country size, internal vs external constraints, wages and income distribution, fiscal and managerial capability of the state, industrial heritage, and finally productivity growth and access to technology. They argued that there is a peculiar asymmetry in the DUP model. While they successfully presented the argument that 'market failure' is not automatically a justification for government intervention, because it may produce even worse results, they neglected to state that 'government failure' cannot justify the argument for a free market.

Taylor's (1991) expectation is that the development strategy of the next decade will be inward-looking. Lack of access to external sources of capital, particularly for heavily indebted countries, and a growing protectionism in the Northern countries may deprive developing countries, especially small and poor ones, of the necessary stimulus for their development process. Thus, there is a need for more government investment in the agricultural sector to encourage private investment (Taylor, 1993). Adelman (1984) argues that a strategy of agricultural-demand-led industrialization (ADLI) might prove to be more efficient than a strategy of export-led growth, after the initial stages of industrial development, in most middle-income countries and large low-income countries. The role of the state through direct investment programmes can enhance the supply of the domestic agricultural sector (surplus creation rather than surplus extraction).

A second dimension in the literature of counter-counter-revolution is a *theoretical* one. Krugman (1993) believes that recent neoclassical literature has neglected the importance of externalities and linkages for the economy.[11] The blind advocacy of free market policies and the emphasis on 'government failure' in development has directed the literature away from the high development theory of the 1940s and 1950s. In fact the theoretical ideas of external economies, strategic complementarities, and economic development, which have been forgotten, may continue to have practical applications and should be revived. On the other hand, the failure of formalizing models in support of the high development theory and the failure of the industrialization idea as the essence of development were the major reasons for neglecting the 1940s and 1950s theories of development.

Krugman's model of forward and backward linkages shows that the concentration of manufacturing industries in one region is due to factors of allocation (interaction of economies of scale with transportation costs) in the larger market (backward linkages) and the desire of workers to have access to goods produced by other workers (forward linkages) (Krugman, 1991). The greater the degree of economies of scale, the stronger the tendency towards concentration (Krugman, 1993). This model helps to emphasize the important role of government promotion policies in directing investment towards rural areas in order to induce the development of such regions, which depends on the strategic complementarity argument.

Another model, introduced by Murphy, Shleifer and Vishny (1989), has emphasized the important role of pecuniary externalities in escaping the no-industrialization trap in small economies. This model explored Rosenstein-Rodan's idea of the 'big push' and introduced it in a formal model. It explained how economies with small domestic markets could expand their markets in order to escape the no-industrialization trap. The model indicated that the industrialization of one sector leads to the expansion of the market for other sectors. This allows the state an important role in coordinating investments across sectors, which is essential for industrialization. The argument of the model is that the profit factor alone cannot induce firms to invest as they lack the advantages of economies of scale (the market size constraint). The result is a no-industrialization trap. On the other hand, a firm which employs labour from the traditional sector will enlarge the market of other firms by increasing wage income and consequently the demand for manufactured goods. As a result 'a programme that encourages industrialization in many sectors simultaneously can substantially boost income and welfare even when investment in any one sector appears unprofitable' (Murphy *et al.*, 1989, p. 1024).

The second theme of the argument concerns another important pecuniary externality, namely the one generated by investment in 'jointly used intermediate goods' such as infrastructural investment and investment in training facilities (ibid., p. 1006). State provision of such investment is necessary, and its high fixed cost is reduced if industrialization takes place because many firms will use the facilities and thus enable the government to recover costs, if not necessarily show a profit. The spirit of this model is consistent with that of high development theory.

Part of the counter-counterrevolution literature can be related to the importance of knowledge in achieving growth. In the new growth theory Romer (1986) assumes that the social returns on investment are higher than private returns because of external economies. In this model, technological externalities are the driving force for long-term growth. However, these externalities arise through the accumulation of knowledge (endogenous technological change). Exogenous technological change is ruled out of the model. Consequently any intervention by the state which results in shifting 'the allocation of current goods away from consumption and toward research will be welfare-improving' (Romer, 1986, p. 1026). The role of the state in raising beneficial technological externalities is important for long-term growth, by fostering investment in knowledge and human capital. Such an argument contradicts the minimal state argument of neoclassical political economy.

The implication of these models is that the economic theory of the free market is not always the best but that 'there is an intellectually solid case for some government promotion of industry' (Krugman, 1993, p. 32). There is a need for a reorientation of research towards failures of both market and government rather than just 'government failure' alone.

Streeten (1993) pointed out Adam Smith's admission that rent-seeking is also common in the private sector and that government action may contribute to its elimination. Anti-monopoly and anti-cartel legislation, import liberalization and the introduction of competition in the public sector are examples of such anti-rent-seeking. Streeten also refers to Bhagwati's argument that the creation of new rents can reduce or altogether destroy existing rents and existing rent-seeking activities (Streeten, 1993, p. 1292).[12] In addition, there is a rent-avoiding process which runs in parallel with rent-seeking behaviour. Lipton (1989) in his study of rural villages in Asian countries revealed that villagers can reduce the rent payable to the local monopolistic moneylender by searching for alternatives which reduce their dependency on rents (e.g. by adopting a less credit-intensive product mix). Thus, the rent would be reduced.

The evidence, empirical and theoretical, asserts the necessity of creating an active state which possesses a strategic capacity: 'for the proper working of markets, strong, and in many cases expanded state intervention (of the right kind, in the right area) is necessary' (Streeten, 1993, p. 1281). What is needed is a fundamental structural change, a redistribution of assets and of access to power which neither the market alone, nor a neutral state, can provide (ibid.).

It is surprising that agencies such as the World Bank have been advocating free market policies, and arguing for the simultaneous eradication of poverty and an increase in participation in growth by the poor (World Bank, 1990). The first requires a minimalist state and the second an active state. The poor lack access to assets and particularly land. This implies a need for the state to initiate a better and more equitable distribution of assets. Bhagwati (1988) argued for this when he advocated a minimalist state.

The following quotation from Banuri (1991) suggests a reason for 'government failure' in development.

The failure of a state does not derive from its refusal to adhere to a theoretical dogma. On the contrary; it derives, in the short run, from its abandonment of the goal of governance in favour of theoretical certitudes; and in the long run, from its inability or unwillingness to create or modify institutions to facilitate the management of conflicts which are forever changing in form and intensity (Banuri, 1991, p. 36).

## 2.5  CONCLUDING REMARKS

A survey of the literature on the role of the state in development suggests that the theoretical analysis is problematic. This derives from the complexity of the subject itself. However, it is possible that the literature is moving into a cyclical pattern, as observed by Hirschman (1982) and Pereira (1993).

During the 1940s and 1950s, development economists explained the process of development in terms of growth, industrialization and capital accumulation but there was no analysis of the institutional context for such development. The failure to carry out successful industrialization in developing countries has led the literature of high development theory to be put aside in favour of the neoclassical approach to development. The problem with this approach is that it provides a generalized approach based on the belief in a minimalist state. However, the introduction of the NIE has provided a good analytical framework for understanding the role of the state as one of several institutions which has to be included in the theoretical argument. The problem was that the state in some of the schools (i.e. public choice and DUP) became an exogenous rather than an endogenous actor in development. In other theories such as transaction costs and property rights, the state was employed in the analysis of institutional change. The result was an abandonment of the concepts of externalities and strategic complementarity towards one concentrated on government failure caused by competitive rent-seeking and the collective action of special interest groups. The consequences of this analysis became apparent in forcing developing countries to adopt free market policies as a reaction against the government interventionist approach.

The literature of the 1990s shows that a minimalist state cannot provide the conditions required by the neoclassical political economists. The emphasis has been placed on understanding the reason behind the development success of the East Asian countries. Free market policies appear to have been not the only reason for such success; other interventionist policies have also been required. It is necessary to understand each country's special circumstances because the latecomers' conditions and challenges may be entirely different from those which have already achieved successful development. A revitalization of the economic concepts used in the high development theory of the 1940s and 1950s might provide a good guide for a new role of the state in development. It will be different from the previous role and better in the quality of actions. However, decision-makers should look for long-term objectives rather than depend on policies for short-term goals. The role of the state then becomes strategic rather than crisis-driven.

# 3 Public vs Private Ownership: The Economic Rationale for Privatization in Developing Countries

## 3.1 INTRODUCTION

In the preceding chapter it was asserted that the role of the state in development has expanded, partially, through the intellectual dominance of the 'developmentalism' ideology. Another reason for the expansion of the state, and its enterprises, can be explained through the theory of public economics; the theoretical justification for the allocative role of the state is given in Section 3.2.

Section 3.3 looks at the reasons behind the expansion of state-owned enterprises (SOEs), and asks whether they were identical in all developing countries or not, and why.

In order to examine the economic rationale for privatization in developing countries, this chapter defines privatization as the transfer of ownership and/or control (whole or partial) from the state to the private sector; it therefore excludes deregulation and liberalization policies because these necessitate neither a change in control nor a change in the source of supply for goods and services.

The chapter's main argument is that the really significant differences in efficiency lie not in the realm of ownership change but in the institutions which affect the degree of competition in the market.

To achieve this objective Section 3.4 provides a review of the empirical evidence regarding the performance of public enterprises in developing countries with the aim of establishing whether the record of public enterprise performance world-wide provides solid and conclusive evidence for the superiority of private ownership. It will also examine whether profitability means being economically efficient. The second area of investigation (Sections 3.5, 3.6, 3.7 and 3.8) will study the economics of privatization within the context of ownership change.

## 3.2 'MARKET FAILURE' AND THE ALLOCATIVE ROLE OF THE STATE

Traditionally, the economic analysis of SOE pricing and investment policies was concerned with allocative efficiency and thus had a welfare economics orientation. The theory of public economics justifies the allocative role of the state in those activities which escape market logic. This is referred to as Pareto efficiency.

Pareto efficiency is the optimum allocation of resources where no one individual can be made better off without another individual being made worse off. When the market of any economy fails to meet the conditions required for Pareto efficiency (first-best solution), government intervention, at least in principle, will be justified to correct the failure of the market (the second-best solution). Thus, government will intervene when the competitive market mechanism fails to provide an efficient allocation of resources.

The causes of 'market failure' are grouped into four main categories, namely the existence of public goods and externalities, economies of scale, information symmetries, and uncertainty. These four causes of 'market failure' imply two different kinds of state intervention, leading to state ownership in the first two groups and regulatory intervention in the second two. However, it is difficult to draw the demarcation line separating state intervention through direct production from intervention through regulation because this will depend on the judgement of policy-makers as to what is appropriate to correct a 'market failure'.[1]

Traditionally, state ownership has been justified on the grounds of public good. The main characteristics of public goods and externalities are 'non-excludability' and 'non-rivalness' in consumption. These characteristics lead to the free-rider problem where individuals cannot be excluded from the consumption of such goods (e.g. a lighthouse). Non-rivalness derives from the indivisibility character of these goods as well as the zero opportunity cost for the marginal user, which means that the price of public goods should be nil (e.g. a non-crowded bridge). Governments will provide these goods because the market itself will fail to allocate them efficiently as they are unattractive to private entrepreneurs.

In the case of externalities, the market will fail to produce goods associated with external economies (e.g. health, education, infrastructure) while over-supplying goods which imply external diseconomies (e.g. pollution). The reason for 'market failure' in these cases derives from the high transaction costs of introducing voluntary agreement between individuals and the lack of well-defined property rights which can preclude the free-rider problem (Demsetz, 1967; 1988).

The second reason for state or public ownership derives from economies of scale or what is called the existence of decreasing cost industries. In this case the market solution of production through several producers would be inefficient (bearing in mind the size of the market) because marginal cost pricing in such industries will not cover the cost. As a result, producers will cut production and increase prices, leading to a departure from the first-best conditions of Pareto efficiency. As a result, governments will act directly on such industries through direct ownership in order to employ pricing policy rules which can achieve a more efficient allocation of resources. However, this solution is inferior to the direct regulation of monopolies (Rees, 1989, pp. 29–44). The direct provision of public utilities (e.g. water, electricity) is an example of such an allocative role for the state. However, in addition to economies of scale, many natural monopolies possess economies of scope which arise from the joint use of a central facility for the production of different products. Governments invest in infrastructure facilities because of such characteristics.

The theoretical justification for state ownership therefore rests on allocative efficiency considerations rather than those of technical or productive efficiency. The latter are concerned with minimizing input requirements or costs for a given level of output. However, allocative efficiency will be violated in the absence of technical efficiency although the converse does not hold. In other words technical efficiency is a necessary condition for allocative efficiency, but the latter is not a necessary condition for the former.

Privatization has been, therefore, introduced mainly as a means of achieving technical efficiency based on the assumption that SOEs do not operate in a cost-minimization manner.

## 3.3 THE ORIGINS OF PUBLIC SECTOR GROWTH

There is a difference between the approach advocated by the theory of public economics, as discussed in the previous section, and that of development theories. In the theory of public economics, public sector activities are subjected to the achievement of Pareto efficiency and its aim, therefore, is to define the minimum position that the public sector should occupy in a market economy. Such a context, by contrast, cannot be found in the high development theory, which is concerned with generating economic surplus, filling the gaps in private investment, and pursuing economic and social objectives. Nevertheless, there are activities where both theoretical approaches are allowed to be provided through the public sector (i.e. infrastructure, public utilities). However, the theory of public economics excludes the historical background to the formation of the public sector as well as the dynamic play of the institutional factors which were behind its creation in different developing countries.

*1. Nationalization*
After political independence, many developing countries nationalized enterprises owned by foreigners and the wealthy upper classes. Nationalization was seen as a major component in the drive towards economic independence. However, in Latin America the process started during the 1930s (e.g. Mexico and Bolivia) while in Africa and Asia it began after political independence following the Second World War; thus, the age of the public sector in those countries is not the same.

The economic case for nationalization was based on increasing the saving ratio and obtaining the rents derived from natural resources which had previously been absorbed by foreign companies. When nationalizing local private enterprises the aim was to reduce the consumption of the upper class elite and redirect the resources towards public investment (Yaffey, 1995, pp. 202–3). Also, nationalization assisted in increasing the net capital inflows and foreign investment in developing countries, particularly before 1982 (Andersson and Brannas, 1992).

## 2. The Ideological and Political Factors

Many Third World leaders were influenced by socialist thinking, and particularly by the Soviet model of industrialization. The expansion of SOEs was seen as the only way to achieve industrialization and economic independence. Investment in heavy industries and increasing state intervention in other economic sectors were justified on the grounds of building a new national identity and self-sufficiency as well as an apparatus for the new rulers to exercise control and obtain legitimacy. Government was seen as the representative of the people and its owning the means of production was a notion of anti-capitalist exploitation.

However, it may be inappropriate to generalize such rationale to all developing countries because most Latin American states, for example, did not believe in socialism.

## 3. The Commanding Heights of the Economy

Controlling the commanding heights of the economy represents another reason for creating SOEs. These heights are the key sectors of the economy which can stimulate industrialization and growth and facilitate long-term economic planning. They therefore cannot be left to market forces or to the private sector (Vernon, 1988, pp. 10–11; Rees, 1989, p. 5). In infrastructural activities (such as the generation and distribution of energy, transportation and communication) and the heavy industries (such as oil and petrochemicals) control of the public sector is seen as essential for the provision of external economies and strategic complementarities which can encourage investment in other sectors (Powell, 1987, p. 6). In some countries a distinction was made between strategic sectors, where the public sector obtained exclusive monopoly (e.g. oil extraction, refining, basic petrochemicals), and priority sectors, where the state acted as the driving force (e.g. different medium industries) (Bouin and Michalet, 1992, p. 38).

Controlling the commanding heights is an application of the theory of 'market failure' in the provision of public goods and externalities as well as the ownership of natural monopolies. However, it is difficult to be sure whether the leaders of developing countries were in fact influenced by this theoretical justification provided by the theory of public economics.

## 4. Industrialization and Modernization

The creation of a modern and diversified economy was analogous to breaking the bonds of dependence, saving and earning more foreign exchange and enhancing employment opportunities so as to provide income and promote the living standards of the population (Nixson, 1990, pp. 312–13). Large investment was needed to build a modern industrial sector, for which the private sector possessed neither the resources nor the willingness to take risks. The consequence was heavy investment in capital-intensive industries. As a result SOEs in developing countries were characterized by higher rates of capital intensity ratio (CIR).[2] While it was 1 for the SOEs in 17 industrialized countries, it was 3 for the SOEs of 55 developing countries during the period 1974–77.[3] Moreover, there were differences between Third World regions. In Asia and the Western Hemisphere the capital intensity ratio was about 3.5 while in the African countries it was about 2.

Another dimension lies in the distinctive features and circumstances under which industrialization was adopted in different developing countries. In Latin American countries, for example, there was a unique combination of early political independence and early integration into the international capitalist economy through the production and export of primary products. Their economies before the end of the 1930s were managed on the basis of *laissez-faire* and export-led growth. The ISI policy was adopted because of the negative consequences resulting from such integration, namely the severe impact of the 1930s Great Depression on those countries. ISI and the subsequent expansion of the public sector were a reaction aimed at reducing a vulnerable dependence on the international market. In other words, industrialization was seen as a way of survival in an unstable world. In Africa and Asia, on the other hand, states were dependent on foreign exchange from agricultural and/or mineral exports. Industrialization was seen as a way of ending their economic dependency whether on cash crops, such as cocoa and coffee, or minerals such as copper, bauxite and oil. The fluctuation in the prices of such primary products was the main reason behind government policies of economic diversification through industrialization.

As a result, the share of public enterprises in total output and investment increased in most developing countries but in varying proportions, as Table 3.1 depicts. The differences might support Gerschenkron's (1962) thesis regarding the relationship between the role of the state and the relative backwardness of a country.

### 5. The Lack of Local Private Enterprenuers

While in advanced capital countries private entrepreneurs were in sufficient supply, developing countries lacked individuals with 'economic resources such as funds, risk absorption, managerial talent and (Schumpeterian) entrepreneurship' (Trebat, 1983, p. 31). As a result, political leadership took the initiative by converting the state into a big entrepreneur. In

*Table* 3.1   Public enterprises: share of GDP and investment in developing countries, 1976–82

| Indicator | PEs share (%) | Range (%) | No. of countries |
|---|---|---|---|
| **GDP** | | | |
| Africa | 15 | 4–48 | 18 |
| Asia | 3 | 1–7 | 6 |
| Latin America | 12 | 2–28 | 8 |
| **Investment** | | | |
| Africa | 25 | 8–54 | 12 |
| Asia | 17 | 10–56 | 9 |
| Latin America | 19 | 7–47 | 17 |

*Source*: Swanson and Wolde-Semait (1989, p. 8).

addition, foreign lenders and aid agencies were more willing to lend and assist governments and their SOEs than private entrepreneurs (Herbst, 1990, p. 951). In sub-Saharan Africa, for example, direct foreign loans to private enterprises at the end of 1984 represented only 0.6 per cent while foreign loans to development finance institutions, which finance private and public investment, accounted for only 0.8 per cent of the total loans to those countries (Marsden, 1990, p. 19).

Socially, private entrepreneurs in some countries were aliens and expatriates, which created a popular call for state control. Thus, people's attitudes revealed a strong mistrust of the private sector and with it the motivation of profit maximization in the marketplace. This derived from the historical links between such groups and colonialism, which was associated with exploitation of the poor (Nellis, 1986, p. 13; Bulter, 1986, p. 22; Evans, 1990, p. 103).

## 6. Employment Generation

One of the main merits of SOEs in developing countries is that they employ a large number of educated people. Such an objective was categorized as urgent by the leaders of developing countries. In addition, it was supported by the high development theory, which emphasized the importance of generating wage labourers in order to generate demand in the economy and thus enable the economy to escape the no-industrialization trap (Romer, 1986). Table 3.2 shows that the African public sector has employed more than half the

*Table* 3.2   Public sector share in non-agricultural employment in comparative perspective, 1979–82 (%)

| Region<br>Levels of public sector | OECD | Africa | Asia | Latin America |
|---|---|---|---|---|
| Central government | 8.7 | 30.4 | 13.9 | 20.7 |
| State–local government | 11.6 | 2.1 | 8.0 | 4.2 |
| Non-financial SOEs | 4.1 | 18.7 | 15.7 | 5.5 |
| Total public sector employment | 24.2 | 54.4 | 36.0 | 27.4 |

*Source:* Heller and Tait (1983, p. 7).

workers in the formal sector while non-financial SOEs employed about 19 per cent of the total. By comparison, Asian SOEs absorb about 16 per cent while in Latin American countries the absorption factor lies at about 6 per cent.

The 1980–86 figure for the African countries shows that SOEs absorbed between 25 and 30 per cent of total employment in the formal sector (Swanson and Wolde-Semait, 1989, p. 8). However, the direct effect on employment is not analogous with the SOEs' total role in generating employment because investment in SOEs generates forward and backward linkages. That means the enhancement of opportunities for employment in other sectors of the economy. This goal has to be related to the incidence of poverty and low income levels characterizing the economies of many developing countries.

## 7. Balanced Regional Development

One of the heritages of colonialism was the unbalanced development of the regions.

Japanese colonialism of Taiwan (1895–1945) and Korea (1910–48) led to the development of rural regions in those countries, particularly the development of a highly productive agricultural sector. In the case of western colonization, however, the expansion of urban centres was the main feature. This was related to the economic gains generated from the extractive industries. The establishment of new projects in underdeveloped regions was seen as a way of stimulating investment by the private as well as the public sector. Although such investment projects were not viable, the state invested through its enterprises in order to achieve this goal.

There were other objectives behind the creation of SOEs in different developing countries. Goals such as the control of inflation through underpricing of SOEs' products, stabilization of the economy and equal distribution of income and opportunities can all be included in the reasons and objectives for establishing SOEs. In the case of Indian SOEs:

> there are at least 28 national objectives state-owned enterprises are expected to pursue, ranging from building

up surpluses and providing competition with the private sector to developing backward areas, developing indigenous technology, working as a model employer, and promoting a socially desirable pattern of consumption (Mulji, 1990, p. 143).

Such a wide range of objectives is quite different from those pursued in the private sector, where the main goal is profit-maximization. They may appear desirable on an individual basis, but when combined, they are often in conflict with one another. For example, inflation control seldom creates employment, underpricing policies cannot create profits, regional balances might be inconsistent with economic viability. On the other hand, the economic strategy itself may be different among different countries. In Latin America, for example, the main objective of ISI was the reduction of vulnerability to foreign economic shocks. In Asian countries, however, the main motive was to establish an industrial sector similar to the one existing in advanced countries (Banuri, 1991) although in India, the main reason was to achieve self-sufficiency through a pattern similar to that adopted in the former USSR.

In summary the political, social, historical and economic objectives behind the establishment of public enterprises were complex, and they are far away from the simple efficiency and profitability debate regarding the economic rationale for privatization. Despite that it is important to examine the performance of SOEs to determine if the empirical evidence provides support to the privatization advocates who believe in the superiority of private ownership.

## 3.4 THE PERFORMANCE OF SOEs

The proponents of privatization often argue that the financial record of public enterprises world-wide is in itself evidence for the necessity of privatization.

Between 1989 and 1991, public enterprises' financial losses as a percentage of GDP constituted 9 per cent in Argentina, 8 per cent in Yugoslavia, and on average more than 5 per cent in some African countries. Also, 30 per cent of SOEs in China incurred losses in 1991 (Kikeri *et al.*, 1992). As a result of the heavy losses of SOEs, government transfers (including subsidies) to these enterprises accounted for 4 per cent of GNP in Turkey in 1990, and 9 per cent of the GDP in Poland.

Studies of African SOEs reported that a large number of public enterprises (PEs) showed net losses, and negative net worth because of constraints imposed by their respective governments on pricing decisions, investment policies, and other factors such as employment policies. Despite these constraints there were enterprises which achieved positive financial results (Nellis, 1986; Swanson and Wolde-Semait, 1989).

Evidence from individual countries' studies in Africa is also mixed. In the case of Ghana, a cross-debts study on 18 SOEs (about 8 per cent of all Ghana's SOEs) in 1987 revealed that the cross-debts between SOEs totalled around $58 million in 1986 while their indebtedness to the government was around $450 million[4] (as cited in Adda, 1989, p. 306).

In the Egyptian SOEs, a study revealed the contrast between poor financial performance and positive economic performance. According to Ott (1991), the overall deficit of PEs in Egypt as a percentage of GDP rose from 3.9 per cent in 1979 to 8.4 per cent in 1983–84 while the estimated rate of return on revalued assets was –5.7 per cent (Ott, 1991, pp. 204–6). On the other hand, a study of seven public firms in the Egyptian industrial sector showed that four of them had a negative rate of return in 1984–85 while the indicators of total factor productivity (TFP) change, which could be a reliable measure of economic efficiency against that of financial efficiency, indicated a positive TFP change ranging from 0.5 to 11.1 during the period 1976 to 1984–85 (calculated from ibid., Table 10.13, p. 211).

There is also a number of studies which indicate the mixed stories of success and failure in some of the Western Hemisphere countries. According to Guerra (1992), the operational results of the public sector in Brazil have on average run at around –6 per cent since the beginning of the 1980s. In 1990, the 50 largest SOEs lost $6.4 billion or 12 per cent of their net worth and 15 of the 20 largest deficit companies in the country were SOEs. On the other hand, nine of the largest profitable enterprises were SOEs. Such mixed results indicate the importance of studying SOEs on a case-by-case basis so as to understand the factors impeding the profitability of some enterprises against the success of others.

The assessment of good performance through financial measures may also bring with it many misgivings, particularly where some SOEs are important for generating positive externalities in the economy. Schmitz and Hewitt (1991), in their study of government investment in the computer industry in Brazil, observed that questioning the opportunity cost of government unprofitable investment may be misleading. The reason for this is that one of the main problems in the Brazilian economy during the 1970s and 1980s was the flow of capital into financial rather than manufacturing operations because profits in the former were easier and higher than in industry. On the other hand the Brazilian national computer industry, for example, was employing over 40 thousand people by 1987. Their social opportunity cost could be measured if there had been full employment in the economy, but that was not the case. Other benefits, such as cumulative learning, innovation, and adaptation to local demands and other positive externalities are not included in the account of financial performance. Thus, state efficiency in some enterprises might be increasing despite short-run costs. However, it is not possible to make generalizations applicable to all SOEs.

It is necessary to explore the reasons for bad performance. Transforming poorly performing SOEs into successful ones could be achieved, as Schumacher and Hutchinson (1991) show in their study of Jamaican SOEs, by adopting a package of reforms which increase accountability through efficient monitoring and control systems and by increasing the prices of the products to competitive levels. While 21 public enterprises were unable to finance their operating expenditure, taxes and debt service in 1980–81, by 1988–89 they had succeeded in generating operating profits amounting to J$ 752.6 million and had financed about 90 per cent of their capital expenditure (ibid., pp. 239–41).

A study of the 1986 profitability of 56 SOEs in Peru reported that 46 per cent obtained no profits, 37.5 per cent achieved profit rates of less than 15 per cent, and 16.5 per cent of the SOEs earned more than 20 per cent profits (De Zevallos and Ortiz, 1989, p. 362).

## Public vs Private Ownership

The above evidence establishes that the dangers of privatization derive from the sweeping belief in its merits. Privatization became a matter of belief rather than one option in a general programme of economic policy reform (Shackleton, 1986; Starr, 1990). If the aim is to increase profitability *per se* there are many options for SOEs. For example, Jones (1991, p. 16) reported that in one case a large industrial public firm in South America moved from large losses to a significant profit within one year by changing the shape of the firm's accounts (i.e. debt and interest payment) rather than increasing efficiency.

In Pakistan's 195 SOEs, the pre-tax return on capital in 1985–86 for 37 per cent of them was negative, for 32 per cent average profits were between 0 and 15 per cent, while the remaining 31 per cent achieved pre-tax profits equal to or more than 15 per cent (Bokhari, 1989, p. 167).

Evidence from India reveals that public enterprises employed about 2.2 million people out of a total public workforce of 16.8 million workers. In 1988, the share value of all Indian public sector enterprises was about $22 billion while that of the private corporate sector was $6.7 billion (Waterbury, 1990, p. 295). However, against expectation, the rate of return on all investment in public enterprises in 1986 was 12.54 per cent. Even, after exclusion of the petroleum sector, the rate exceeded 7.5 per cent. A comparison of this rate with comparable private sector enterprises revealed that the latter's rate was 13.6 per cent (Reddy, 1989, p. 181). So, the difference between private and public investment rate of return was only 1 per cent, an unexpected result considering the literature criticizing the public sector in India. However, that does not mean that all public sector enterprises are financially viable.

In the case of Malaysia, there were more than 1000 SOEs in 1990. It was found that 60 per cent of the SOEs had achieved profit during 1980–88 while the remainder were unprofitable. Adam and his associates (1992, p. 223) ranked Malaysian SOEs' general performance based on enterprise profitability relative to capitalization during the period 1980–88. In 1988 16.7 per cent of SOEs were 'sick', 24.1 per cent 'weak', 14.4 per cent 'satisfactory' and 44.8 per cent 'good'.[5] The scholars in this study argued that privatization has had a benefit impact not necessarily through the implementation phase but through what they called the 'threat effect' where SOEs' managers improve their performance in order not to carry out actual privatization on their enterprises.

Recent figures of the estimated losses of public enterprises in a number of countries or regions provided by UNDP (1993) show that the arguments for the privatization of SOEs can be divided between the belief in private sector technical and allocative efficiency superiority, irrespective of the institutional factor of a country, and the argument of the social opportunity cost of public enterprise losses (for example, in the context of education and health spending) which is also within the dimension of allocative efficiency.

As illustrated in the analysis of 'market failure', Pareto efficiency (i.e. allocative efficiency) cannot equal profitability on all accounts. For example in decreasing cost industries a profit-maximizing producer has to produce an output less than the Pareto-efficient level and sell at a price higher than that which the consumer is willing to pay. That is because, as the average cost declines, Pareto efficiency (i.e. allocative efficiency) will result in net losses on the part of producers since they have to produce more and charge less. This contradicts the rationality of profit maximization for a private producer. In this case, as we said earlier, the product could either be produced through the public sector or the private sector can produce the product with the government subsidizing the losses incurred in order to achieve a more efficient allocation of resources. Thus, profitability is not a sufficient indicator of efficiency since both alternatives can lead to losses in order to achieve allocative efficiency.

The other side of the argument is that Pareto efficiency does not indicate any bias towards private against public ownership. The important factor is competition in the market. Thus, as many services provided by the public sector imply a natural monopoly character, the monopoly rent after privatization will fall to private monopolists, which reduces consumer welfare and imposes losses on society. This means that competition, rather than change in the geometry of ownership, is the critical factor.

The UNDP (1993) argument presented in Table 3.3 is a rule of thumb. The assumption is that all financial losses in

Table 3.3  The social opportunity cost of public enterprise losses, 1988–90

| Country or region | Estimated losses of PEs as % of GNP | Public education and health spending as % of GNP | Potential increase in education & health spending if PEs losses are eliminated (%) |
|---|---|---|---|
| Argentina | 9 | 5.5 | 164 |
| Poland | 9 | 7.6 | 118 |
| Bangladesh | 3 | 3.1 | 97 |
| Turkey | 4 | 4.6 | 87 |
| Egypt | 3 | 11.0 | 27 |
| Philippines | 2 | 8.3 | 24 |
| Sub-Saharan Africa | 5 | 6.5 | 77 |

Source: UNDP (1993, Table no. 3.4, p. 48).

public enterprises will be directed towards education and health spending if they are to be eliminated. But since many of the losses occurred in the utility sectors, the question becomes: who will provide transportation, health, education and other services? If it is the public sector, then the losses will continue. On the other hand, if it is left to the private sector, then the allocation of resources toward such services will decline if not cease (the profit maximization constraint).

The conclusion drawn in a World Bank study in 1993 revealed that cuts in spending as a result of structural adjustment policies occur 'for important but politically less visible operations and maintenance (O&M) – such as providing drugs and supplies for health clinics and repairing roads' (Pradhan and Swaroop, 1993, p. 29). Also, the squeezing of spending has affected investment in important infrastructural projects with high returns because such investment was seen as the 'softer' option for the governments of developing countries.

Ramirez's (1993) assessment of the austerity measures in Latin American countries during the 1980s is that it led to a significant reduction in public spending on health and education. For example, in Brazil expenditure on health and education as a percentage of total public expenditure decreased from 12.4 per cent in 1982 to 10.3 per cent in 1989; in Argentina such expenditure declined from 17.2 per cent in 1982 to 11.3 per cent in 1989; in Mexico it deteriorated from 22.6 per cent to only 8.5 per cent between 1980 and 1988 while in Chile it decreased from 21.5 per cent to 16 per cent between 1982 and 1989. This leads us to the important question of what is the economic rationale for privatization. Does ownership affect the productive or X-efficiency of an enterprise, and if the answer is yes, then why?

## 3.5 THE FIRM AND THE THEORY OF X-EFFICIENCY

In the analysis of the neoclassical theory, there is no direct investigation of the internal factors affecting economic efficiency within the firm. That is because the neoclassical theory treats the firm as an impersonal and anonymous entity. It is assumed that the owner is rational and will thus minimize costs in order to maximize profit (the residual). The major assumptions are: there is no separation between ownership and control, and zero transaction costs (costs of obtaining information about alternatives and of negotiating, policing, and enforcing contracts). Thus, the economic behaviour and performance of different organizational forms, such as 'public' versus 'private', have no place in neoclassical analysis (Jensen and Meckling, 1976, p. 306).

In the traditional neoclassical analysis it was assumed that the entrepreneur is a coordinator or auctioneer in the marketplace. Thus, price mechanism will solve the problem of market transactions.[6] But Coase (1937) observed that there are costs of transactions in the marketplace; that is why firms exist. These costs arise from imperfect information and uncertainty which can be eliminated through the hierarchical organization of the firm. In addition, the separation between ownership and control became the dominant feature of the new corporations.

The development of the behavioural and managerial theories provided new understanding to the objectives of the firm which deviated from the neoclassical assumption of profit maximization; a result derived from the different and sometimes conflicting goals between managers' and owners' utility functions which are subject to constraints.

It is now established that the main factors behind the establishment of the firm are to minimize the transaction costs of exchange in the marketplace as well as the establishment of different organizational forms in order to minimize the transaction costs within the organization. Williamson (1985) noted that uncertainty, idiosyncracy, complexity, informational asymmetry, and opportunism were inherent to transactions, which made coordination between highly independent production and distribution processes through the market alone costly and difficult.[7] The unequal distribution of knowledge and information is a result of the specialization and division of labour, which leads all individuals to possess specialized knowledge in their area of skill (Scitovsky, 1990, p. 137). Internalizing transaction costs does not mean their elimination, and their existence introduces what is known as X-inefficiency.

The degree of X-inefficiency is the degree to which actual output is less than the maximum output for a given input or the excess of actual over minimum costs for a given output. The differences between the neoclassical theory and X-efficiency theory are summarized in Table 3.4.

*Table* 3.4   The differences between X-efficiency theory and the neoclassical theory

| Components | X-efficiency theory | Neoclassical theory |
|---|---|---|
| 1. Psychology | Selective rationality | Maxim. or Minim. |
| 2. Contract | Incomplete | Complete |
| 3. Effort | Discretionary variable | Assumed given |
| 4. Units | Individuals | Household & firms |
| 5. Inert areas | Important variable | None |
| 6. Agent–principal | Differential | Identity of interests |

*Source*: Leibenstein (1978, p. 129).

Leibenstein observed that the deviation of real effort given by the individual to the firm from the optimal one expected by the firm determines the degree of X-inefficiency. The other important factor is the amount of pressure operating on the effort variable. An individual whose behaviour is influenced by the context of selective rationality will not try to maximize profit or minimize cost because contracts are incomplete and there are differences of interest between the principals (owners) and agents (managers and workers). There is also discretion among firm members in their efforts to conduct the contractual activities and there are inert areas which are determined by the inertia costs of individual movement from one effort position to another. These inertia costs depend on individual personality and it is clear that the motivation of workers and the quality of managerial decisions are the major constraints on the productivity of modern firms (Leibenstein, 1978). Thus, X-inefficiency results from the existence of positive transaction costs which are themselves the products of bounded rationality, opportunistic behaviour and information impactedness.[8]

X-efficiency theory was criticized for its failure to emphasize the importance of different property rights structures, particularly since any reduction in the degree of X-inefficiency depends on monitoring and incentive factors, both dependent on introducing different structures of property rights.[9] In 1989 Leibenstein noticed the importance of environmental pressure factors, which implies an indirect relationship with property rights structure. He argued that there are two kinds of pressure, the first 'from below' because of competition with other producers and the second 'from above', namely from the firm's owner or representative. Thus, 'different institutional arrangements will involve different sources of pressure' Leibenstein, 1989, p. 1364). Accordingly, the possibility of X-inefficiency is real in typical public enterprises because of the absence of pressure from either direction (above and below). He therefore suggested a number of options for the reform of public enterprises, such as using a franchise approach in order to reduce costs.

The question is: does privatization, as a change in ownership *per se*, enhance X-efficiency or not?

## 3.6 THE ECONOMIC THEORY OF PROPERTY RIGHTS

The economic rationale for privatization within the context of ownership change is based on two fundamental theories; the first being the economic theory of property rights.

The main argument of this theory is that ownership matters on the basis that the transfer of property rights from the public to the private sector will increase the efficiency of the enterprise, particularly that of X-efficiency.

Within the privatization debate, the comparison of efficiency with that of alternative property rights structures rests mainly on three factors, namely ownership specialization, risk bearing, and the transferability of ownership. The significance of these factors stems from their effect on the *incentive* (cost–reward) and *monitoring systems* which result in different alignments of resources and different input–output mixes.

*1. Ownership Specialization*
Under private ownership, people will choose to be owners of an organization if they possess a sufficient knowledge of its activities (Alchain, 1965, p. 821). Such specialization will lead to a better decision-making structure. It is preferable for decisions related to the operation of the enterprise to be taken by specialized individuals who have an interest and stake in its development as this will also increase their capacity to monitor management behaviour and decisions.

In the case of public ownership there is no such specialization because each member of the public has only a minute stake in the enterprise. Thus, even if it is assumed that individuals from the public have a stake in the efficiency of the enterprise, they will not possess a comparative advantage of ownership similar to that which exists under private ownership.

However, this argument may not constitute a decisive difference in the effects of ownership form. In most modern corporations shareholders are neither specialists nor knowledgeable in the activities of the organization; rather, the owners' objective may be to spread the risk of their investment by building up investment portfolios among different enterprises.

## 2. Risk-Bearing

The possession of private property is a voluntary risk-bearing decision based solely on individual choice. By contrast, public ownership is not voluntary, thus individual members of the public have no risk-bearing function in the context of individuality. Hence, the most significant difference is that the incentive for the owners as risk-bearers will be most apparent in the case of private ownership; consequently, the motivation for taking correct decisions, introducing an efficient system of incentives, and monitoring the performance of the enterprise will be greater (Hanke and Walters, 1990). However, the separation of ownership and control in private corporations also enhances the opportunistic behaviour of managers and employees. Thus, 'the condition of residual risk bearing is fully determinative of organization form' (Williamson, 1983, p. 356). In this case the use of a U-form (unitary) structure within a private organization may result in a worse outcome than the use by an organization of the multi-divisional M-form structure. This is because the decentralizing feature of the M-form structure offers more incentives to management and provides better control mechanisms and therefore efficiency increased in a number of British public enterprises as a result of the employment of such institutional change (Bishop and Thompson, 1992). Privatization by itself cannot resolve the problem of risk-bearing.

## 3. Transferability of Ownership

By and large, the most significant difference between public and private ownership lies in the transferability of property rights. In public ownership the rights of the individual as shareholder do not include the right of saleability or exchange of rights because this right is purely 'nominal' (Alchain, 1965; Millward and Parker, 1983). Therefore, politicians and, to a lesser extent, managers possess 'control rights' over SOEs. Cash-flow rights, by contrast, are officially held by the public but without an exchange right to make it effective (*The Economist*, 18 November 1995, p. 136). In other words, if members of the public are not satisfied with or do not approve of the performance of a public enterprise, they cannot sell their shares. This denotes less pressure on the management of a public enterprise, which Leibenstein (1989) called pressure from the top or from above. In contrast, the contestability of ownership represents one of the major monitoring devices for managers of a private corporation. Where there is a high level of opportunism and shirking behaviour, the value of the enterprise's shares will fall on the stock market, on the one hand providing a signal to shareholders to sell their shares and on the other putting pressure on management to increase their efforts. Both outcomes will lead to more X-efficiency.

Likewise, Niskanen (1971, 1973) in his bureaucracy model argued that bureaucrats prefer greater present budgets in order to increase their non-pecuniary consumption, such as their tenure period or prestige and power. As government bureaus are the agents responsible for proposing new projects, they tend, in the absence of ownership contestability, to reflect their own interests (James, 1989).

In summary, the theory of property rights argues that a transfer of ownership from public to private will enhance the efficiency of the firm because of the better incentive systems and control mechanisms associated with private ownership which derive from the benefits associated with residual claimants. Public assets are not owned, there are no clear rights for residual claimants and the exchange of rights does not exist. This lack of ownership contestability means that decisions formulated by public enterprise managers do not translate into a change in market prices and consequently there are no risk-bearers of decisions.

The main criticism of the theory of property rights is that it has established the differences between public and private ownership on the presumption that there is an existing and well-defined system of property rights. This is true mainly in the advanced capitalist countries but such an assumption is not valid in a large number of developing countries or in the former socialist countries.

In advanced countries such as Britain, 'the legal system has created property rights that can be exchanged in an expanded market' (De Soto, 1993, p. 8). Such a system is yet to be institutionalized in many developing countries and the comparison between public and private becomes meaningless without such an important ingredient. The success or failure of privatization in achieving economic efficiency 'depends critically on the creation of the most essential elements of a competitive environment, including effective control mechanism, and the recognition in principle of the validity of all alternative property rights' (Brabant, 1995, p. 78).

Although the comparison between public and private ownership, as in the case of property rights theory, seems to be compatible with any case of comparison in the real world, such a context may vary widely between different countries. In addition, even differences in the form of public ownership will determine the simplicity or complexity of any subsequent privatization (Lipton and Sachs, 1992).

Western advisers should understand that a distinction should be made between the legalization of private property and its institutionalization. The latter means providing the 'social legitimacy' of property rights. In the words of Koslowski:

> For the use of property rights to become a settled practice as in established market economies, a newly established system of property rights must become legitimate. If the rules regulating the recognition of property rights are not initially acceptable to the polity, the permanence of those property rights is questionable. Although exchange of such property rights is possible, reproduction of exchange on a routine basis is less likely (Koslowski, 1992, p. 684).

In the final analysis, the differences between the context in which property rights theory was developed, and the lack of a clear and institutionalized structure for such property rights in different developing countries may weaken the argument for privatization presented by this theory.

## 3.7 THE PRINCIPAL–AGENT THEORY

The theory most fundamental to privatization is the principal–agent theory, which focuses on the informational and incentive differences between private and public enterprises.[10]

The agency problem arises from contracting with asymmetric information when the principals (owners) delegate other parties, the agents (managers), the right to act on their behalf, or as their representatives, in a particular set of decisions regarding the functioning of the organization. If both the principal and the agent are maximizers of their utilities, there will be a conflict of objectives. Although the principals' aim is to induce their agents to act in their interests and maximize wealth this will result in additional agency costs being imposed (Ross, 1973, p. 134).

Agency costs are the costs of writing and enforcing contracts. They include the costs of structuring, monitoring, and bonding a set of contracts with conflicting interests. They also include the value of output loss where the costs exceed the benefit yield from the full enforcement of contracts (Jensen and Meckling, 1976, p. 308). In other words, the principals will face a monitoring problem because of a lack of adequate information about the efforts and behaviour of their agents (Strong and Waterson, 1987, pp. 18–20).

In a simple relationship between one principal and one agent, the principal can reduce the agency costs by observing the change in the level of output. In this case, the optimal contract would be to compensate the agent in relation to the output level (Diamond and Verrecchia, 1982, pp. 275–6). Because of the specialized nature of such a small firm, there would be no observability problem, or even if there were, it could be solved with minimum effect on the firm's efficiency (Fama and Jensen, 1983, p. 307).

As privatization deals with large enterprises, the agency problem becomes more complicated. The separation between owners (principals) and managers (agents) is a characteristic of such organizations, the agency costs will rise in both types of organization. The *ex ante* costs arising from the 'adverse selection' and *ex post* costs arising from 'moral hazard' will increase the total agency costs derived from the problem of asymmetrical information and observability.[11] As the number of shareholders (principals) is large in both public and private organizations, the difference between them lies in their ability to provide the optimal contractual agreement (the incentive constraint) and the monitoring devices (the information constraint).

In contractual agreements there is no decisive difference between public and private organizations if it is assumed that 'bounded rationality' is a problem for the principals of both organizations. The difference between them lies in their ability to design contracts which induce the agents to act according to the principals' objectives. For example the use of pecuniary and non-pecuniary reward schemes can be found in both types of organization. However, if the differences in the principals' objectives are taken into account, important differences can be assumed between the two.

Under public ownership, public enterprises are run by ministers or bureaucrats who are maximizers of their utility functions, a weighted average of social welfare and their personal objectives. These personal objectives satisfy the goals of 'public management', such as large budgets, high wages and employment levels in particular enterprises or sectors, patronage, and the redistribution of income and wealth to favoured interest groups (Shapiro and Willig, 1990). It is sometimes argued that the result of these goals will be the absence of efficiency-promoting incentives, because this, even if sought by political decision-makers, 'is frequently a low-ranked priority' (Prager, 1992, p. 307). In contrast, the private owners of an enterprise are usually eager to pursue the goal of profit maximization, and efficiency as a means of achieving it, which is one component of the social welfare function. Others may be derived from the firm's activities such as the effect on consumer surplus and, for example, other distributional and non-distributional effects. Thus, in both cases, there is a divergence between the principals' objectives and social welfare (Shapiro and Willig, 1990; Vickers and Yarrow, 1991).

What can decide the advantages of one form of enterprise against the other is the design and functioning of the political system versus the structure of the market. If there is an optimal political system, where managers cannot pursue their personal goals, then public enterprises are at an advantage in a non-competitive market structure. On the other hand, private enterprises will be at an advantage in a competitive market structure with an inefficient political system (Vickers and Yarrow, 1991). In reality both assumptions rarely exist, particularly in developing countries. Thus, the comparison will depend on the speciality of each case to determine the differences between the contractual arrangements in both forms of ownership. For example, Bishop and Thompson (1992) claim that the introduction of management remuneration schemes in some of the British public enterprises, such as the Post Office and British Steel, during the 1980s contributed significantly to an improvement in the performance of those enterprises without a change in the ownership structure.

The other most important determinant of agency costs is the monitoring problem. This is based on the available information for each form of organization. It is argued that there are several control mechanisms which can provide information and subsequently a disciplinary system to private enterprise managers.

The first is the Annual General Meeting (AGM) of the shareholders. Although shareholders delegate the power of decision-making to the managers of the enterprise, they still retain the power to vote on important decisions. In large private corporations, the influence of internal managers is immense because of the wide range of information they hold which affects the decisions taken during the AGM (Demsetz, 1986). Yet, in public enterprises, there is no meeting between the public and the managers. Ministers or representatives of other government agencies are the principals responsible for discussing the achievement of enterprise goals, which are often asymmetrical. The agency costs in such enterprises tend to be high.

The other monitoring device is change in the value of shares on the stock market. The difference, as mentioned earlier, between private and public ownership is the transferability or contestability of ownership. In private ownership, changes in share prices provide a less costly mechanism for understanding the implications of internal decisions for current and future net cash flows. Thus, in the case of declining share prices, the owners will either change managers or encourage them to correct their policies. Nevertheless, where there is unresolved conflict, the shareholders will sell their shares as a reflection of their dissatisfaction with the managers' performance. This puts pressure on managers to increase their efforts. A firm in continuing decline will be in danger of takeover by another corporation, or of bankruptcy if the firm's assets fall below outstanding liabilities, or when, at least in the case of fallen share prices, the firm is unable to obtain access to additional capital (Vickers and Yarrow, 1988). In public enterprises none of these control devices exist. This leads to an increase in their agency costs and increased inefficiency.

Nevertheless, none of the above devices can succeed in disciplining private enterprise managers and thereby reducing the agency costs. Stiglitz (1985) suggested that the three most important mechanisms are: control of the enterprise by the banks, when they are major lenders; the concentration of equity ownership; and the factor of managerial reputation. In addition, the financial markets may not be the perfect mechanism by which shareholders can control their agents.[12] Stiglitz (1985, 1993) argued that credit rationing may not provide a clear signal about the performance of managers in some enterprises. In other words, if the banks adopt a policy of credit rationing, they may refuse the finance of long-term projects and thus reduce the future performance of an enterprise.

The problem of asymmetric information in SOEs, as the proponents of privatization put it, leads to a greater provision of capital from the principals (planners or government) and less profit from the enterprise. This is because the principals cannot obtain full information about market and technology conditions and so are unable to give instructions to the agent about first-best level of price, output, labour and wage rates and generally inefficient allocation of resources, particularly when there are no penalties in the public sector for unrealistic forecasting (Rees, 1988). Agency costs will be high in such enterprises because agents might give information about the level of production below the actual level, or the government may use past performance in setting future goals. Hence, the achievement of such targets will be rewarded while there is no incentive mechanism to induce the agents to perform up to their potential (Sappington, 1991).

The World Bank's (1995, p. 93) assessment is that private organizations tackle this problem by employing four methods which governments find difficult to employ. One is the 'identification method' in which the principal convinces the agents to take the goal of the firm as their own goal. A second method is by using 'authority' to order agents to conduct specific tasks. A third solution is by transferring responsibility of monitoring from managers to workers in the group. This is called the 'peer pressure' method. A fourth approach is the 'reward' approach in which management induces the workers to achieve the goals of the organization. However, Vickers and Yarrow (1991) contended that loss-making public enterprises might face tightened state budgets which may limit managerial discretion. Others believe that managers in public enterprises may consider the value of their expertise and reputation as important factors in reducing agency costs (Vining and Weimer, 1990). Also, there is no one reason why governments in Third World countries cannot adopt any of the principal–agent solutions mentioned by the World Bank in its *World Development Report* (*WDR*).

What differentiates public from private regulated enterprises is the nature of private information. If private information about the agents in both enterprises cannot be revealed, there will be a major impact from privatizing public enterprises; however, if there is no hidden information, which diverges public and private interest, there will be no major impact from privatization (Shapiro and Willig, 1990). On the other hand, as agency costs are major components in the total transaction costs, privatization will be beneficial through reducing the transaction costs derived from government intervention in enterprise decision-making (Sappington and Stiglitz, 1987). But, even after privatization, according to Boycko, Shleifer and Vishny (1996), politicians may intervene in a privatized firm to achieve political ends; they may even provide subsidies to such firms in order to maintain the level of employment.

Therefore, there is no major argument in the principal–agent literature that can stand without challenge to the primacy of private over public ownership. Even the argument regarding the existence of the capital market as a signalling device might fail to stand in developing countries because most of them lack such capital markets. However, the threat of takeover and bankruptcy may put more pressure on private managers.

On theoretical grounds, the differences between the two are not analogous with ownership, but rather information and incentives which are based on the main objectives of each organization. Simon (1991) summarized the above context in the following words:

Large organizations, especially governmental ones, are often caricatured as 'bureaucracies', but they are often highly effective systems, despite the fact that the profit motive can penetrate these vast structures only by indirect means (Simon, 1991, p. 43).

## 3.8 CONCLUDING COMMENTS

By examining the allocative role of the state, this chapter suggests that developing countries are not a homogeneous group. Each region, and sometimes each country, has had different reasons for the creation and expansion of its public sector. Such conclusions have to be taken into account when the proponents of privatization (i.e. international agencies and advisers) attempt to enforce privatization policies on developing countries. That is to say, the argument of private versus public ownership seems to be, in general terms, irrelevant in a large number of developing countries because many of the reasons behind the creation and expansion of the public sector are still valid. Objectives such as the control of the commanding heights, the creation of high-tech industries, the control of natural resources, employment generation, balanced regional development and many others continue to be listed as high priorities in many developing countries. These are a translation to the theoretical context of public economics.

While the argument of private versus public ownership rests on cost-benefit analysis, it is suggested that profitable does not mean economically efficient. The empirical evidence from the three main regions of the developing countries revealed that public ownership is not synonymous with loss. On the other hand, the empirical evidence asserts that many loss-making public enterprises were economically efficient when parameters such as total factor productivity were employed in the analysis.

Arguments such as those based on opportunity costs were also found to be misleading because the losses themselves are related to the special character of the industry, or to the kind of policies enforced by the government on its enterprises in order to achieve specific goals (i.e. learning, employment, subsidies). However, there is no suggestion here that all public enterprises are efficient, only that it is necessary to study each case on its own in order to reach a more accurate conclusion about whether to privatize or not.

The theoretical presumption that private ownership is superior was, when investigated, also found to be misleading. While bounded rationality, opportunistic behaviour and information impactedness are found in both public and private organizations, the level of transaction costs seems to depend on the structure of the organization rather than on the type of ownership *per se*.

Although the economic theory of property rights presents several arguments in favour of private ownership, such a theory depends on the existence of stock markets where shares can be transferred from one shareholder to another. In the majority of developing countries, however, such markets do not exist or, if they do, they lack the necessary institutions and codes which protect, enforce and legitimize property rights.

Within the context of principal–agent theory, the arguments have shown that incentive and information structures are the major factors determining the level of agency costs and consequently X-efficiency. Better incentives and information are not characteristics of private ownership alone. Factors such as tight government budgets, appropriate control mechanisms and efficient reward–penalty systems can be employed to the benefit of public enterprises as well. The existence of factors such as managerial expertise and reputation can minimize agency costs in both public and private enterprises.

Finally, all the above theories share the belief that competition in the market is the single most important factor in enhancing efficiency and reducing agency costs. Thus, it is not ownership, but market structure which determines the success or failure of privatization.

The question of efficiency at the enterprise level is whether efficiency will be improved under private ownership. In such a context the investigation of the competitiveness of the firm will play a more important role in the analysis of efficiency than the simple test of profitability. However, even if there are efficiency gains from divestiture, these should be compared with the transaction costs of the divestiture itself.

On the macro-level the reasons for privatization in developing countries might not be related to the question of efficiency alone but to other factors. However, describing this will be the task of the next chapter, which will review the empirical evidence regarding the different dimensions of privatization in developing countries.

# 4 Review of the Empirical Evidence on Privatization in Developing Countries

## 4.1 INTRODUCTION

Until 1987 details on privatization transactions in developing countries were not available. However, a World Bank study in 1988 reported the number of privatization cases underway, planned and completed during 1980–87. Tables 4.1, 4.2, and

*Table* 4.1  The number of SOEs (1986) and cases of privatization (1980–87) in the low-income countries

| Country | No. of non-financial SOEs | No. of financial SOEs | Total number of SOEs | No. of privatization cases underway | No. of planned privatization cases | No. of completed privatization cases |
|---|---|---|---|---|---|---|
| 1. Nepal | 37 | 9 | 46 | ... | 6 | ... |
| 2. Bangladesh | 34 | 16 | 50 | ... | 7 | 8 |
| 3. Malawi | 25 | 1 | 26 | 1 | ... | 1 |
| 4. Zaire | 40 | 5 | 45 | 1 | ... | 9 |
| 5. Mali | 28 | 7 | 35 | 1 | 6 | 5 |
| 6. Uganda | 67 | 7 | 74 | ... | 5 | 7 |
| 7. Tanzania | 204 | 8 | 212 | n.a. | n.a. | n.a. |
| 8. Togo | 47 | 8 | 55 | 4 | 22 | 16 |
| 9. Niger | 23 | 10 | 33 | 10 | 9 | 14 |
| 10. Benin | 52 | 7 | 59 | 2 | 13 | ... |
| 11. Somalia | 51 | 6 | 57 | ... | ... | 2 |
| 12. Cent. African Rep. | 15 | 5 | 20 | ... | ... | 1 |
| 13. Rwanda | 29 | 8 | 37 | ... | ... | 1 |
| 14. China | n.a. | n.a. | n.a. | ... | 6 | ... |
| 15. Kenya | 110 | 22 | 132 | 1 | ... | 2 |
| 16. Zambia | 304 | 12 | 316 | ... | ... | 6 |
| 17. Sierra Leone | 22 | 7 | 29 | ... | ... | 2 |
| 18. Pakistan | 88 | 25 | 113 | 10 | 3 | 1 |
| 19. Ghana | 50 | 11 | 61 | 31 | ... | 7 |
| 20. Sri Lanka | 110 | 16 | 126 | ... | 6 | 12 |
| 21. Mauritania | 28 | 12 | 40 | 3 | ... | 5 |
| 22. Senegal | 47 | 10 | 57 | 2 | 33 | 6 |
| 23. Guinea | 184 | 7 | 191 | 8 | ... | 39 |
| Total | 1595 | 219 | 1814 | 74 | 116 | 144 |

*Table* 4.2  The number of SOEs (1986) and cases of privatization (1980–87) in the lower-middle-income countries

| Country | No. of non-financial SOEs | No. of financial SOEs | Total number of SOEs | No. of privatization cases underway | No. of planned privatization cases | No. of completed privatization cases |
|---|---|---|---|---|---|---|
| 1. Liberia | 16 | 5 | 21 | 1 | 10 | 2 |
| 2. Indonesia | 155 | 109 | 264 | ... | 1 | 3 |
| 3. Philippines | 41 | 13 | 54 | ... | ... | 5 |
| 4. Morocco | 73 | 11 | 84 | ... | ... | 11 |
| 5. Bolivia | 35 | 16 | 51 | 1 | ... | 1 |
| 6. Nigeria | 83 | 31 | 114 | ... | 98 | ... |
| 7. Dominican Rep. | 8 | 4 | 12 | 1 | 2 | 1 |
| 8. Papua New Guinea | 16 | 4 | 20 | 8 | 5 | 1 |
| 9. Côte d'Ivoire | 57 | 6 | 63 | ... | ... | 36 |
| 10. Honduras | 11 | 6 | 17 | ... | 14 | 2 |
| 11. Egypt | 468 | 31 | 499 | ... | ... | 2 |
| 12. Thailand | 497 | 131 | 628 | 2 | 5 | 2 |
| 13. Jamaica | 117 | 18 | 135 | 4 | 3 | 34 |
| 14. Cameroon | 58 | 9 | 67 | ... | 1 | 5 |
| 15. Turkey | 31 | 10 | 41 | 7 | ... | 2 |
| 16. Tunisia | 106 | 19 | 125 | ... | ... | 8 |
| 17. Colombia | 345 | 67 | 412 | ... | ... | 1 |
| 18. Chile | 21 | 7 | 28 | 4 | 4 | 40 |
| 19. Costa Rica | 28 | 16 | 44 | 5 | 1 | 1 |
| 20. Jordan | 19 | 9 | 28 | ... | 4 | ... |
| **Total** | 285 | 522 | 2707 | 33 | 148 | 157 |

4.3 present statistics on the number of SOEs and the number of privatization cases for 57 developing countries classified by income groups.[1]

Out of 391 cases of completed privatization, 38 per cent took place in the low-income group, 40 per cent in the lower-middle-income countries, and the remaining 22 per cent occurred in the upper-middle-income countries. According to the tables, sub-Saharan Africa, Latin America and the Caribbean were the most active privatizers in developing countries in terms of number of sales. In fact seven countries from both regions accounted for 53 per cent of total completed privatization transactions (Togo, Niger, Guinea, Côte d'Ivoire, Jamaica, Chile, and Brazil).

*Table* 4.3   The number of SOEs (1986) and cases of privatization (1980–87) in the upper-middle-income countries

| Country | No. of non-financial SOEs | No. of financial SOEs | Total number of SOEs | No. of privatization cases underway | No. of planned privatization cases | No. of completed privatization cases |
|---|---|---|---|---|---|---|
| 1. Brazil | 561 | 14 | 575 | 53[a] | ... | 28 |
| 2. Malaysia | 73 | 10 | 83 | 3 | 21 | 10 |
| 3. Mexico | 243 | 75 | 318 | 5 | 4 | 10 |
| 4. Portugal | 244 | 36 | 280 | 1 | 12 | ... |
| 5. Panama | 218 | 5 | 223 | 1 | 3 | 5 |
| 6. Argentina | 233 | 42 | 275 | 14 | 7 | 3 |
| 7. Korea, Rep. | 144 | 10 | 154 | ... | 9 | 7 |
| 8. Venezuela | 66 | 27 | 93 | 1 | 4 | ... |
| 9. Gabon | 33 | 9 | 42 | ... | ... | 3 |
| 10. Oman | 21 | 4 | 25 | ... | ... | 4 |
| 11. Trinidad & Tobago | 58 | 9 | 67 | ... | 4 | ... |
| 12. Israel | 166 | 15 | 181 | 1 | 2 | 1 |
| 13. Singapore | 15 | 8 | 23 | 3 | 36 | 15 |
| 14. Iraq[b] | 267 | 9 | 276 | 1 | 1 | 3 |
| **Total** | 2342 | 273 | 2615 | 30 | 103 | 90 |

*Note*: For Tables 4.1, 4.2 and 4.3 privatization cases may include privatized branches of the same SOE.
(a) This number is the sum of both privatization cases, both underway and planned.
(b) The number of SOEs in Iraq as cited in Abu Shair (1988).
*Sources*: Data for Tables 4.1, 4.2 and 4.3 are calculated from: (1) SOEs figures from IMF (1987) [Supplement on public sector institutions] (2) Privatization figures from Candoy-Sekse (1988).

The 1980–87 privatization data, however, have many deficiencies because methods of collection were uneven. Also, privatization cases in sub-Saharan Africa and other countries included small privatization transactions where the number of transactions was the determinant factor rather than their value. The main conclusions from Tables 4.1, 4.2 and 4.3 are: first, the number of privatization cases underway and planned outweigh the completed cases: 144, 157, and 90 completed cases in the three income groups against 190, 181, and 133 planned and underway cases. Second, there is no apparent relationship between the number of privatization cases and the number of SOEs in the country because many examples were in branches of the same SOE. Third, the data, although indicating sub-Saharan Africa as a major privatizer in developing countries, appear misleading given the value of privatization transactions globally between 1988 and 1994 (see Table 4.4).

Globally, privatization is an invention of the industrialized countries. The percentage of the total value of SOE sales[2] between 1988 and 1994 in the OECD countries alone amounted to 70.5 per cent (US$214.3 billion) of the total sales world-wide. Low and middle-income countries, which comprise the majority of developing countries, on the other hand represented less than 30 per cent. In fact Figure 4.1 shows that there is a clear pattern of association between the value of

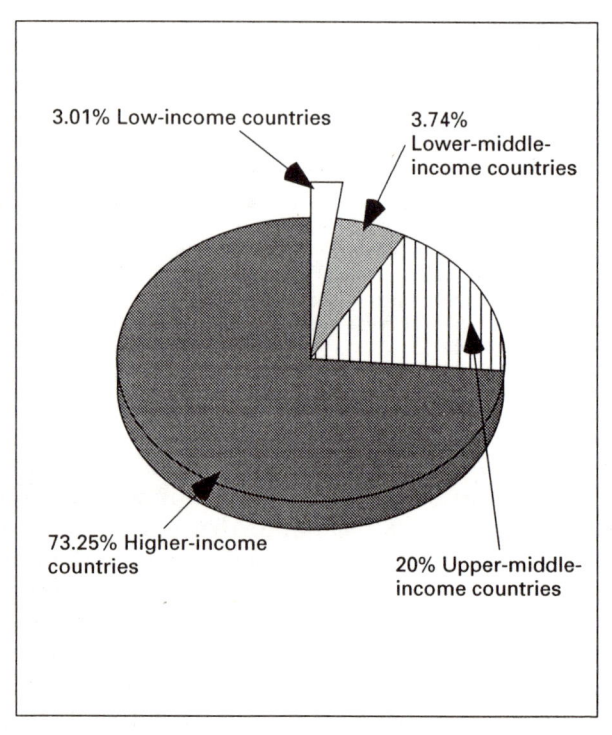

*Figure* 4.1 Total privatization proceeds in the world according to income groups (1988–94)

Table 4.4  Total major privatization proceedings in the world by income groups and geographical regions (1988–94) ($ million)

| Income Groups | 1988 | 1989 | 1990 | 1991 | 1992 | 1993 | 1994 | 1988–94 |
|---|---|---|---|---|---|---|---|---|
| **Low-Income** | | | | | | | | |
| Sub-Saharan Africa | 8 | 0 | 25 | 0 | 0 | 0 | 410 | 443 |
| East Asia & Pacific | 0 | 0 | 0 | 0 | 543 | 781 | 3167 | 4491 |
| South Asia | 0 | 0 | 0 | 13 | 343 | 775 | 2737 | 3868 |
| Middle East & N. Africa | 0 | 0 | 0 | 0 | 0 | 209 | 122 | 331 |
| Total | 8 | 0 | 25 | 13 | 886 | 1765 | 6436 | 9133 |
| **Lower-Middle-Income** | | | | | | | | |
| Sub-Saharan Africa | 0 | 0 | 0 | 0 | 0 | 0 | 0 | 0 |
| East Asia & Pacific | 0 | 165 | 325 | 190 | 608 | 276 | 743 | 2307 |
| Eastern Europe & Central Asia | 0 | 0 | 32 | 350 | 720 | 739 | 598 | 2439 |
| Rest of Europe | 0 | 105 | 267 | 0 | 304 | 364 | 333 | 1373 |
| Middle East & N. Africa | 0 | 0 | 0 | 0 | 0 | 157 | 249 | 406 |
| Latin America & Caribbean | 189 | 337 | 42 | 117 | 143 | 139 | 3873 | 4840 |
| Total | 189 | 607 | 666 | 657 | 1775 | 1675 | 5796 | 11365 |
| **Upper-Middle-Income** | | | | | | | | |
| Sub-Saharan Africa | 0 | 1435* | 0 | 0 | 0 | 0 | 0 | 1435 |
| East Asia & Pacific | 0 | 2100 | 928 | 190 | 1619 | 650 | 1047 | 6534 |
| South Asia | 0 | 0 | 0 | 0 | 0 | 0 | 0 | 0 |
| Eastern Europe & Central Asia | 0 | 130 | 32 | 180 | 845 | 1011 | 227 | 2425 |
| Rest of Europe | 0 | 494 | 838 | 1246 | 1671 | 698 | 990 | 5937 |
| Middle East & N. Africa | 0 | 0 | 0 | 0 | 0 | 0 | 0 | 0 |
| Latin America & Caribbean | 2165 | 148 | 4597 | 14666 | 14866 | 6195 | 1763 | 44400 |
| Total | 2165 | 4307 | 6395 | 16282 | 19001 | 8554 | 4027 | 60731 |
| **Higher-Income** | | | | | | | | |
| *OECD Countries* | | | | | | | | |
| East Asia & Pacific | 26096 | 956 | 3803 | 1620 | 2349 | 8427 | 4627 | 47878 |
| Rest of Europe | 8715 | 17730 | 13204 | 32645 | 16647 | 28380 | 41479 | 158800 |
| North America | 1962 | 824 | 990 | 1574 | 1217 | 543 | 518 | 7628 |
| *Non-OECD* | | | | | | | | |
| East Asia & Pacific | 0 | 285 | 177 | 472 | 1363 | 3967 | 910 | 7174 |
| Middle East & N. Africa | 95 | 53 | 74 | 0 | 235 | 345 | 141 | 943 |
| Total | 36868 | 19848 | 18248 | 36311 | 21811 | 41662 | 47675 | 222423 |
| **World Total** | 39230 | 24762 | 25334 | 53263 | 43473 | 53656 | 63934 | 303652 |

* Only in South Africa.
Source: Calculated from *Privatisation International Yearbook* (various issues), Privatisation International Ltd, London.

privatization proceedings and the income groups of the geographical regions. The lower the income the fewer the sales and vice versa. Such an association can be linked to Gerschenkron's (1962) thesis on the role of the state in backward economies where the state has to do more in order to substitute for the lack of private entrepreneurs.

Within developing countries, as Table 4.5 asserts, the expansion of privatization activities tends to concentrate on particular regions. Without any doubt the market revolution in Latin America and the Caribbean countries, particularly in Argentina, Brazil, Chile and Mexico, has had a major impact on the total value of assets transferred from the public to the private sector and, therefore, in 1988 nearly all major privatization sales took place in this region. Major divestitures also took place in East Asian and Pacific countries, and the former socialist countries, particularly in 1992, when the privatization wave entered the implementation phase in Eastern Europe. The regions with the fewest transactions were sub-Saharan

Table 4.5  Total privatization proceedings in developing countries by geographical regions, 1988–94 (US$ million)

| Years Regions | 1988 | 1989 | 1990 | 1991 | 1992 | 1993 | 1994 | Total 1988–94 |
|---|---|---|---|---|---|---|---|---|
| Sub-Saharan Africa | 8 | 1435* | 25 | 0 | 0 | 0 | 410 | 1878 |
| East Asia & Pacific | 0 | 2550 | 1430 | 852 | 4133 | 5674 | 5867 | 20506 |
| South Asia | 0 | 0 | 0 | 13 | 343 | 775 | 2737 | 3868 |
| Middle East & North Africa | 95 | 53 | 74 | 0 | 235 | 711 | 522 | 1690 |
| Latin America & Caribbean | 2354 | 485 | 4639 | 14783 | 15009 | 6334 | 5636 | 49240 |
| East Europe & Central Asia | 0 | 130 | 64 | 530 | 1565 | 1750 | 825 | 4864 |
| Rest of Europe | 0 | 659 | 1105 | 1246 | 1975 | 1062 | 1323 | 7370 |
| Total | 2457 | 5312 | 7337 | 17424 | 23260 | 16306 | 17320 | 89416 |
| % of World Total | 6.26 | 21.45 | 28.96 | 28.96 | 53.50 | 30.39 | 27.09 | 29.45 |

* Only in South Africa.
Source: As Table 4.4.

Africa, apart from South Africa in 1989, the Middle East and North Africa, and South Asia, as Figure 4.2 shows.

Despite the increase in the sales of SOEs in developing countries, their contribution to the total output has not changed. According to a recent study by the World Bank (*Bureaucrats in Business: The Economics and Politics of Government Ownership*) 10.2 per cent of the total GDP in developing countries was produced by SOEs in 1991 in comparison with 9.1 per cent in 1978. In the case of sub-Saharan Africa the share was even higher than the average (17.3 per cent in 1991 in comparison with 18.6 per cent in 1978) (World Bank Policy Research Report, 1995, Table A.1, p. 268).

In short, the scope of actual privatization in developing countries, particularly the poorest, is limited although the

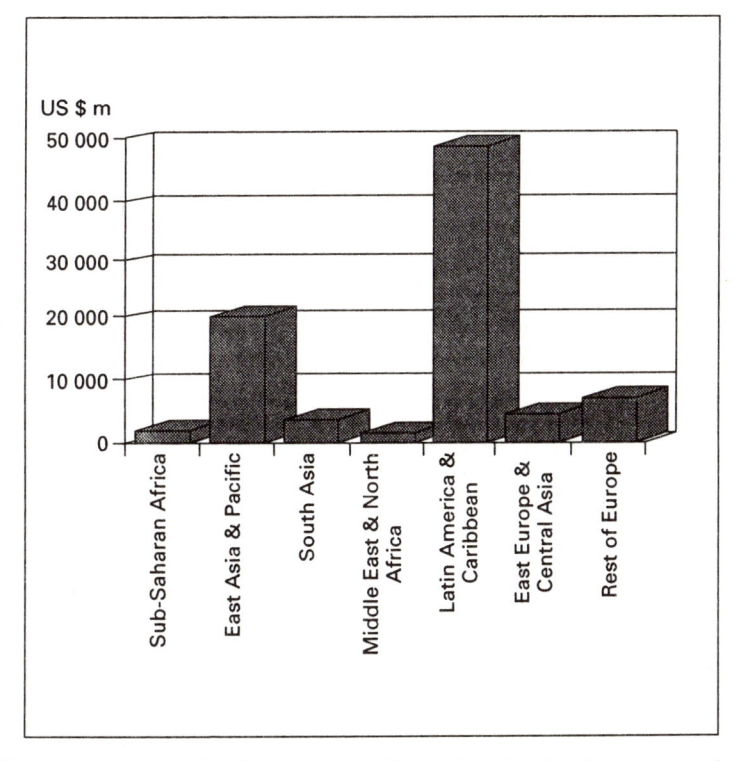

*Figure* 4.2 Privatization proceedings in developing countries, 1988–94, by geographical regions

governments of those countries are trying to convince international aid institutions and donor governments that they are transferring their enterprises to the private sector. In reality however, the *implementation phase* is the harder for the decision-makers because economic, social, and political conditions are far from stable.

After these introductory insights we now turn to the empirical work conducted by different scholars regarding privatization in developing countries. They are rarely brought together in the literature, hence this review.

At the microeconomic level, Section 4.2 answers the most important question in the privatization debate: is there solid empirical evidence to support a belief in the superiority of private over public ownership?

The macro-level, on the other hand, raises a number of questions. First, what are the factors determining private investment in developing countries and in particular the effects of public investment on private sector investment? Second, is there conclusive evidence of an adverse relationship between government size and economic growth? Third, what is the impact of public enterprises on budgetary deficits in developing countries? Fourth, is there a correlation between privatization and development in its wider definition (including the human development index). Fifth, what are the reasons for privatization in developing countries? Is privatization domestically motivated by the desire for efficiency or is it imposed by external factors? There are also the distributional consequences of privatization. Who are the major winners and the losers from such a policy?

## 4.2 EFFICIENCY COMPARISON

Advocates of privatization argue that private ownership restores incentives which promote productive efficiency. To examine this claim, this section brings together evidence from about 15 empirical studies that have attempted to compare public and private enterprise performance. One of the countries studies is Levy's (1981), which investigated private and public enterprises in three industries in Iraq and found that public firms were more technically efficient while private industries were more allocatively efficient than their counterparts. The study concluded that there is a significant possibility for economic growth if an increase of allocative efficiency in the public sector is accompanied by an increase of technical efficiency in private industry. Likewise, Abu Shair (1988) found that, although the productivity of labour in both private and public industrial enterprises increased in Iraq over the period 1970–85, the annual growth for labour productivity in the private sector was 6.7 per cent while in the public industrial sector it was only 5.3 per cent.

Aylen (1988) compared two publicly-owned steel enterprises, one (POSCO) in South Korea and its counterpart (SAIL) in India, and found that labour productivity per worker in SAIL was only one-tenth that in its counterpart. Trying to identify what specific aspects influenced performance, Aylen confirmed that it is not ownership but rather market environment, firm organization and managerial incentives which determine a firm's performance.

Millward (1987) studied the comparative performance of public and private enterprises in less developed countries (LDCs) in terms of productivity and cost effectiveness over the period 1976–86. There was no statistically significant evidence that private enterprises in LDCs functioning at the same scale of operation as their counterparts in the public sector are technically more efficient.

Ilokwu (1991) carried out a comparative analysis of 24 enterprises in Nigeria (12 SOEs and 12 private enterprises) across four industries over the period 1980–89 and reached the conclusion that public enterprises produced a lower performance (return on investment) and were less efficient (annual turnover ratios). Across the four industries (airline, insurance, banking and manufacturing), public enterprises were 1.9 percentage points lower than private enterprises in the return on investment ratio and 12.2 percentage points lower in the annual turnover ratios. However, public insurance companies outperformed their counterparts in the private sector.

Perera (1991) compared the performance of the public and private bus systems in Sri Lanka. The study revealed that the average operating cost of the private bus sector was 2.5 times lower than in the public transport system. Likewise, the productivity ratios for cost efficiency asserted the superiority of the private bus system. The same results were found when comparing labour efficiency between the two types of ownership.

Ruangrong (1992) examined the efficiency parameters of the monopoly state-owned electric utility in Thailand (EGAT) and proclaimed that productivity growth rose around 1.15 per cent annually during the study period. There was also no divergence in total factor productivity (TFP) growth between EGAT and the private industrial manufacturing sector.[3] Ruangrong concluded that there was no justification for the privatization of EGAT because it was fulfilling its objective of cost minimization.

Balassa in 1987 reviewed eight previous studies which had compared the relative efficiency of public and private enterprises in developing countries. The author, one of the strongest advocates of privatization, concluded that private enterprises are more efficient than their counterparts in the public sector and that therefore privatization will enhance efficiency. However, Millward (1987), who made use of a number of the same studies reviewed by Balassa, such as Tyler (1979), Hill (1982), Gupta (1982, cited in both Balassa, 1987, and Millward, 1987) reached a different conclusion.

Dollar (1990), in an econometric analysis, studied the change in TFP growth and the change in allocative efficiency of 20 Chinese industrial SOEs. In comparison with the pre-reform period (before 1978) these enterprises experienced in 1982 a rapid growth in TFP as well as an improvement in allocative efficiency. Efficiency gains also exhibited a positive correlation with the share of enterprise profit distributed to workers and managers. The evidence demonstrated that a reform of the incentive system rather than a change in ownership played a significant role in enhancing the efficiency of these enterprises. Within the same context, a study by Park (1987) showed that changing the system for evaluating the performance of public enterprises in South Korea played a major role in enhancing the performance of public managers. The revision not only adjusted the mechanism of accountability but also provided better guidelines for rewarding the efforts of management and employees.

Boardman and Vining (1989) investigated the relationship between type of ownership and economic performance for the 489 largest manufacturing and mining corporations outside the United States operating in a competitive environment. The sample consisted of 409 private companies (PCs), 23 mixed enterprises (MEs) and 57 SOEs. It was found that the average return on equity was only positive (4.3 per cent) in the private companies. The rate of return in PCs on the other hand was 14.5 per cent higher than that in SOEs and 18.4 per cent higher than in MEs. The efficiency indicator of average sales per asset showed PCs to have the highest ratio; however, in terms of sales per employee, MEs outperformed SOEs and PCs. The conclusion of the study was that partial privatization is worse than either complete privatization or complete state ownership.

A number of financial ratios taken from a large sample of public and private enterprises in Chile during the period 1980–87 were studied by Hachette and Luders (1992, as cited in Luders, 1993, p. 114). They concluded that private enterprises as a group were slightly more efficient than SOEs. The reasons behind this efficiency were a minimum of political interference in SOE operations during the period and the positive effect of a hard budget on the opportunistic behaviour of SOE managers. The first factor reduced transaction costs while the second reduced agency costs. However, by employing a different methodology to analyse efficiency Hachette, Luders, Tagle and others claimed that in five out of six large privatized enterprises, internal efficiency had increased as a result of privatization (Luders, 1993, p. 114).

Cakmak and Zaim (1992) for their part studied the comparative efficiency of public, private and mixed enterprises in the Turkish cement industry. The examination of the 41 cement plants comprising 17 SOEs, 18 private enterprises, and 6 mixed enterprises in 1990, revealed that the ownership factor had no effect on the economic efficiency of the different plants. Market structure or competition was the driving force behind improvements in the productive efficiency of the 41 plants. Efficiency gains from divestiture policies, the scholars concluded, are likely to be negligible unless accompanied by enhanced competition in the marketplace.

Likewise, in the case of Malaysia, Mohamed (1992) measured the average percentage growth rate of productivity in public versus private firms in 31 industries and found that there were only four cases in which the private sector appeared to be more efficient: fish canning and preserving; cocoa, chocolate and sugar confectionery; sawmills; and structural clay. On the other hand, there were 12 industries where public enterprises performed better than the private ones. The structural features of the market in which the industries operate are more important and the study, therefore, rejected the property rights hypothesis which suggests that SOEs are inherently less efficient than their counterparts because of the transferability constraints in public ownership.

Potts (1995), in his study of the nationalization and denationalization of estate agriculture in Tanzania over the period 1967–90, claimed that 'there is no conclusive empirical evidence to suggest that the economic performance of the public sector estates in Tanzania has been worse than that of the private sector in general' (Potts, 1995, p. 194). He observed that during the period 1970–85, the production performance of estates deteriorated significantly in both the private and public sectors while those owned by foreign companies performed better than the national ones. The reasons behind the deterioration lay outside the ownership effect. Factors such as institutional change, access to foreign exchange, the exchange rate effects, taxation policies, and the general economic environment played a major role in determining overall performance. Potts concluded that privatization would not be able to solve problems of productivity without the injection of new external resources into the agricultural estates.

Weiss (1995) examined the effect of ownership on performance for the largest 500 industrial enterprises in Mexico. Three measures of firm performance – sales, sales per worker, and sales per total assets – were estimated for these enterprises for the period 1985–90. After constructing a cross-sectional regression model to explain the changes in the performance indicators brought about by variables reflecting scale, industrial structure, general industry trends (measured by changes in nominal protection) and ownership, the evidence showed that there was no relationship between economic efficiency and ownership type. According to Weiss's estimates, performance was strongly influenced by industry-level trends, with some influence from market structure, as measured by concentration and protection. However, foreign companies, in the same industry, were more efficient than national firms after size differences were taken into account. The empirical study concluded that there was no support for the view that state ownership *per se* implies a poor performance. The scholar emphasized, however, that such a finding may have been due to the privatization of many poorly performing SOEs in Mexico before 1985. Nevertheless, he stressed that factors such as economies of scale, market structure and industry trends may be more important in explaining a firm's performance than ownership type.

Broadly, then, the international empirical evidence is consistent with the theoretical material presented in Chapter 3. Reviewing the empirical work at the micro-level in developing countries has produced no conclusive evidence to confirm the superior efficiency of private enterprises over their counterparts in the public sector. Generalizations derived from property right and principal–agent theories about the effects of ownership on efficiency are not evidenced in all the empirical work. On the contrary, factors such as organizational and market structure, enterprise size and other institutional factors have been found to play an important role in determining the efficiency of an enterprise whether it is in the public or the private domain. It is also important to note that the different methodologies for the calculation of efficiency employed in the various empirical studies can in themselves lead to different conclusions from similar sets of data. Privatization, therefore, might not be beneficial unless it is accompanied by competition in the marketplace.

## 4.3 THE FACTORS DETERMINING PRIVATE INVESTMENT

This group of studies concentrates on the factors which determine private investment in LDCs; in particular, the hypothesis of public investment 'crowding-out' private investment.

An econometric study by Greene and Villanueva (1991) analysed the economic factors determining the average levels of private investment in 23 developing countries over the period 1975–87. The econometric evidence indicated that the rate of private investment was positively related to the rate of public sector investment. The researchers made reference to the importance of categorizing public investment into two kinds, long-term investment (in infrastructure) and short-term investment (other activities) but the study found no statistical evidence to support the argument of 'crowding-out'.

The International Finance Corporation (IFC) of the World Bank undertook a study of private investment in 30 developing countries during the period 1970–88 (Madarassy, 1990). In order to examine the 'crowding-out' hypothesis the IFC looked at 31 episodes when public investment was increased by more than half a per cent annually over a three-year moving average period. In nearly 55 per cent of the cases private investment (as a percentage of GDP) also grew while in the remaining cases it declined. Thus, there is no conclusive evidence that in developing countries public investments support private investment or that they compete with it.

Blejer and Khan (1984) examined the impact of government economic policy on private investment in a sample of 24 developing countries over the period 1971–79 and concluded that there was a quantitatively important role for public investment in the process of private capital formation. However, although the researchers advocated the 'crowding-out' hypothesis, their study was not able to provide any powerful evidence for it.

Rodrick (1991) investigated the relationship between policy uncertainty and private investment in developing countries and established that the uncertainty deriving from reform policies in developing countries may have a more harmful effect on private investment. After developing a model to measure the effect of uncertainty on private investment he reviewed more than 10 empirical studies which supported his hypothesis and concluded that economic liberalization and 'getting the price right' might have a negligible effect on private investment in developing countries when compared with policy stability and continuity.

A study by Pradhan, Ratha and Sarma (1990) dealt with the relationship between public and private investment in India under different modes of allocation and financing public investments. The research group used an 18-sector computable general equilibrium model and demonstrated that, although public investment crowds out private investment the economy is better off with increased public investment in terms of its effect on total investment, growth and distribution of income. As a result they took the view that the 'crowding-out hypothesis, when considered in a wider perspective, need not be undesirable' (Pradhan *et al.*, 1990, p. 115).

In the case of Latin American countries Cardoso (1993) investigated the issue of private investment from different perspectives. He drew attention to the argument of the 'over-extended' public sector and its poor performance and stated that 'even though the performance of the public sector has been strongly criticized, the empirical evidence shows that there is an important complementarity between public and private investment' (Cardoso, 1993, p. 842). In his regression model for the relationship between public and private investment in six countries he estimated that a one-percentage-point increase in the share of public investment in GDP increases the share of private investment in GDP by more than half a percentage point. Nevertheless, he also observed that the crowding-out hypothesis may hold if there is an increase in budget deficits since government borrowing from the local credit market is likely to crowd out private investment because of the subsequent increase in interest rates and the reduction in the availability of credit to the private sector.

In a similar econometric study covering 15 developing countries Serven (1993) investigated the effect on the private investment/GDP ratio of a one-point increase in five variables; public investment/GDP, foreign debt/GDP, real GDP growth, inflation instability, and the real exchange rate instability. The regression results indicated that an increase in the ratio of public investment/GDP by one percentage point raised the private investment ratio by 0.257 per cent. More significantly, a reduction in the public investment ratio contributed to a deterioration in the private investment ratio of about a half per cent. The main upshot was, government investment is necessary because 'even if austerity and liberalization consolidate, the market equilibrium may not bring renewed investment and growth' (Serven, 1993, p. 137).

Fontaine and Geronimi (1995) in their examination of the crowding-out and -in hypothesis in sub-Saharan Africa established that public investment in infrastructure has a long-term complementarity rather than a substitutability effect on private investment due to its backward and forward linkages. However, in the short term an inverse relationship may exist due to financial factors (sensitivity to the rate of interest). By using a time-series analysis on a country-by-country basis for eight African countries, the results suggested that six countries obtained significant but contradictory results. In Kenya, Gambia and Malawi there was a direct 'crowding-out' effect while in Burundi, Côte d'Ivoire and Gabon there was a 'crowding-in' effect and in two countries (Mauritius and Senegal) there was a 'crowding-nil' effect. Therefore, the scholars suggested that policy-makers cannot rely on such a hypothesis to determine policy because they need to be cautious. Even when they analysed the effect of privatization on private investment in three groups of African countries (non-, limited and strong privatizers) they discovered that privatization itself does not bring about a significant increase in private investment: rather 'it should follow the restoration of private investment', which is more related to incentives within the economic environment (p. 158).

Although there is a widespread belief that there is an 'overextended' public sector or investment by this sector in developing countries, a calculation of the trends in private investment provided by Pfeffermann and Madarassy (1992) revealed a different conclusion. An analysis of the data for 47 developing countries indicated that during the period 1981–85 private investment, as a share of total investment, amounted to about 56 per cent while during the period 1986–91 it increased to about 59 per cent. However, there was a wide gap between different developing regions. For example, private investment in eight East Asian countries was on average about 68 per cent of total investment during the period 1980–91 whereas in 18 Latin American countries it stood at about 60 per cent for the same period. In other words, despite the weight of private investment in the Latin American countries their economic performance was still below that achieved in the East Asian countries. The reasons for good or bad economic efficiency shift therefore from the traditional vision of the effect of ownership geometry to other institutional factors differentiating the two regions. These have not been taken into account by the advocates of privatization.

## 4.4 THE RELATIONSHIP BETWEEN GOVERNMENT SIZE AND ECONOMIC GROWTH

Seven empirical studies are available which have examined the relationship between government intervention and/or government size and the economic growth of developing countries.

Singh (1985, as cited in Shackleton, 1986, p. 434) carried out an econometric analysis of 73 developing countries aiming to assess the impact of government intervention (regulatory role of the state, its level of nationalization on a numerical scale) on economic growth. The study pointed out the significant negative effect of such intervention on a country's rate of economic growth (other factors constant).

Landau (1983) took a sample of 104 developed countries and LDCs (including 8 major oil-exporting countries) over the period 1961–76 and found that the size of government (share of government consumption expenditure in GDP) was negatively correlated to the rate of growth in per capita GDP. He confirmed that the relationship was negative and statistically significant for both lower- and higher-income countries.

Another study by Nunnenkump (1986) assessed the effect of public enterprises (their share in output and investment) on economic performance (real growth in GDP, gross fixed investment, industrialization level and the growth of employment) but was unable to detect any statistically significant cross-country relationships between the role of public enterprises and general economic performance with the exception of the industrialization level, which showed itself to be positive.

An econometric study by Scully (1989) covered 115 market economies including 93 LDCs in the period 1960–80. The analysis indicated that the size of the state (measured by government expenditure as a fraction of national output) was negatively correlated with economic growth (growth rate of real GDP), with each one percentage increase in the size of government in 1960 or during the 20-year period of study reducing the growth rate by roughly 0.1 per cent. The same negative trend was found in the size of government and economic efficiency (technical or production efficiency).

Khan and Reinhart (1990) separated the effects of private and public investment on economic growth in a sample of 24 LDCs over the period 1970–79. After developing a simple growth model that allowed private and public investment to exercise differential effects on output, the study found that private investment plays a more important role than public investment in increasing long-term economic growth. Public investment appeared to have no statistically significant effect on growth. Nevertheless, the researchers indicated that their conclusion was related only to the direct effects of public investment, stating that 'it is quite possible that public investment has positive indirect effects on growth' (Khan and Reinhart, 1990, p. 25). In other words government investment in infrastructure and human capital may have a complementary effect on long-term investment in the private sector as well as a positive effect on the long-term growth of the economy. The policy implications are:

> governments should aim at creating conditions which make private investment attractive. These conditions can range from the most general – establishing a stable macroeconomic environment, provision of adequate legal and institutional arrangements for the protection of private property – to more specific ones, such as adequate access to credit and to imported inputs by private investors (ibid., p. 25).

Kirkpatrick (1986) looked at a sample of 23 LDCs and established a negative, but statistically insignificant, relationship between the share of public enterprise output in GDP and the growth in income in these countries during the 1970s. Cook and Kirkpatrick (1988) pointed out that the argument for an 'overextended' public sector in LDCs is empirically unproven and the evidence of a negative relationship between the size of the public sector and macroeconomic performance is inconclusive.

Finally Ram (1986) analysed the effect of government size on economic growth for 115 market economies over the period 1960–80 and found a positive correlation between the two variables. Productivity in the government sector, moreover, appeared to be higher when compared with the private sector, particularly during the 1960s.

So, the relationship between government size and economic growth, although negative in most of the empirical studies, is insufficient to support an absolute rejection of government intervention and investment in the economy. The difficult question is: is there an *ideal* size of the state that supports economic growth and sustains development? Economists have yet to come up with a definitive answer. The significance of the above studies, then, derives from their recommendation of a higher-quality government intervention. In other words, it is no longer right to assume, for example, that public spending is bad, because public resources can be mobilized for selective activities (e.g. infrastructure, technology transfer, R&D, training, etc.) where such spending can encourage and support private investment.


## 4.5 THE RELATIONSHIP BETWEEN PUBLIC ENTERPRISES AND BUDGETARY DEFICIT

One of the main arguments for privatizing public enterprises in developing countries is their negative impact on the budgetary balance. Short (1984), in his international statistical comparison, found that the overall deficit of public enterprises in the mid-1970s in a sample of 12 industrial countries was only 1.7 per cent of GDP as opposed to 3.9 per cent of GDP in a sample of 25 LDCs. After the deduction of government transfers (subsidies) the public enterprises' overall deficit increased to 3.5 per cent and subsequently 5.5 per cent. His conclusion was that public enterprises in LDCs are a major cause of stabilization problems (inflation and balance of payment difficulties).

Likewise, the World Bank in its 1988 *World Development Report* (*WDR*) asserted that the net budgetary transfers to state-owned enterprises in eight developing countries ranged during 1983–88 from more than one per cent of GDP in the Dominican Republic to more than 5 per cent in Sri Lanka.[4] However, the Report claimed that there were public enterprises which made sizeable positive contributions to the budget. According to the Report the reason behind the negative budgetary impact of public enterprises was that 'budgetary transfers have thereby been the unintended outcome of poor decisions in investment, pricing, and management' (World Bank, 1988, p. 169).

Waterbury (1992) studied the relationship between public enterprises and the adjustment process in LDCs by focusing on the problems of public enterprises in four countries: Egypt, India, Mexico and Turkey. Part of his work was devoted to the effect of the public enterprises in those countries on the budgetary deficit. He asserted that as a percentage of GDP the public enterprise budgetary deficit was 9.0 per cent in Egypt

(1986–87), 3.2 per cent in India (1988–89), 2.0 per cent in Mexico (1987), and 2.7 per cent in Turkey (1990). The scholar noted that according to the figures above, 'Turkey and Mexico run SOE deficits that are proportionately as large as the total public deficit of the United States' (Waterbury, 1992, p. 197). However, in the case of Egypt the public enterprise deficit cannot be compared with that of other countries. His conclusion, derived from his introductory argument, was that 'the SOE sector in developing countries is the major cause of the public deficit, which in turn fuels inflation, reduces international creditworthiness, crowds out private borrowers, and impedes export promotion' (ibid., p. 183).

In his study of public enterprise reform programmes in developing countries Galal (1991) emphasized that there have been many attempts to reduce the budgetary burden of public enterprises in a number of countries. In Thailand, for example, the reform of the public enterprise sector has remitted to the government more than it received during the period 1983–88. Likewise, in Mauritius, government transfers to public enterprises declined from Rs 290 million in 1983 to Rs 160 million in 1985. However, in other countries such as Malawi and Senegal the net transfers from the treasury to public enterprises increased. Thus, the evidence of the budgetary impact resulting from the reform of public enterprises, as the researcher contended, is inconclusive. Failure, however, was the result of three factors: subsidy reductions were not accompanied by a programme of restructuring at the enterprise level; reform efforts concentrated only on one element of the equation, that is the transfers from the treasury, while neglecting the second element, namely, the outflow of funds from the public enterprises; finally, the important elements of the budgetary impact of public enterprises are implicit in the pattern of exemptions and preferential treatment of all kinds.

In summary, the studies above have accused public enterprises in LDCs of having a negative impact on the public budget. In a recent study the savings–investment deficit of the SOEs in 45 developing countries was found to be near to zero for middle-income countries while it was about 2 per cent of GDP for the low-income countries (*The Economist*, 2 December 1995, p. 120). Nevertheless, there are success cases where reforming public enterprises proved to have a positive budgetary impact. Privatization will, therefore, not be the only solution to a country's fiscal crisis.

## 4.6 THE RELATIONSHIP BETWEEN PRIVATIZATION AND DEVELOPMENT

Yoder, Brokholder and Friesen (1991), in empirical work based on a sample of 45 Third World countries, aimed to examine whether there exists an association between privatization (measured by private sector spending as a share of GNP) and development (measured by per capita income, life expectancy at birth, literacy rate, infant mortality rate, income distribution, and GNP growth rates). The distinction between this empirical study and all others is that it has explained development as a mixture of growth and other human development indicators rather than concentrating on the GNP growth rates as a meaning of development.[5]

After dividing the sample into three income groups, the researchers concluded that there was no support for the argument of an 'over-extended' public sector in LDCs. The private sector on average contributed 74 per cent of GNP and in no case did the public sector contribute more than 29 per cent to the GNP. Moreover, there was no statistically significant correlation at the 0.05 confidence level between privatization (measured by the size of the private sector) and any of the development indicators. There was a negative, though not statistically significant, relationship between privatization and the development indicators for 21 of the countries included in the sample. At the 0.10 confidence level, there was a statistically significant positive relationship (a) between privatization and average GNP growth rates for the low-income countries, and (b) between privatization and the share of income going to the lowest income groups (in the middle-income and upper-middle-income countries).

Using the empirical findings of this study, the research group concluded that 'the claims of privatization have been overstated and unsubstantiated' (Yoder *et al.*, 1991, p. 432). Rather than concluding that the cure must be in the private sector, the scholars argued that the size of the public or the private sector will not make a significant difference because the difference may be found in the investigation of the regulatory environment, trade policies, and fiscal and monetary policy; in other words, the institutional factors which determine interactions in the complex process of development.

## 4.7 THE REASONS BEHIND PRIVATIZATION

Responses to economic crises are shaped by a range of internal and external pressures, but they are also strongly influenced by the intellectual lenses through which economic advisers and political leaders perceive the crisis and the available options. Ramamurti's study in 1992 tested five hypotheses regarding the reasons for privatization, using a sample of 83 developing countries. Within this sample there were 34 non-privatizers, 21 cautious privatizers, and 28 actively privatizing countries. The hypotheses examined were that privatization occurs in countries characterized by (a) higher fiscal pressure on governments (high budgetary deficit, large domestic public debt, and large external debt), (b) higher dependency on loans from international organizations (World Bank and IMF), (c) a large share of SOEs in total investment, (d) inferior SOE performance in comparison with non-privatizers, and (e) lower long-term growth. The empirical test of these hypotheses revealed that privatization occurs in countries with higher financial problems, such as a large budgetary deficit and external debt, as a percentage of GDP. There is also a positive correlation between privatization and dependency on loans from international organizations. That is to say, the greater a country's dependence on loans from the World Bank and IMF, the greater the probability of its being an active privatizer. However, the econometric analysis does not support the assumption that privatization is related to poor financial performance by SOEs and poorer long-term growth. The researcher pointed out that in Latin American and Asian countries, the increasing trend towards privatization is related to their past 'overuse' of SOEs (larger weight in the economy) and their faster-growing private sector.

In Africa, on the other hand, privatization has been imposed by external factors, particularly the pressure exercised by the World Bank and IMF, even though the conditions for privatization were not necessarily appropriate. In fact, the study found that in African countries 'privatizers did not have significantly larger SOE sectors than nonprivatizers, nor did they experience growth rates that were significantly higher than that of nonprivatizers' (Ramamurti, 1992, p. 241). On the other hand, the set of opportunities provided through privatization to the multi-national corporations (MNCs) has provided the latter with new avenues to gain entry into sectors that were previously barred.

Sader's study of the relationship between privatization and foreign investment in developing countries revealed that privatizing infrastructural services might attract substantial inflows of foreign direct investment (FDI). Over the period 1988–92 FDI was the most common method of foreign participation in privatization transactions in the Third World. About 10 per cent of FDI inflows was linked to privatization transactions during 1988–92, that is US$14.5 billion (Sader, 1993, p. 22). Although the sale of SOEs in sub-Saharan Africa is relatively low in global terms, this area depends more than other developing regions on foreign investors to privatize. Foreigners contributed about 37 per cent to the total privatization revenues generated in Africa (excluding South Africa) during the five-year period. The reasons are mainly linked to the conditionality attached to structural adjustment loans given by the World Bank and the IMF and shortage in domestic finance and heavy debt, just as Ramamurti concluded.

Recent statistics also show that almost $70 billion of FDI flew into Latin American countries between 1990 and 1994, and a large part of this was attracted in by privatization, as utilities such as telecoms, electricity, as well as airline firms were put up for sale (*The Economist*, 9 December 1995).

The problem is that a government's desire to sell enterprises and raise revenue from asset sales to balance the budget means that no objectives, and in particular economic efficiency, can effectively be attained. Governments must be clear about their objectives: receiving maximum income from privatization, attracting foreign capital and investment into the economy, improving the management and efficiency of the enterprises to be privatized or, rolling back the state's role in the economy.

## 4.8 THE RELATIONSHIP BETWEEN PRIVATIZATION AND THE DISTRIBUTION OF GAINS AND LOSSES

Whether privatization benefits the poor or the rich is a question of considerable importance because far more than in any other industrialized countries, developing countries' privatization has benefited vested interests.[6] There are three studies which have investigated the effects of privatization on the distribution of gains and losses between domestic consumers, shareholders, employees and foreigners.

Jones and Abbas (1992) studied three cases in Malaysia; Malaysian Airlines, Kelang Container Terminal and Sports Toto. In the first case the domestic consumers lost around 600 million Ringgit and the major beneficiaries were foreign consumers (3196 million Ringgit) (ibid., Table no. 12-31). In the second case, the domestic consumers benefited by only 58 million Ringgit, and foreigners by 29 million Ringgit, while the major beneficiaries were the domestic concentrated shareholders (109 million Ringgit) (ibid., Table no. 13-17). In the case of the gambling company Sports Toto, the society gained 121 million Ringgit, the government 147 million Ringgit and private buyers 112 million Ringgit, while the main losers were the formal and informal gambling sectors (−69 million Ringgit). Thus, it appears that the consumers lost in one and gained in the other two.

In the case of Chile, Galal (1992) selected three privatized companies for his empirical study of the consequences of privatization. The privatization of the electricity generating company (CHILGNER) had no benefits for consumers because the company was a price taker; however, the private domestic shareholders benefited by Ch$3.8 billion and foreign shareholders by Ch$2.7 billion (ibid., Table no. 8-27). In the second case, the electricity distribution company (ENERSIS) shareholders were the biggest winners (Ch$42.9 billion) while consumers were better off by Ch$7.7 billion (ibid., Table no. 9-27). According to Galal, the sale of the telecommunication company (Compañia de Teléfonos de Chile) resulted in gains to consumers of Ch$516 billion while private shareholders benefited by Ch$8 billion and foreign shareholders by Ch$39 billion (ibid., Table no. 10-26). In total, two out of these divestiture cases were distribution-enhancing in relation to impact on consumers while one was neutral.

Tandon (1992) examined three Mexican privatized companies. The privatization of the telecommunication company (TELEMEX) resulted in large reductions in consumer gains because of large price increases during 1988–91 (ibid., pp. 18–19). This may have been related to the fact that more than 50 per cent of the company is owned by foreign shareholders, who were the main winners (ibid., Table no. 16-15). In the second case, the privatization of Aeroméxico led to a net loss on the side of consumers while the government and the buyers of the company gained the most (ibid., p. 35). The third case demonstrating the effect of privatization on distribution is that of Mexicana Airline. An analysis of distributional impact reveals net losses on the side of domestic and foreign consumers while the major winners were the government and domestic shareholders (ibid., Table no. 18-17). Thus, in total, privatization led to consumer net losses in all three cases although the first two might indicate total gains after taking into account other parties such as shareholders and the government.

In summary, these nine cases reveal that shareholders are the main winners while consumers, in most cases, were the main losers. This contrasts with the conclusion of the three researchers, who argued that the welfare effect should be taken into account rather than the distributional impact on the part of consumers alone. Their studies, which formed part of the 1992 World Bank Conference on 'Welfare Consequences of Selling Public Enterprises', concluded, as the conference did, that privatization can enhance welfare rather than reduce it.

Another dimension of privatization is its impact on employment. In Bangladesh, for example, the government privatized 31 jute mills out of the 62 existing in 1983. Bhaskar and Khan (1995) reported that average employment in the state sector was 5693 workers in 1983. This increased to 5754 workers in 1988. In contrast, with the initiation of privatization, the private mills employed only 3112 workers and reduced their workforce further to 2948 workers in 1988. Although much of the difference in the state sector was due to the giant Adamjee mill, which accounted for 20 per cent of state-sector employment, the percentage change of employment in the two sets of mills established that privatization has had a negative impact on employment: 'privatization had a large negative effect on white-collar employment, and a smaller but still significant negative effect on the employment of permanent manual workers' (p. 271). Likewise, the privatization of the railroads in Argentina laid off 70 per cent of the prior workforce (*Civil Engineering*, April 1995, p. 24).

Despite the contradictions between the findings of the World Bank and others on the social impact of privatization, the problem is whether the state possesses the capacity and the will to examine such impact or not. While such tendencies exist in countries such as South Korea (Kim *et al.*, 1994), many governments may overlook this dimension and therefore run the risk of accumulating resistance to reforms. States in developing societies typically seek to preserve the fundamental elements of the socio-economic order and to promote powerful elites. Thus, privatization tends to favour capitalists because it promotes a new division between capital and labour. This means that state elites in charge of the policy-making machinery as well as powerful members of the capitalist class are likely to be very important players in the politics of privatization and its social impact.

## 4.9 SUMMARY AND CONCLUSIONS

From this review of the empirical evidence there is no conclusive evidence on the microeconomic level to support the argument for private-ownership superiority.

Likewise, on the macro-level, there is no clear-cut evidence that public investment is 'crowding out' private investment, but in many studies it has been found that there is a complementarity effect between public and private investment.

Most of the empirical evidence reviewed suggests that the relationship between government size and economic growth is negative but such a relation is vague and dependent both on the circumstances of each country and the methodology employed by the different scholars. There are no empirical grounds either for a rejection of government intervention or for an increase in its size. The studies appear to indicate that what is important is the quality and type of government intervention. Where SOEs proved to be a heavy burden on the budget, as is the case in many low-income countries in particular, a comprehensive programme for reforming the public sector would be pivotal. Without such an approach privatization might prove to be a more attractive cure for this problem, from the government point of view, as has been the case in many developing countries.

On the correlation between privatization and development, the empirical work concluded that there was no statistically significant correlation at the 0.05 confidence level between privatization and all the other development indicators. The work directed attention to the study of the impact of the institutional factors that may affect development. The reasons behind privatization, where investigated, suggest that higher fiscal difficulties and dependence on external finance are the main factors driving privatization in developing countries. This means that conflicts in government objectives regarding privatization have made economic efficiency subordinate to the goal of easing the budgetary deficit.

Consumers and employees, unless protected, may become the victims of privatization because ownership change also gives more power to capital over labour. Thus, foreign investors and other international financial agents may overlook the fact that privatization is a means to an end; where the means become the final objective, there is need for a more cautious approach in advising the application of such a policy in developing countries.

# 5 Privatization, Decentralization, Participation and Development

## 5.1 INTRODUCTION

Privatization is often described as the transfer of state assets and/or control (partial or full) to the private sector. The implication for development is derived from the belief that private ownership or control brings greater economic efficiency, more innovation, improved responsiveness to consumer demands, and wider choice for individuals (i.e. shares, goods). The argument of maximizing profits also implies increased savings and greater investment, which in their turn produce rapid growth and higher incomes, both symbols of development. This approach can be called an 'income-centred' approach to development.

Privatization can also be defined as decentralizing decision-making away from the monopolistic centralized bureaucracies and back to the market. Taking this definition in retrospect, this chapter will investigate the relationship between privatization and development using concepts such as 'choice', 'participation', 'voice', 'appropriate technology', 'linkages', and 'territorial decentralization' or 'devolution'. Such an approach embraces a wider concept of development and in particular looks at human development centred on enhancing capabilities as the ultimate objective of development rather than simply growth in GNP.

The World Bank identified poverty alleviation and an increase in equity among the first considerations among its economic policy priorities for the 1990s. Is privatization, as one component of the free-market-oriented strategy strongly advocated by the Bank, able to make a positive contribution to the achievement of these goals? What is the relationship between privatization and the poor within consumer-choice perspectives?

It is often argued that privatization is the final phase of decentralization with the latter a means of achieving the former (World Bank, 1988, p. 10; Rondinelli and Nellis, 1986). Is decentralization in the context of 'giving power to the people' symmetrical with the privatization lessons experienced by LDCs?

The globalization of economic policy choices is a feature of the current economic environment, particularly after the collapse of the former Soviet Union and the end of the Cold War. Can such a globalization be of advantage to LDCs in adapting appropriate technology, internal innovation, and balanced regional development? Would privatization promote development, or would a bottom-up approach offer a genuine alternative?

## 5.2 THE MEANING OF DEVELOPMENT: GROWTH VS HUMAN DEVELOPMENT

Since the 1940s economists have been trying to reach a consensus on the meaning of development. During the 1950s and early 1960s, economic development was associated with economic growth in per capita income but in the 1970s it was redefined from the liberal aspect as growth with equity. Its new wider definition implied the reduction or elimination of poverty (basic needs), inequality, and unemployment within the context of a growing economy. The emphasis during the 1980s and 1990s has been on growth and efficiency as a way of reducing poverty, unemployment and inequality.

Development literature provides us with a number of both old and new meanings of development: historical growth; structural change; modernization; political change; decentralization and participation; redistribution and basic needs; human development; sustainability; ethics and morals (Ingham, 1993). Of these, human development and poverty reduction are the most valuable objectives of development which can be achieved by increasing political and civil liberties.[1] In the words of Ingham, 'countries whose citizens enjoyed greater political and civil liberties also performed better in people-centered measures of development, in life expectancy at birth, in real income per head and in infant survival rates' (ibid., p. 1819).

Ingham's conclusion related more closely to the 'capability approach' to development, as developed by Sen (1988, 1989, 1990) and adopted by the United Nations Development Programme (UNDP) in its Human Development Reports (HDR), than to that embodied by the World Bank in its *World Development Reports* (*WDR*), particularly that on poverty (1990).

This divergence between the World Bank and UNDP views on the meaning and objectives of development is pivotal to the analysis of privatization within a framework of decentralization. The difference of view is important for two reasons; the first is the influential role the World Bank has played, particularly from the late 1980s, in advocating and forcing the drive towards privatization in LDCs, which complemented the Bank's vision of development; the second is the Bank's income-centred and growth-dependent view of development. This separates it from the capability approach to human development, which measures development by the Human Development Index (HDI) taking into account factors such as the quality of life, life expectancy, literacy and adjusted income.

Only 13 per cent of structural adjustment loans (SALs) provided by the Bank to 21 LDCs, up to the beginning of 1986, were specifically attached to conditions of privatization of public industries or agricultural marketing facilities while 62 per cent required various forms of deregulation (Mosley, 1988, p. 134). By the first half of 1992, however, the Bank's figures reveal that 70 per cent of all SALs and 40 per cent of all sectoral adjustment loans (SECALs) were in support of privatization. In total 182 Bank operations, between 1981 and the first half of 1992, implied privatization in 63 countries, half of them in sub-Saharan Africa (Kikeri *et al.*, 1992, p. 32). Thus, there is a significant influence from the Bank in the restructuring of economic policies in developing countries.

The main differences between the capability approach to human development and the income-centred approach favoured by the World Bank lie in their means and ends. In the capability approach, Sen (1989) criticized the use of opulence measurements such as income, wealth or commodity possession and other utility measurements such as happiness, desire fulfilment, or even the simple utility of choice. Capability itself derives from the freedom to be well, which in simple terms is about the ability to live longer, be literate, be healthy and well-nourished and generally enjoy a higher quality of life. To be capable would be an end in itself.

In contrast, the World Bank approach, based on mainstream income-centred evaluation, looks exclusively at the investment in human capital (education, health, and nutrition) as a way of increasing productivity so as to increase income and growth which in turn will reduce poverty. In this case the calculation is based on the viability of the *rate of return* on such an investment. The following quotations from the *WDR* (1990) describe the means and ends.

> The principal asset of the poor is labor time. Education increases the productivity of this asset. The result at the individual level, as many studies show, is higher income. Most recent research also points to a strong link between education and economic growth (World Bank, 1990, p. 80).

> The effect of better health and nutrition on productivity is less well documented than the effect of education. An increasing number of studies, however, show a positive effect on agricultural productivity (World Bank, 1990, p. 81).

Such different approaches to the means and ends of development will subsequently affect the policies employed. The capability approach views the public provision of social services as the principal medium for human development. Even markets, according to the United Nations, are the means and human development is the end (UNDP, 1992).

The World Bank, on the other hand, 'supports privatization in the context of its broader goals of economic development and the reduction of poverty' (Kikeri *et al.*, 1992, p. 1). In this context economic development is a synonym for growth using the trickle-down argument. By contrast, the United Nations is concerned about the effects of privatization on reducing social services to the people.

In the face of rising unemployment and poverty, social security systems are finding it increasingly difficult to cope.

State-owned enterprises used to distribute most social benefits, from child care to health care to pensions. But over the past three years, these widespread automatic benefits have been dramatically curtailed and are being replaced by 'social safety nets' whose services are targeted more narrowly – and thus risk missing millions of people in desperate need (UNDP, 1993, p. 48).

In short, the meaning of development should be understood within the context of increasing human capabilities. This requires an increase in freedom through a participatory approach in which the people's well-being is the end and empowering them through decentralization represents the means.

## 5.3 PRIVATIZATION, CHOICE AND PARTICIPATION

The essence of 'public ownership' is that it provides people, as owners or as consumers, with a theoretical right to intervene in the production process. In practice, however, they do not. Therefore, according to the public choice theorists, public ownership reduces social welfare, and privatization can cut 50 per cent of the total social costs associated with public ownership (Hanke and Walters, 1990).

Privatization proponents often argue that 'choice' is the main value of privatization because the marketplace enhances the ability of individuals to choose their own share of the goods and services they demand. In other words, public choice theory believes in 'consumer sovereignty' where the market can aggregate individual choices, thus bringing about an accountable and effective means of allocating and producing goods.

The important question is whether more choice for shareholders and consumers provides everyone with an equal opportunity to participate in the markets of developing countries or not.

Privatization as a phenomenon is almost the novelty of the western countries and one of its components is the concept of 'people capitalism' as a way of broadening the ownership base, as was the case in Britain (Marsh, 1991, p. 474). In developing countries the same slogan has been adopted but with far less impact. In most developing as well as in some developed countries there are two main restrictions on the effectiveness of 'people capitalism'. The first is the relatively small size of the middle-income group who can acquire shares, and the second is the thin spread or non-existence of capital markets (Suleiman and Waterbury, 1990, p. 15). Acording to the World Bank, privatization transactions in 90 countries showed that there were 530 recorded transfers to single buyers in the countries of sub-Saharan Africa, Brazil, Italy and Spain (Nankani, 1990, p. 44). More recent data which records individual privatization transactions (over $100 million in value) between 1988 and 1991, reveals that out of 28 divestiture cases in 11 developing countries, of $41.979 billion in total value, only five, with a mere value of $3.5 billion, were transferred through public offerings while the remainder were divested through private sales (Kikeri *et al.*, 1992, Table no. 1, p. 26). This indicates that ordinary people, and the poor in particular, were excluded from the opportunity of share ownership and consequently from participation. Furthermore, even if there were such a wide share-owning base, it is likely that small shareholders would quickly sell their shares on to larger shareholders in order to generate short-term profits via the market. If privatization by broadening share ownership is unlikely to make an impact on equity ownership in Britain, as Marsh (1991, p. 475) noted, how can one expect it to have a better impact in LDCs? Carlsen, writing about Mexico said:

> Few nationals have the money or international contacts to buy government-owned companies. This constrains the number of eligible bidders, weakens bids and means that the few who are able to purchase previously state-owned enterprises can extend their economic reach, an unwelcome prospect given the extreme concentration of wealth and power in Mexican society (Carlsen, 1992, p. 19, as cited in Martin, 1993, p. 100).

In Sri Lanka 70 per cent of all shares is concentrated in the hands of about 2000 people while in Pakistan some 6000 persons hold about 80 per cent of all shares. Likewise in India less than 0.4 per cent of the total number of shareholders (in companies with capital above 50 000 Rs) held about 70 per cent of the total paid capital (Ramanadham, 1989, p. 41). Powerful political elites and the privileged are directing the process of privatization to their benefit in many countries: in Indonesia, for example, the government sold 70 per cent of the Indonesian state-owned Tyer Maker (Intirub) in 1990 to a local conglomerate, Bimantara Citra, controlled by Suharto's son (Montagu-Pollock, 1990, p. 35). The experience in Eastern European countries suggests that old communists have become the new powerful capitalists. *The Economist* (18 November 1995, p. 136) summed up the privatization efforts in Russia as 'quick and dirty'.

These examples demonstrate that unless privatization of SOEs is well designed it neither increases choice nor alleviates poverty. On the contrary, it concentrates power in the hands of the marketplace elite. This runs contrary to the objectives of development as a participatory approach to human well-being. The term 'well designed' privatization may include schemes which target specific groups, such as employee participation (e.g. employee ownership, profit sharing, and participation in decision-making) within the privatization plan. Employee participation fulfils many objectives, such as: increasing productivity; avoiding enterprise bankruptcy; broadening the distribution of ownership; and facilitating privatization procedures. For example, the People's Share Programme in South Korea allowed low-income individuals and 20 per cent of employees to purchase 75 per cent of shares (Lee, 1991, p. 15). In this way the government achieved many goals. It enhanced the distribution of income, reduced the opposition to privatization, and increased efficiency. However, only four developing countries have experienced such schemes (Argentina, Poland, Sri Lanka, and Jamaica), and until now the assessment of the experience has revealed mixed results (ibid.). On the other hand, we must not forget that opposition to such schemes may be generated from different interest groups such as managers of the same SOEs, as was the case in eight medium-sized industrial plants in Bangladesh (Ali *et al.*, 1992).

The second argument of choice is based on the belief that consumers make *rational choices* and will exercise their power by choosing among competing suppliers in the market. Here the argument of relative prices, in which the prices will determine the demand and consequently the supply, might not apply in all cases, particularly as many privatized enterprises in developing countries sustain their monopolistic position in the market. In societies with different cultures and values as well as extremely uneven income distribution, the assumption of rational choice from the western point of view might not apply because the aspirations of real individuals are shaped by the assumptions, traditions, and ideals of their society (Slater, 1989, p. 522). In other words the rational-choice assumption might be incompatible with the 'power of belief'. However, even if it were compatible, it would be the richer classes of the developing countries who would enjoy the benefits, unless privatization is well designed to enhance equal opportunity and equal access. As Sinha (1995, p. 561) puts it: 'Those who favor privatization for reducing rent-seeking would certainly be disappointed by what has happened in the cases of recent privatization.'

Another important aspect of choice according to the public choice theory and most proponents of privatization is the belief in only 'individual choice'. It might be important to recognize that choice in itself remains desirable as a value for the individual although in traditional societies, as is the case in many developing countries, 'collective choice' and 'instrumental choice' are what society is looking for in order to improve well-being and capability rather than choice as an end in itself as is the case in privatization (Higgins, 1988, p. 203; Marglin, 1990, p. 4).

So, as privatization leads to growth, choices would only expand in some dimensions, as the economic history of developing countries reveals. Thus, privatization would reduce the concepts of 'freedom of choice' and 'collective choice' to the narrower notion of 'individual choice' if it were pursued as a reaction to a financial crisis. While some people will be better off, the vast majority of the poor will be worse off and therefore 'privatization would leave development to the vagaries of exploitative forms of primitive exchange' (Riddell, 1985, p. 215). However, another explanation of choices could be derived from Hirschman's concepts of exit and voice.

## 5.4 PRIVATIZATION: EXIT OR VOICE

In his theory of *exit, voice, and loyalty* Hirschman (1970) emphasized that economists tend to use the option of market forces as the only option available to achieve equilibrium in the market. It had long been thought that the more elastic the demand, the better the economy was functioning. This option, according to Hirschman, means the *exit* option where customers of a firm or members of an organization choose to stop buying the firm's product or quit from the organization as a demonstration of their dissatisfaction with the firm's product or the organization's policies. As a result, revenue drops and a decline in membership forces management to correct their inadequate performance.

The argument against the use of the exit option alone is based on the inability of competition to lead firms/organizations to 'normal' efficiency, performance, and growth standards after they have lapsed from them. Non-market forces are not necessarily less automatic than market forces, particularly in the world of quasi-perfect competition. In this case *voice* would mean a mechanism for change from within rather than escape (exit). Voice means

> any attempt at all to change, rather than to escape from, an objectionable state of affairs, whether through individual or collective petition ... or through various types of actions and protests, including those that are meant to mobilize public opinion (Hirschman, 1970, p. 30).

In retrospect, Hirschman is advocating a participatory approach similar to that emphasized by the United Nations. The superiority of voice over exit is due to the voice option's capability of evolving in different and new directions. No such capability is available for the other option (exit). Participation, which is in this case a synonym for voice, gives people access to a 'much broader range of opportunities' (UNDP, 1993, p. 21). Hence, the justification for introducing privatization policies on their own would be as a way of employing the exit option rather than exit and voice together. So, while voice denotes an opportunity for 'change from within', exit seems to offer its supporters little challenge.

The lessons drawn from this theory can provide reformists with a new direction of thinking replacing the traditional method of using the financial discipline or the market (exit) option to introduce the recuperation initiative. The use of the two combined (exit and voice) in different proportions would depend on the environment and the history of each case under investigation. But non-market forces are no less automatic and efficient than market forces in bringing about recuperation if there is a commitment on the side of decision-makers to enhance the possibilities for 'change from within', particularly when the latter can be induced through *decentralization and democratization.* Privatization is a government reform movement rather than a social one and therefore one should be cautious because of the seven sins that may coincide with its implementation. According to the UNDP (1993, p. 50) they are:

1. Maximization of revenue rather than creating competition.
2. Replacing public monopolies with private monopolies.
3. Corruption and nepotism through non-transparent procedures.
4. Using sale proceeds only to finance budget deficits.
5. Crowding the financial market with public borrowing at a time of public disinvestment.
6. Making false promises to the workforce.
7. Relying on executive orders rather than political consensus.

We should understand that people (and their organizations) resist privatization, using the voice option (i.e. protests and riots), not because they are in favour of bureaucratization, but because they demand a reform that will give them more participation in the progress and development of their communities. The 'interest groups', as the neoclassical political economists termed them, in developing countries, especially non-governmental organizations (NGOs) (e.g. trade unions, women's movements, farmers' cooperatives, religious organizations, and the like), are the same people who elsewhere take part in 'anti-systematic' movements (referring to movements against centralization and bureaucratization) as in the case of Latin America, India, and Africa (Slater, 1989, p. 522; Wallerstein, 1974, cited in Banuri, 1990a, p. 53). The same people, with different nominations, request one important right, namely 'popular participation' through decentralization of power to them and not to the market or representatives at the centre.

## 5.5 DECENTRALIZATION AND PARTICIPATION

Decentralization is a concept with different definitions, meanings and benefits. No overwhelming consensus has been reached regarding it. The belief that decentralized development could be seen as a genuine future alternative for development in developing countries started as a reaction to the economic difficulties developing countries have faced during the last three decades, in particular the 'unbalanced development' as witnessed by uneven rural development, poverty and inequality in the distribution of income (Griffin, 1981, p. 225). Moreover, as Banuri argued (1990b, p. 98), it has been seen as a vision of the future in most developing countries. The question is whether privatization or another meaning of decentralization is seen as a vision of the future.

There are two main definitions of decentralization. The first is *functional decentralization*, which means the decentralization of production or/and services to parastatal or non-government organizations. Thus, privatization policies are included in a definition which deals with functions only. The second definition is *territorial decentralization*. This means the decentralization of government to sub-national levels such as local governments or authorities (Conyers, 1984, p. 187).

The advocates of privatization and market-oriented paradigms in general are consistent in their belief in the first definition of decentralization. Moreover, they use the two concepts of decentralization and privatization as synonyms although privatization is sometimes seen as the ultimate phase of decentralization.[2]

> The problems of providing and maintaining public services and infrastructure have brought increasing calls for decentralization and privatization, and many governments are now decentralizing responsibilities for service and infra-

structure provision, financing and management (as quoted in Rondinelli *et al.*, 1989, p. 58).

Rondinelli and his associates also believed in decentralization as 'a situation in which public goods and services are provided primarily through the revealed preferences of individuals by market mechanism' (Rondinelli *et al.*, 1989, p. 59). However, in theory at least, they emphasized that concepts such as people participation, empowerment and local democracy were included in their vision of decentralization.

The World Bank concept of decentralization is restricted to *fiscal decentralization*: where 'decentralizing both spending and revenue authority can improve the allocation of resources in the public sector by linking the cost and benefits of local public services more closely' (World Bank, 1988, p. 154).

In practice the World Bank does not advocate empowering the poor to restore the unbalanced nature of the decision-making processes and the powerful position of the government elite. Its suggestion is that poverty should be alleviated not through the *devolution* of power or territorial decentralization but by designing poverty-reduction policies that would not be resisted by the non-poor (which is not the right word) or, in real terms, the rich and powerful elite who guard the gates of the decision-makers.

> The nonpoor [sic] are usually politically powerful, and they exert a strong influence on policy. Giving the poor a greater say in local and national decision making would help to restore the balance. But since political power tends to reflect economic power, it is important to design poverty-reducing policies that would be supported, or at least not actively resisted by the nonpoor (World Bank, 1990, p. 52).

The interesting point is that the same *WDR* identified privatization among the factors that have contributed to poverty in rural areas (ibid., p. 32). As Cardoso and Iielwege (1992, p. 19) stated, 'economic poverty reflects political poverty: the poor lack the means for voicing their demands'. In this case poverty-reduction programmes will not empower the poor but rather sustain the existing power structure.

It seems that there is a consistency in the argument adopted by the international agencies and the advocates of market-oriented policies, namely that privatization should be the ultimate goal of decentralization. It is for this reason that the emphasis has to be placed on territorial rather than functional decentralization. The question to be asked is, why?

## 5.6 PRIVATIZATION VS TERRITORIAL DECENTRALIZATION

The proponents of privatization are concerned with transferring state-owned enterprises to the private sector as well as introducing competition in the market. But there are two factors which have been neglected in the analysis of privatization. The first is *space* and the second is the *structure of government.*

### 5.6.1 The Space Factor

One of the major differences between market-oriented strategies and those of territorial decentralization is that the first (without solid evidence) considers shifting the production functions from SOEs to the private sector for purely economic reasons (see Chapter 4).

In the case of territorial decentralization, development requires not only the production of goods and services but also the production of complex political, social and economic goods. Such a concept requires complex and coordinated efforts by diverse people across a large area of space. Space includes not only the geographical meaning of the word but also rules, behaviour and the institutional factors (i.e. history, politics) within this space (Miller, 1992). It is a territory where people can communicate as well as struggle to achieve prosperity within the context of their satisfaction with the process itself. The importance of this factor is that it can explain the rationality of human actions because the latter 'varies systematically and unpredictably according to the context in which the action occurs' (Barnes and Sheppard, 1992, p. 18). The dimension implies complexity, people's capacity, control of technology, innovation, participation, linkages, flexibility, and development from below and within. It refers therefore, to the territorial distribution of power:

## Decentralization and Participation

It is concerned with the extent to which power and authority are dispersed through the geographical hierarchy of the state, and the institutions and processes through which such dispersal occurs. Decentralization entails the subdivision of the state's territory into smaller areas and the creation of political and administrative institutions in those areas (Smith, 1985, p. 1).

Devolution enhances political participation or democracy as well as economic participation by increasing local entrepreneurial activities. This is not what happens to the notions of deconcentration and delegation where the central authority retains effective control and power at the local level, thereby neglecting the needs of local people.

Where privatization occurs, there is no space factor within the context of a local community, but a market where rational individuals, consumers and producers compete to maximize their utility functions, whatever they are. There are standard and quantitative ends which draw the line between efficient and inefficient. A universal approach to growth and relative unity in implementation is required. Thus, it could be described as an approach to 'development from above'.

### 5.6.2 The Structure of Government

A factor not included in the privatization prescription is the structure of government. Privatization requires a powerful and authoritarian government in order to withstand the voices of discontent. Privatization does not discuss the legislation and judiciary rules of the state intended to implement it. It does not discuss the creation of grassroots organizations (GROs) outside the bureaucratic structure or the institution-building requirement. Nor does it look into possible reforms within the existing structure itself. Both these are, however, important if activation of the voice option is to be enhanced and the hierarchical structure of the centralized state broken down.

Opposition to privatization in developing countries is derived from its inability to deliver participation and freedom, factors which increase the capability of individuals at the local level. Privatization transactions have been limited in developing countries because governments are trying to maximize sales revenues and they do not possess either the 'institutional capacity' or the will to study the sales carefully as is the case in western countries. Changes of government become the norm in countries embarking on major reform programmes because privatization creates new empires where the majority is excluded from participation in the market. One may ask why the communists were elected in Russia's December 1995 general election only four years after rejecting communism. Some commentators believe that the privatization process in developing countries might be reversible as happened in Chile (1983) and in Japan in the second half of this century (Suleiman and Waterbury, 1990, p. 19). Privatization as a form of functional decentralization has led other economists to believe that the developing countries would stay in the hands of the public sector, at least for the foreseeable future, even though that might not be the most efficient means of achieving sustainable development (Ikenberry, 1990; Kone, 1990; Low, 1990; Ramanadham, 1989).

## 5.7 PARADIGMS OF DECENTRALIZED DEVELOPMENT

There are three major paradigms of decentralized development all of which consider territorial decentralization to be the main apparatus of development: the first is 'development from below' (bottom-up and periphery-inward) (Stohr and Taylor, 1981); the second the 'strategy of reversals' (Chambers, 1991); and the third, an extension of the previous two, is 'development from within' (Taylor and Mackenzie, 1992).

### 5.7.1 Development from Below (Bottom-Up and Periphery-Inward)

This strategy, introduced by Stohr and Taylor (1981), was influenced by the dependency school ideologies. The latter believe that the deterioration of development in the underdeveloped world is an outcome of the expansive and exploitative development of the industrial market economies and that the status of underdevelopment is not a temporary stage leading to development, but a continuous one resulting from the pattern of centre–periphery exploitative relationships (Street and James, 1982, p. 681).

The strategy had its roots in the populist ideas of the nineteenth and early twentieth centuries where 'development from below' was to be internally generated from the grass roots as represented by rural villages away from the power and influence of the development bureaucracies. In the words of Robertson this strategy would

> articulate the need to secure the cooperation of 'ordinary simple people' in reformist endeavour, and usually do so by making the generous assumption rest with them (the people) – rather than with other more clearly identifiable groups and interests like businessmen (Robertson, 1984, p. 222).

According to Stohr, there are five major dimensions of policies which have to be followed and these form the cornerstones of this paradigm: territorially organized basic-needs services; rural and village development; labour-intensive activities; small and medium-size projects; and the application of a notion of technology which can permit the full employment of regional human, natural and institutional resources on a territorially integrated basis (Stohr, 1981, p. 43). As a result, development should be achieved through spatial mobility and diversity rather than unitary solutions dependent on externally imposed functional goals such as privatization and free-market oriented policies:

> There are many concepts of development depending on the natural and social environment of different communities and the development over time of specific culture and institutional conditions. In fact, these represent major factors of development potential and should not be subordinated to the short-term pressures of any externally dominated or anonymous market mechanism (Stohr, 1981, p. 44).

However, the criticism of this paradigm arose from its lack of feasibility under the international conditions which prevailed. Stohr (1990, p. 22) had three major doubts about the feasibility of 'development from below'. The first concerned the weak position of most local economies (i.e. few resources and scale economies) to absorb the international wave of economic restructuring processes. The second was political in that local communities did not possess enough power or momentum successfully to confront the powerful international and government elites. The third reason was the lack of evidence of successful local or regional development initiatives whether from developing or developed countries. However, the paradigm has recently restored its credibility because of increasing evidence of successful locally based development initiatives which have emerged from developed and developing countries.[3]

### 5.7.2 The Strategy of Reversal

Over the period 1983–91 Chambers developed what he called 'A Counter-ideology of Reversals' taking 'as its starting-point the conditions and priorities of rural people, especially the poorer, and the problems and opportunities which they face; and it leads to a different constellation of prescriptions' (Chambers, 1991, p. 265).

This strategy counters the neo-Fabian school, where the state should do more, and the neo-Liberal school, where the state should do less, in that they are prescriptions for development from above, centre-outwards and top-down. While functional decentralization was the main weapon of the two earlier schools, the 'counter-ideology of reversals' was based on territorial decentralization: 'Near the core of this paradigm is decentralized process and choice' (ibid., p. 276). Its main focus is the rural poor and the realities of field administration (i.e poorly-paid staff). The reversals of the strategy are: location, learning, explanation, values, control, authority and power, and the major goal is first to put people on the periphery. For the state to be able to function effectively it should be open to *indigenous pluralism* and the mix of ideas. The state functions proposed by Chambers are: first, maintenance of peace and the democratic role of law; second, provision of a basic infrastructure and services; and third, management of the economy (ibid., pp. 267–8).

As far as privatization is concerned, the strategy emphasized the importance of studying each case independently rather than attempting to generalize from the experience of other countries. However, it is always important to ask the questions, who will be better off and who will be worse off?

The Technical Centre for Agriculture and Rural Cooperation (CTA) in its monthly bulletin (*Spore*) reported that privatizing the supply of fertilizers in Senegal resulted in a sharp decline in fertilizer use, thus affecting land fertility (*Spore*, 1992, p. 2). Likewise, the privatization of state monopolies in the field of vaccines and the treatment of animals 'crowded out' poor livestock producers in Chad as they became unable to pay the high charges following privatization. Merchants have taken over the most favourable sections of the agro-chemical supply business in Africa, neglecting in the process the needs of the less crowded rural areas. Similar problems arose after the privatization of the African marketing boards in Mali. The big business men deal with capitalist farmers while small farmers are unable to access the market (ibid., p. 2). The uncontrolled policy of privatizing state monopolies as well as state lands in the agricultural sector has been shown to represent a risk for peasant farmers, who are often insecure and who have to learn to adapt to the new rules of the game (ibid., p. 4). Thus, identifying winners and losers should form an important part of any privatization programme.

In brief, the strategy aims to transform what is called the *unable state* into an *enable state*, so that equity and efficiency can be achieved through reversal and diversity. A further aim is equitable development through raising the voice of the poor and enabling them to become more efficient in the sense of mobilizing their creative energy. Providing incentives for long-term self-reliant investments by the poor should lead to more sustainable development. There is no simple medicine such as 'getting the price right' or 'rolling back the state'.

### 5.7.3 Development from Within

This paradigm is based on both previous models of decentralized development. The heart of the strategy is to maximize the utilization of the resources (physical and human) to meet the needs of a local territory. The framework is based on actual experience drawn from eight case studies in rural sub-Saharan Africa. This strategy can be a 'strategy for survival' in cases of short-term needs and a 'strategy of development' when it emerges as a complete institutional building process mobilizing the capacity of local people. The basic goal is 'to allow local people to become the subject, not the object, of development strategies' (Taylor, 1992, p. 257).

This runs contrary to privatization because the latter minimizes people's capacity to one characterized by a rational actor without any space and place dimensions. Privatization focuses more on isolated individuals than on social interaction within local communities. For this reason 'development from within' cannot be understood through systemic processes, as is the case in privatization, because the moral considerations appearing through the case studies at the micro-level are incompatible with rationality at the macro-level.[4]

This paradigm demonstrates a local community's understanding of communal bonds and constructive collective identities based on time and place. Such a relationship is difficult to quantify through a mathematical model without simplification of the various factors operating in reality. However, it can be assessed through analysis of the general results on the ground.

The two main building stones of this strategy are *participation* and *territoriality*. In participation, the paradigm adopts Goulet's participation concept (1989) as both goal and means where participation is 'not induced from above but is generated from below by the populace itself; it can also be generated by the catalytic action of some external third agent' (Taylor, 1992, pp. 236-7). Goulet (1989) and Taylor (1992) agree that different kinds of development require different forms of participation. Thus, in the case of survival, action will not depend on permeation by the state or a bureaucratic organization. On the other hand, if the aim is 'people-centred development', there will be a need for a form of participation in which the elites play no active role (territorial decentralization). In the case of growth-oriented policies, such as privatization and free-market policies which are based on a top-down approach, participation will be imposed and monitored in order to achieve the functional goal of growth with a major and active role for the elite.

The second key component is the territoriality concept. This includes 'place and social relations and power interaction which take place within the bounded space' (Taylor, 1992, p. 241). However, territory has a variety of scales, the most efficient one being the 'local scale' where people can interact and coordinate within their life-space bounds (these include values and morals within given institutional conditions). Such a scale of local territory may appear to be small and not to utilize the advantages of economies of scale.

The problem of equating participation with decentralization, as perceived by governments through the delegation of their powers to local-level organizations, is that it does not mean empowering people or meaningful participation by the rural or urban masses. Instead, the distribution of political and economic power determines the magnitude of participation because it is based on a top-down approach to development (Ghai, 1990, p. 216; Ingham, 1993, p. 1810). The value of participation should be derived by empowering the people who are deprived and excluded. This requires local organizations to be democratic, independent and self-reliant (Ghai, 1990, p. 216). In this way decentralization becomes an approach to human development, with participation denoting the cornerstone.

Territorial decentralization will be judged on whether participation is authentic empowerment of the poor or a manipulation of them. This requires an examination of the 'elite domination hypothesis' where the elite deprive the poor of the fruits of territorial decentralization and depend upon them for employment, loans and gaining access to the administration (Griffin, 1981; Echeverri-Gent, 1992, p. 1409).

That is why privatization cannot be discussed within the same fabric of territorial decentralization: because the first enhances the power of the elite itself, while the latter needs to heighten people's consciousness and awareness in order to raise their voice. Thus, privatization is a functional decentralization which, when imposed on people in a conventional top-down and centre-outward approach, may not imply participation. It is a continuation of the policy of monocentric reliance on traditional large-scale market-driven, large-organization and central-government initiated development processes.

### 5.7.4 The Differences between Functional and Territorial Decentralization

There are a number of major differences between privatization and territorial decentralization.

- One of the differences lies in the origins of the ideas and initiatives. Privatization originated in the West and is initiated from the capital city whereas territorial decentralization is initiated from villages or towns.
- Privatization may include participation but in bottom-up territorial decentralization, participation is essential; without it decentralization has no meaning.
- The implementation of privatization is relatively rapid once decided upon whereas territorial decentralization is gradual, local, and at the people's capacity and pace.
- Evaluation is external in privatization but internal and continuous in territorial decentralization.
- A further difference is the standardization of privatization policies, which in territorial decentralization are diversified.
- The scope of privatization is limited to the achievement of quantitative goals (i.e. technical efficiency, profitability), whereas territorial decentralization offers more scope for institutional growth, which can often be qualitative.
- Privatization benefits the dominant elite while territorial decentralization benefits everybody, particularly the poor.
- A final difference is the level of knowledge or what Banuri (1990a) called 'epistemological decentralization'. Territorial decentralization depends on shared nature and experience whereas in privatization the knowledge forms are alien and can generate counterproductive ends (Bardhan, 1993, p. 636).

We may note that while the public sector represents a centralized approach to development, the private sector or the market also represents a functional decentralization. In rural areas 'people-centred' development requires a third sector (local level) in which the grassroots organizations (GROs) operate and provide the best approach to sustainable rural development (see Table 5.1). The impact of the organizations emerging from each approach will lead to a negative-sum game in the state sector, a zero-sum game in the market, and a positive-sum game in the case of GROs (Uphoff, 1993, p. 612).

'People-centred' projects cannot be limited to projects only in the social sectors (education, health, family planning, nutrition, and the like). People must be central to all projects and the latter need to be sustainable because sustainability is a necessary condition for 'replicability' (Gaude and Miller, 1990, p. 212). This is contrary to the privatization experience in the majority of developing countries, which have deprived the poor of the capacity to participate in the development process.

Devolution of power to the local level increases economic efficiency because projects and services are planned, implemented, monitored, and evaluated by local people who

*Table* 5.1 Alternative approaches to rural development

| *Details* | *First approach* | *Second approach* | *Third approach* |
|---|---|---|---|
| Principal mechanisms | Bureaucratic organizations | Market processes | Voluntary associations |
| Decision-makers | Administrators and experts | Individual producers, consumers, savers and investors | Leaders and members |
| Guides for behaviour | Regulations | Price signals and quantity adjustments | Agreements |
| Criteria for decisions | Policy – and best means to implement it | Efficiency-maximization of profit and/or utility | Interests of members |
| Sanctions | State authority backed by coercion | Financial loss | Social pressure |
| Mode of operation | Top-down | Individualistic | Bottom-up |

*Source*: Uphoff (1993, Table 1, p. 610).

understand their needs and priorities better than the centre. It also increases political freedom and enhances democracy if initiated within a package of institutional reform (UNDP, 1993, pp. 77–8).

In contrast privatization and free-market-oriented advocates are mainly concerned with increasing revenues and using them efficiently at the local level within the context of decentralization. According to Rondinelli and his colleagues (1989, p. 70), 'user charges are likely to become a major source of financing local services in developing countries'. Although it may be important to raise local government revenues to finance expenditure, their generalization to primary health care and education will 'deter many of the poorest users and cause considerable hardship – while raising relatively little money' (UNDP, 1993, p. 73). An assessment of the user charges effect can be derived from the empirical evidence provided by Weissman (1990) in a visit to two public health clinics in one of the low-income areas in Accra (Ghana). He noted that user charges have benefited the rich and crowded out the poor.[5] In his words,

> A major aspect of structural adjustment policy has been the introduction of health fees to ease budgetary burdens. Those now amount to 12% of the allocated recurrent budget. But according to available data, the use of health services declined in many areas following the introduction of fees in 1985. While utilization increased for the more advantaged populations, the level of use remained depressed among the poorer groups (Weissman, 1990, p. 1627).

The difference between the World Bank/IMF vision of functional decentralization, and the human development approach to decentralization can be traced to the following quotation from the HDR of 1992.

> The World Bank and the IMF must ... assess projects and programmes with a vision that extends beyond economic and financial feasibility. They must take into account the effect such projects and programmes will have on the human being concerned (UNDP, 1992, p. 81).

In short, empowering people at the local level might be the only viable alternative for sustainable development during the twenty-first century. Such development cannot be achieved by macro-instruments (Clark, 1995) or by a single decision, as is the case in privatization, but requires commitment to an institutional building process beyond the magnitude and objectives of privatization. This means also that within a privatization programme the interests of the underprivileged groups must be articulated at all stages of the divestiture process. Through the promotion of a more open and interactive process an environment can be created which is more conducive to improving public confidence in the state privatization programme and more favourable to its implementation. Privatization, however, is only one aspect of the solution to the economic problems of developing countries. Others, such as the reform of SOEs within a context of increasing autonomy and accountability, are further components. Instead of withdrawing from ownership of state enterprises, particularly in the social services, the government may decide to reform and rehabilitate an increasing number of them.

## 5.8 DECENTRALIZATION IN PRACTICE

Decentralization in developing countries during the 1970s and 1980s was seen as a partial cure for excessive centralization and as a response to the inability of the centralized state to plan and implement development agenda. The concept was vague, and the results of its implementation in developing countries were received with 'guarded optimism', as Rondinelli and Nellis (1986, p. 4) called it. However, the experience as reviewed by the World Bank (1984), Cheema and Rondinelli (1983), Rondinelli and Nellis (1986) put privatization at the end of the decentralization scale, while during the late 1980s, the privatization position jumped into the lead (Rondinelli *et al.*, 1989, p. 72).

Privatization in its current context will not reduce centralization, increase empowerment and people participation, or alleviate the poverty which is the cancer of developing countries. This is because the financial crisis in developing countries following the debt crisis in 1982 enabled the international aid agencies such as the World Bank and the IMF to play a major role in the international political economy. Their visions as financial institutions are more related to factors of financial feasibility and solvency. This is symmetric with their organizations' objectives. Thus, it is not surprising that they may be in conflict with the capability approach to development. Furthermore, those aid agencies themselves are currently behind the increasing trend towards centralization because their provision of aid and conditional loans to central government is linked with policy advice and the design of the current reform policies in many developing countries, particularly the poorer ones which lack the administrative ability to design reforms.

The data on decentralization measurements in developing countries represent a major obstacle when assessing the extent of decentralization and its impact on human development. The HDR of 1993 provided different measurements of financial decentralization and social-expenditure decentralization ratios in developing and industrial countries.

Table 5.2 indicates a wide difference between developing and industrial countries in the expenditure and revenue decentralization ratios. On average the expenditure decentralization ratios are below 15 per cent in developing countries, except for South Korea, Zimbabwe and Nigeria. In Latin American countries, such as Chile and Brazil, the ratios are below 10 per cent while for other sub-Saharan African countries and Pakistan the expenditure ratios are below 5 per cent.

Local governments in industrial countries, by contrast, spend a larger proportion of the total expenditure. Except for Australia (5 per cent), the expenditure decentralization ratios of other industrial countries ranged between 15 and 45 per cent. Even with the deduction of military expenditure and debt servicing in the modified ratios, developing country indicators of expenditure decentralization do not improve significantly. Similar indicators could be found in the revenue decentralization ratios of developing countries where local governments do not possess the power to raise revenue from local taxes. The only decentralization ratios in which developing countries appear to be equal to those in the industrial ones are the financial autonomy ratios (about 60 per cent). However, in reality the difference is immense because local

Table 5.2  Financial decentralization in local governments in selected countries (percentage)

| Country | Year | Total expenditure decentralization ratio* | Modified expenditure decentralization ratio** | Revenue decentralization ratio*** | Financial autonomy ratio**** |
|---|---|---|---|---|---|
| **Developing countries** | | | | | |
| Korea, Rep. | 1987 | 33 | n.a. | 31 | 99 |
| Zimbabwe | 1986 | 22 | 29 | 17 | 58 |
| Nigeria | 1988 | 17 | n.a. | n.a. | n.a. |
| South Africa | 1988 | 10 | 11 | 10 | 70 |
| Chile | 1988 | 8 | 10 | 6 | 61 |
| Brazil | 1989 | 7 | 14 | 1 | 33 |
| Morocco | 1987 | 6 | n.a. | 8 | 108 |
| Paraguay | 1989 | 4 | 5 | 3 | 88 |
| Kenya | 1989 | 4 | 5 | 7 | 134 |
| Pakistan | 1987/88 | 4 | n.a. | 6 | 100 |
| Costa Rica | 1988 | 3 | n.a. | 3 | 123 |
| Ghana | 1988 | 2 | n.a. | 2 | 71 |
| Côte d'Ivoire | 1985 | 2 | n.a. | 2 | 115 |
| **Industrial countries** | | | | | |
| Denmark | 1988 | 45 | 51 | 31 | 58 |
| Finland | 1989 | 41 | 43 | 29 | 63 |
| Sweden | 1989 | 37 | 42 | 30 | 78 |
| United Kingdom | 1989 | 26 | 31 | 16 | 55 |
| Czechoslovakia | 1990 | 26 | 27 | 19 | 61 |
| Ireland | 1989 | 23 | 28 | 10 | 33 |
| Switzerland | 1984 | 22 | 24 | 22 | 87 |
| USA | 1989 | 21 | 26 | 16 | 65 |
| Hungary | 1990 | 19 | 21 | 11 | 53 |
| Austria | 1990 | 16 | 18 | 17 | 89 |
| Canada | 1989 | 16 | 18 | 11 | 53 |
| Australia | 1990 | 5 | 6 | 5 | 83 |

\* Local government expenditure as a percentage of total government expenditure.
\*\* Local government expenditure as a percentage of total government expenditure less defence expenditure less debt servicing.
\*\*\* Local government revenue as a percentage of total government revenue.
\*\*\*\* Local government revenue as a percentage of local government expenditure.
Source: Countries have been selected from the UNDP (1993, Table no. 4.2, p. 69).

government autonomy derives from its expenditure ability. This ability is narrow in developing countries and consequently a high financial autonomy does not mirror the size of local spending as a proportion of total government spending, but rather the percentage represents 60 per cent of an already small percentage of spending.

Other indicators of decentralization which relate to human development such as social expenditure at the local level revealed that developing country local governments spent only about 5–6 per cent on social spending while in developed countries the ratio was around 25 per cent (UNDP, 1993, p. 71). As was argued earlier, the decentralization of social spending may be more efficient at the local level but, despite that, developing countries' governments still control a large proportion of expenditure. However, the decentralization of expenditure at the local level does not in itself secure the provision of local needs. The experience of building prestigious projects such as expensive colleges and hospitals, as was the case in Pakistan in 1985, may provide counter-evidence of the rocky road to decentralization (ibid., p. 74).

There is a need to empower the poor and enhance the democratic polity at the local level before the delegation of power can proceed. This requires government commitment rather than government withdrawal. The overall assessment of decentralization practices in developing countries undertaken by the United Nations found that there was not much evidence of full devolution; where there was some kind of decentralization, it has generally increased efficiency and produced better priority spending ratios. However, decentralization requires state intervention to reduce the disparities between poor and rich regions as well as some sort of mechanism to remobilize the structure of power towards the excluded people (UNDP, 1993, p. 83).

Although there is pessimism rather than optimism about the benefits of decentralization in developing countries, the growing body of literature on the subject proves that decentralization and democratization in the context of enhancing people's capabilities is gaining ground. Scholars such as Slater (1989), Marglin and Marglin (1990), Ingham and Kalam (1992), Uphoff (1993), Lipton (1993) and Nugent (1993) are only a few examples among many.

## 5.9 THE EFFECT OF PRIVATIZATION ON TECHNOLOGICAL CHOICE AND THE INFORMAL SECTOR

The proponents of privatization and free-market policies argued that market prices, through competition in internal and international markets, would help producers to choose the 'appropriate technology' for the nation. An investigation of the recent technological history of developing countries reveals that economic policies in general and industrialization policies in particular, adopted from the 1950s until the present, have led to a deterioration in the use of 'appropriate technology' or 'orientation'. Imported technology from the West following the adoption of the ISI has left developing countries with huge problems in continuing the use of such technology. Most of the projects have been a kind of 'Master-Key project' which employees are unable to maintain. These have led to greater dependency on the West, and more foreign-exchange expenditure. The results are more debt and more unemployment because most of this technology is capital-intensive in nature and origin. Nevertheless, this does not mean that segments of this technology have not contributed positively to development efforts, in particular, in the areas of communication and marketing.

Why does privatization in its current international context not provide an incentive to enhance the adoption of 'appropriate technology' in LDCs? It is well known that efficient technology means a cheaper and more technically efficient process. So, allowing developing countries to make technological choices within an integrated international market (globalization) will logically induce producers in developing countries to purchase the form of technology that matches the factors of cheapness and technical efficiency in order to compete internationally. According to the argument presented by the World Bank (1991a, pp. 88–90) the integration of developing countries into the global economy means that producers in LDCs will continue to choose western technology. Recent experience in Eastern Europe and the former Soviet Union is positive witness to this. Even organization theories, such as the principal–agent theory, X-efficiency theory, and the transaction costs theory, will induce producers to favour technologies which reduce agency costs, opportunism and shirking, which mean less employment of the labour factor in production. Such logic cannot alleviate poverty in LDCs.

Where centralization as well as commercialization has led rural people into the trap of dependency, participatory development would produce 'self-reliance' and foster self-sufficiency in local organizations. The essential component in this process is 'learning by doing', as well as the efficient 'mobilization' of local resources. Territorial decentralization provides economic operators in rural areas with the incentives to engage in new activities leading to 'inside linkages' (Hirschman, 1984, p. 75). One of the main factors which determine such linkages is the 'degree of technological strangeness'. When this is increased, inside linkages will meet with special difficulties. Hirschman (1984), Cohen and Uphoff (1980), Uphoff (1991), Banuri (1990a, 1996), Stohr (1981) and Taylor (1992) as well as others all argued that using 'appropriate technology' is far more efficient than using an alien technology because the latter attenuates linkages and establishes cultural resistance. Capital-intensive technologies and modernized ones do not by themselves produce development; people produce development. However, not all modernized technologies are irrelevant to the development of developing countries. Those concerned with infrastructure and communication can support the indigenous development effort.

Control of technology is the condition for inside innovation. Without it, the existing path of dependence and the loss of knowledge continues. Indigenously based knowledge could make a major contribution to sustainable development because it is available locally and is more practical than that in advanced countries, which reflects the institutional factors of its origin.

The alternative approach to decentralization provides a good opportunity for the use of 'appropriate technology'. Through popular participation in decision-making the people would reveal their preferences and ideas subject to deliberation. Inside the production system people who are involved in and affected by the production process would utilize what appropriate technology had to offer. Inside linkages would work in two dimensions; the first would be learning from their own experiences how to adapt appropriate technology to their environmental, economic, and social boundaries and restrictions rather than to more technically efficient, sophisticated, and progressive forms. Innovation would come as a logical result in the second dimension through interaction within the production system. 'Need is the mother of innovation' could well apply in this case. The past history of developing countries is consistent with such an argument. If a clear profile of accelerating benefits emerges, for the employee in particular and the community in general, innovation would be one of the expected outcomes. This is consistent with the institutional-school argument denoted by C. E. Ayres. He emphasized that the efficiency of technology rests on two factors. The first is that it is an autonomous, self-sustaining process and the second is that the potential for innovation will be enhanced in a corresponding environment (Ayres, 1962, as cited in Street and James, 1982, p. 684). This denotes a rejection of the conventional belief that invention and discovery are best explained in market terms. The conclusion stems from the institutional-school belief in the progressive evolutionary character of society as well as the technological history of Latin America and sub-Saharan Africa (Street and James, 1982).

Even if we assume that technological progress will accompany privatization, as the latter's advocates have argued, privatization is by no means the only path to technological progress. At the national level, public enterprises and publicly subsidized private firms can be effective motors for technological change and for the indigenizing of technology, as was the case in Brazil and South Korea respectively (Taylor, 1993, p. 586). Likewise, at the local level, the importance of specific learning will contribute to the overall effort of development, which will enhance people's capacity to control their destiny.

Territorial decentralization or devolution recognizes the importance of the informal sector in generating income and employment for the poor. Micro-enterprises could be highly efficient even though most are unlikely to expand and are not primarily seeking to maximize profit but simply to generate income (self-employment creation), particularly when most workers and particularly women tend to work more in the informal rather than the formal sector in developing countries, as Table 5.3 shows.

*Table* 5.3   Shares of men and women workers in the informal sector to the total workforce (percentage of total)

| Country | Year | Men | Women |
|---|---|---|---|
| Bolivia | 1991 | 42 | 70 |
| Cape Verde | 1990 | 42 | 54 |
| Egypt | 1989 | 46 | 74 |
| El Salvador | 1991 | 28 | 48 |
| Ghana | 1989 | 69 | 92 |
| Indonesia | 1989 | 70 | 79 |
| Korea, Rep. | 1991 | 38 | 43 |
| Pakistan | 1992 | 66 | 77 |
| Peru | 1991 | 39 | 55 |
| Tanzania | 1988 | 84 | 95 |
| Thailand | 1989 | 71 | 76 |
| Tunisia | 1989 | 36 | 51 |
| Turkey | 1991 | 55 | 80 |

*Source*: World Bank (1995, Table no. 11.3, p. 73).

In the right setting, the informal sector can have many advantages over large-scale formal sector firms. These are location, simplicity in the production process, lower costs in local markets, and adaptability and responsiveness to changing demands (Streeten, 1992, p. 98). Thus, macroeconomic policies such as free-market-oriented policies and privatization would promote large-scale private investments, which do not necessarily promote small-scale activities and may even eliminate them, particularly where mergers between large enterprises become effectively a policy for cost reduction and increased profitability.

Theoretically, the contestable market features of free entry and exit and zero sunk costs are more applicable to the microenterprises of the informal sector than to those operating in the formal sector. According to Baumol (1982) contestability gives consumers the benefit of competition while at the same time disciplining producers by making them vulnerable to hit-and-run entry.

Thus, privatization as a transfer of ownership and/or control from the public to the private sector or as a functional decentralization should be accompanied by appropriate microeconomic policies and organizations which are necessary to bring micro-enterprise activities into the mainstream of the economic development process: 'crowding in' the informal sector. There is a need to look at the development process in terms of building a pyramid, which requires a solid foundation before proceeding to the next level; otherwise, the top-down approach will result in a 'shaky tower' (Dessing, 1990).

Privatization and liberalization policies might, therefore, lead to an intensification of the disparities between rich and poor unless accompanied by a package of reforms that brings the informal sector into the heart of the development process. It is argued that liberalization and privatization would encourage foreign direct investment to increase its inflows to developing countries. The data on global investment reveals that out of $181.7 billion invested world-wide in 1989, 89.7 per cent was invested in the OECD and only 10.3 per cent in developing countries, of which the most needy sub-Saharan African countries received only 1.4 per cent ($2.6 billion) [as cited in Steidlmeier (1993, pp. 216–17)]. This demonstrates that international investment responds to profits in international markets rather than to the needs of a country.

## 5.10 SOME CONCLUDING REFLECTIONS

The chapter has suggested that privatization might enhance the participation of the poor and the underprivileged if it was designed and implemented within a framework that could enhance workers' participation in decision-making and ownership as well as that of other people who are excluded from participation in the marketplace (such as the low-income groups). However, the experience of developing countries gives little evidence of such intention.

The alternative is devolution or territorial decentralization. There are two key principles on which this alternative can work: participation and linkages. Participation is defined as 'the organized efforts to increase control over resources and regulative institutions in given social situations, on the part of groups and movements hitherto excluded from such control' [as cited in Goulet (1989, p. 165)]. Thus, participatory development would imply a dependency on *local initiatives* through grassroots organizations rather than a bureaucratic structure. As a result, accountability would be enhanced because local people have a special interest in sustainable development.

The proponents of privatization equate economic freedom with privatization or private ownership. In participatory development, economic freedom should be defined as a decision-making input to the degree that one is affected by the outcome of an economic choice. In the case of privatization, unequal ownership of property is inconsistent with 'equality of opportunity'. It is the notion of property rights rather than participation because the scale of the first determines the size and activation of the latter. Thus, the dominance of the private property concept will reduce, if not diminish, any interest in community projects and result in low participation in decision-making, on which the choice concept stands. It is a case of ignorance and isolation.

The problem of privatization in developing countries is that it promotes the culture of silence and people will not participate in their humanization. Poor people will be marginalized in the name of growth and denied the opportunity to choose in the name of 'equal opportunity'.

Development may mean decentralization, which certainly means participation. However, privatization will not necessarily ensure either. It will depend closely on its design and implementation, neither of which can be severed from the objectives behind its introduction. If privatization within the context of developing countries is to be sustainable and people-centred it has to be a gradual process, relatively crisis-free, untroubled and unforced, marked by the fusion of collective participation from below (e.g. grass roots) and individual participation in the marketplace. Such an approach will depend exclusively on the commitment of the decision-makers and their vision of empowering the people.

# Part II
# The Case of Jordan

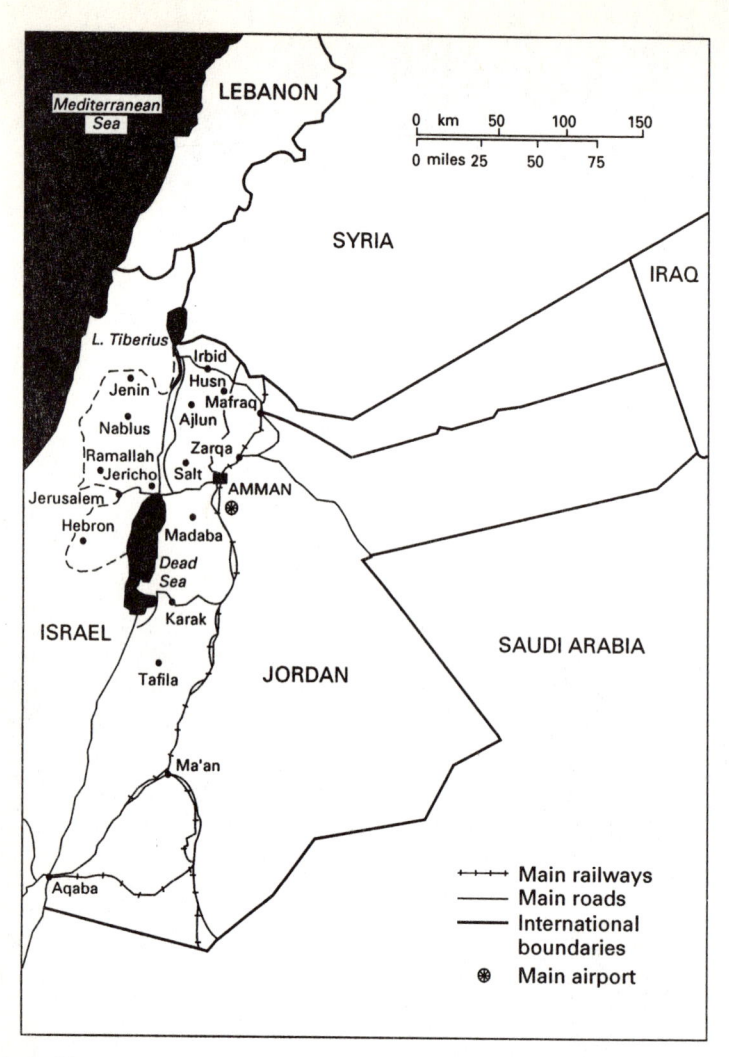

*Map* of Jordan
*Source*: EIU (1992a).

# 6 Privatization in Jordan

## 6.1 INTRODUCTION

In the Middle Eastern economies Jordan represents a distinctive case: a small country of four million people with scarce natural resources, a complex demographic composition (East Jordanians and Palestinians); high vulnerability to internal socio-political factors, because of the 'Palestinian' question following the 1948 and 1967 wars with Israel; and geo-political spillover because of the state of war with Israel until October 1994. All these factors affected its development.

Since its formation in 1950 the Hashemite Kingdom of Jordan has followed a free-market ideology combined with import-substitution and latterly (post-1985) an export-promotion strategy of development. Outcomes, however, have been deficient. Deterioration in the agricultural sector has affected the poor in the rural areas and denied the country its strategic 'food security'. Imports of agricultural products were four times the value of agricultural exports and more than the value-added generated in the sector in 1990 and 1991 (Ministry of Planning, 1994, p. 69). With limited linkages between the productive sectors, the economy became hostage to imports for most of its requirements while its industrial and agricultural export base suffered from unstable regional markets. The average annual value of exports during 1990–94 was JD1843 million while its average annual bill for imports was JD2806 million (Central Bank of Jordan, 1995, Table 49, p. 81).

Dependence on external sources of finance, particularly from the oil-rich rentier states of the Gulf, led the country into a path of instability and consumption patterns which do not reflect real capacity and the opportunities available in the domestic economy.

Both Arab grants and workers' remittances from Jordanians working in the rich Gulf states were the main contribution to the rise of reserves. These enhanced the state's capacity to invest, grow, and achieve a high standard of human development but on a distributive rather than a productive basis. The services sector constituted on average about 60 per cent of the GDP during 1973–94, and 48 per cent of the workforce employed in government activities.

Jordan is a semi-rentier economy, where foreign revenue plays a dominant role, particularly in the composition of government revenues (46 per cent on average during 1973–91). In such an economy, the size and the flow of foreign revenue are not related to productive capacity, but to factors over which Jordan has little or no control. Therefore, decision-makers in Jordan were more reactionary than strategic: external events rather than a long-term strategy of development determined the direction of policies.

Within the above context this chapter will commence by identifying the role of the state sector in the economy (Section 6.2). Such an approach makes it necessary to examine why the introduction of privatization was proposed (Section 6.3).

To establish the relevance of ownership to efficiency and profitability, Section 6.4 will provide a general examination of the performance of Jordanian SOEs, and in particular the case of an SOE in the electricity sector. Jordan Electricity Authority (JEA) will provide further empirical evidence on whether there is a relationship between ownership form and performance.

Privatization through change of ownership has not yet been implemented in Jordan, but the country seems to be nearing a moment of truth. Three industries in principle have been selected for privatization since 1986; Royal Jordanian Airlines (RJ), the Public Transport Corporation (PTC), and the Telecommunication Corporation (TCC), but despite their selection no steps of actual privatization have taken place. In order to prove the difficulties surrounding privatization in Jordan, Section 6.5 will present a complete record for the announcement of government officials about the privatization programme from its first initiative to the end of 1995. Many of these refer to the difficult tasks of design and implementation.

Given the long time since privatization proposals were introduced and the poor financial performance of many enterprises, Section 6.6 will examine the factors which are hindering the implementation of a divestiture programme.

A number of conclusions have to be drawn from the Jordanian experience of suspended privatization. One of these requires emphasis, namely that the merits of privatization should not be judged by its success in developed countries but rather through a study of the economic and non-economic factors affecting the design, implementation and results within a particular context. This can provide a more solid basis for an appropriate understanding of the problems and the right methods of solving them.

## 6.2 THE ROLE OF THE STATE

### 6.2.1 Government Spending

It is often argued that the government spending ratio (or public expenditure ratio) can reveal the level of the allocative role of the government, in particular when the expenditure is divided between current and capital.

Table 6.1 provides statistics on the composition of government spending in Jordan (current and capital) as well as its share of GDP. The first impression is that the ratio of public expenditure during the period 1980–94 was high; on average it constituted about 41.8 per cent of GDP. It is known that government spending affects the demand side in the economy as well as the balance of payments. The government spending ratio increased after the decline in oil prices in 1986 to counter the subsequent recession. However, the high percentage of government expenditure in Jordan must be linked to the external grants and revenues collected by the state during the boom years of the 1970s to the beginning of the 1980s. To draw a comparison with the South-East Asian countries, the average annual government spending ratio in South Korea was only 16.6 per cent while in Malaysia it was about 31 per cent of the GDP during the 1980s. But the problem for Jordan was not the level of government expenditure but the limited capacity of the economy to finance it.

Another important indicator for the presence or absence of a sound economic policy is the share of current and capital expenditure in total governmental spending. Where current

*Table* 6.1  Jordanian government spending and its share of GDP, 1980–94

|  | Government expenditure (MJDs) | Current expenditure (%) | Capital expenditure (%) | GDP (MJDs) | Government expenditure % of GDP |
|---|---|---|---|---|---|
| 1980 | 487.9 | 62.6 | 37.4 | 1151.2 | 40.8 |
| 1981 | 546.2 | 65.2 | 34.8 | 1426.7 | 38.6 |
| 1982 | 632.0 | 71.4 | 28.6 | 1638.1 | 39.4 |
| 1983 | 656.3 | 69.8 | 30.2 | 1765.8 | 37.3 |
| 1984 | 720.8 | 67.7 | 32.3 | 1891.4 | 38.1 |
| 1985 | 805.7 | 67.3 | 32.7 | 1940.6 | 41.5 |
| 1986 | 981.3 | 58.1 | 41.9 | 2114.6 | 46.4 |
| 1987 | 965.8 | 62.4 | 37.6 | 2162.7 | 44.6 |
| 1988 | 1054.0 | 63.5 | 36.5 | 2264.4 | 46.5 |
| 1989 | 1102.3 | 68.0 | 32.0 | 2372.1 | 46.4 |
| 1990 | 1120.1 | 75.1 | 24.9 | 2668.3 | 42.0 |
| 1991 | 1234.2 | 73.2 | 26.8 | 2855.1 | 43.2 |
| 1992 | 1348.8 | 68.9 | 31.1 | 2493.0 | 38.6 |
| 1993* | 1647.7 | 63.4 | 36.6 | 3811.4 | 43.2 |
| 1994* | 1669.1 | 67.0 | 33.0 | 4190.6 | 39.8 |

MJDs: Million Jordanian Dinars.
*Preliminary.
*Source*: Central Bank of Jordan (CBJ), *Monthly Statistical Bulletin* (various issues).

expenditure is large, there is less of a commitment to development and vice versa. The classification itself may not be the same in different countries but with Jordan there is further evidence about the status of developmental or capital expenditure. Current expenditure constituted on average about 67 per cent of the total spent during 1980–94. Government current spending was excessive for two main reasons: a high level of military expenditure, 25 per cent on average (see Table 6.2), and an enormous government wage bill. The latter is so large not because per capita wages are high but because the government employs half the Jordanian workforce in its service sector. This is an example of deficient centralization as more central units of government need more government spending although the economy itself is market-oriented. Further conclusion is that the private sector itself is unable to

Table 6.2  Jordanian government spending by function, 1981–92 (%)

| Years | Defence | General public services | Education | Health | Social Security | Economic Affairs | Others* |
|---|---|---|---|---|---|---|---|
| 1981 | 25.3 | 17.7 | 7.6 | 3.7 | 13.7 | 28.3 | 3.7 |
| 1982 | 24.8 | 12.4 | 10.4 | 3.7 | 16.4 | 28.6 | 3.7 |
| 1983 | 25.6 | 11.2 | 11.5 | 3.6 | 12.5 | 29.9 | 5.7 |
| 1984 | 27.7 | 11.1 | 11.3 | 4.2 | 13.7 | 24.8 | 7.2 |
| 1985 | 26.7 | 12.2 | 12.2 | 3.8 | 7.7 | 22.4 | 15.0 |
| 1986 | 30.3 | 11.4 | 13.7 | 4.2 | 9.0 | 18.1 | 13.3 |
| 1987 | 26.5 | 8.6 | 13.0 | 5.4 | 8.4 | 15.7 | 22.4 |
| 1988 | 25.9 | 6.9 | 15.3 | 4.1 | 8.8 | 14.6 | 24.4 |
| 1989 | 23.1 | 6.4 | 14.2 | 5.8 | 9.7 | 12.9 | 27.9 |
| 1990 | 21.3 | 4.7 | 14.7 | 5.0 | 15.7 | 10.3 | 28.3 |
| 1991 | 26.7 | 5.3 | 12.8 | 5.1 | 13.5 | 10.6 | 26.0 |
| 1992 | 22.1 | 5.5 | 14.3 | 6.3 | 15.1 | 12.3 | 24.4 |

*Others include public order & safety, housing, amenities, recreation & culture and religious affairs.
Sources: IMF, Government Finance Statistics Yearbooks (1991a, 1992a, 1994a).

participate significantly in absorbing the labour force into the economy. Moreover, the lower share of spending on the capital category itself is vital in classifying the merits of government economic policies.

Since income uncertainty has been an important institutional factor in the Jordanian economy, because of its dependence on exogenous sources of finance (52 per cent of total government revenue during 1973–82, and 37 per cent during 1983–91), capital expenditure has been used as a sinking account with much of the spending made in the last quarter of the year. This might explain the reduced commitment of policy-makers to cut current spending while devoting the necessary resources to development. Such commitment is the most necessary ingredient in successful development, as is the case in the East Asian countries (Westphal, 1990, p. 58). One of the challenges for policy-makers in Jordan is to choose policies which suit the needs of the people, particularly the one-third of the population who are poor.

Neo-liberal economic theory suggests that distributional objectives should, as Lal argues (1992, p. 30), be pursued through the use of the fiscal system such as taxes, direct cash transfers and subsidies, but such policies have been lacking in Jordan. Shamaileh (1990) in his study of the impact of government egalitarian policies in Jordan found that four taxes (income, property, gasoline and customs) had no significant impact either on the relative distribution of households among the income brackets (p. 171) or on the poverty gap (p. 176): in real terms income inequality increased in Jordan. The share of the lowest 40 per cent of the population decreased from 18.8 per cent in 1981 to 16.8 per cent in 1991 while the share of the highest 10 per cent increased for the same period from 28.2 to 32.6 per cent of total income (World Bank, 1995, p. 220). This is because of high government dependence on indirect taxation (in particular customs taxes) to maximize revenues, taxes which do not discriminate between the different income brackets.

Over the period 1980–92 indirect taxes were on average about 76 per cent of total tax revenue while the share of taxes on international trade and transactions within total revenue collected from indirect taxes was on average about 65 per cent of total indirect taxes collected by central government (Table 6.3). An explanation for such a phenomenon is that in Jordan revenue maximization is the overriding concern of the state so long as the burden of taxation does not fall on the elite. The desire is for taxes with minimal collection and other transaction costs, particularly where collection is facilitated through certain trade channels (e.g. ports). Johnson (1975, p. 57) denominated such taxes as a 'corruption tax' which does not reflect the relative profitability of the different activities within the economy. They are, therefore, socially inefficient because they do not reflect changes in the social opportunity costs. Table 6.3, however, reveals a marked change in the revenues collected from direct taxation, the result of a government decision to tax the mineral fertilizer industries whose products are priced in dollars and export oriented. As a result, corporate taxes increased from JD29.8 million in 1989 to JD88.7 million in 1990 (IMF, 1992a, p. 318).

In contrast, there was a reduction in the indirect taxes collected from international trade and transactions. The reason

*Table* 6.3  The origins of tax revenues to the Jordanian central government and their relative importance, 1980–92

| Years | Total tax revenues (MJDs) [1] | Direct taxes* (MJDs) [2] | % of total taxes [3] | Indirect taxes** (MJDs) [4] | % of total taxes [5] | Internat'l trade taxes (% of [4]) |
|---|---|---|---|---|---|---|
| 1980 | 164.8 | 43.1 | 26.1 | 121.7 | 73.8 | 83.1 |
| 1981 | 214.2 | 59.8 | 27.9 | 154.4 | 72.1 | 80.0 |
| 1982 | 250.2 | 66.1 | 26.4 | 184.1 | 73.6 | 76.4 |
| 1983 | 274.1 | 69.8 | 25.5 | 204.3 | 74.5 | 68.6 |
| 1984 | 285.8 | 71.0 | 24.8 | 214.8 | 75.2 | 64.3 |
| 1985 | 304.7 | 74.9 | 26.4 | 229.8 | 75.4 | 59.2 |
| 1986 | 291.6 | 64.9 | 22.2 | 226.7 | 77.8 | 57.5 |
| 1987 | 292.0 | 54.7 | 18.7 | 237.3 | 81.3 | 60.5 |
| 1988 | 322.0 | 58.7 | 18.2 | 263.3 | 81.8 | 63.2 |
| 1989 | 354.2 | 77.8 | 22.0 | 276.4 | 78.0 | 55.3 |
| 1990 | 497.2 | 140.1 | 28.2 | 357.1 | 71.8 | 52.4 |
| 1991 | 531.0 | 132.2 | 24.9 | 398.8 | 75.1 | 55.5 |
| 1992 | 829.4 | 164.1 | 19.8 | 665.3 | 80.2 | 60.6 |

*Direct taxes include tax on income, payroll & workforce, profit and capital gains plus property taxes.
**Indirect taxes include domestic taxes on goods & services, taxes on international trade, transactions and others.
*Sources*: IMF, Government Finance Statistics *Yearbooks* (1991a, 1992a, 1994a).

for such a trend in 1989 and 1990 was the effect of the structural adjustment plan. Under this plan, which was signed in 1989, the Jordanian government turned to local indirect taxes as a means of reducing demand on the one hand, and to prove to the IMF its intention of reducing trade barriers on the other. Such policies were imposed on Jordan by the IMF. This analysis is consistent with the argument of Levi (1988) who believed that rulers are revenue maximizers subject to changing constraints. The constraint in the case of Jordan was the IMF structural adjustment programme. This forced the authorities to adjust their ways of revenue maximization because the programme in itself provided a new way of maximizing revenue through the loans given to Jordan.

Another revelation from Table 6.2 is that the share of government spending on social security and welfare was limited, less than 10 per cent of total governmental spending during

1985–89. Such figures reflect the absence of state welfare schemes to provide the poor with effective help parallel to those existing in the welfare states of western countries or those suggested by the World Bank in its report on the problem of poverty in developing countries (World Bank, 1990).[1] Thus, public enterprises are the major means for the state to provide people with income for equity reasons and this fact needs to be taken into account when discussing privatization in Jordan. Nevertheless, the Jordanian state spent a good proportion of its total expenditure on education and health. For example in education it spent on average 12.4 per cent during 1981–90, which constituted 4.8 per cent of the total GNP during the same period. Although no one can argue against such human investment, government policies in education never addressed the real need of the Jordanian economy, middle-level practical skills, but concentrated more on professional academic skills. As a result the highly educated people in the country suffer from unemployment: the rates of unemployment in 1990 and 1991 were 16.8 and 18.8 per cent respectively (Khasawneh *et al.*, 1993, p. 13). If modernization is based on imitating the trends in advanced countries, as is the case in education, any country, not only Jordan, will fall into the trap of cultivating the unemployment of a highly educated workforce.

In health, the proportion of expenditure was about 4.3 per cent of total government expenditure during the period 1981–90 and only 1.7 per cent of the total GNP for the same period. Thus, the social allocation ratio, which is the relative importance of health and education expenditure to the GNP, seems to be low. The problem in health, however, is not the spending but the quality of the spending. The health system is hospital-oriented. Expenditure on hospitals accounted on average for 70 per cent of total annual health expenditure over the period 1983–92 (IMF, 1994a, p. 383), while expenditure on primary health care constituted only 12.5 per cent. About 90 per cent of total health expenditure in Jordan (including that by the military medical services, university hospitals and the private sector) was directed towards the non-primary health services (Kharabsheh, 1990, p. 141). Further worry is the uneven distribution of such services among the rural and urban areas. Such evidence demonstrates the inability of a centralized policy to match the needs of people desperate to enhance their range of choices and entitlements. This implies that health services should be directed towards primary services and to a more even distribution among the regions.

Although capital expenditure is not the same as government fixed capital formation (GFCF) (or government investment), it is closely related to it. Table 6.4 provides the statistics for government as well as private investment and its share of GDP. A number of observations can be made: firstly, private investment constituted an important share of total investment,

*Table* 6.4  Jordanian gross fixed capital formation (governmental and private) and its relative importance to the GDP, 1980–94

| Years | Total GFCF (MJDs) [1] | Government share of GFCF (%) [2] | Private share of GFCF (%) [3] | Government GFCF/ GDP (%) [4] | Private GFCF/ GDP (%) [5] | Total GFCF as (%) of GDP [4+5] [6] |
|---|---|---|---|---|---|---|
| 1980 | 397.8 | 33.2 | 66.8 | 11.1 | 22.2 | 33.3 |
| 1981 | 564.8 | 33.2 | 66.8 | 13.3 | 26.6 | 39.3 |
| 1982 | 597.0 | 30.5 | 69.5 | 11.3 | 25.8 | 37.1 |
| 1983 | 502.8 | 33.2 | 66.8 | 9.4 | 19.1 | 28.5 |
| 1984 | 530.4 | 25.1 | 74.9 | 7.9 | 20.1 | 28.0 |
| 1985 | 455.6 | 30.6 | 69.4 | 7.2 | 16.3 | 23.5 |
| 1986 | 417.1 | 35.0 | 65.0 | 7.1 | 12.9 | 19.8 |
| 1987 | 468.4 | 37.8 | 62.2 | 8.2 | 13.4 | 21.6 |
| 1988 | 513.4 | 35.0 | 65.0 | 8.0 | 14.7 | 22.7 |
| 1989 | 554.1 | 33.2 | 66.8 | 7.7 | 15.6 | 23.3 |
| 1990 | 694.0 | 19.2 | 80.8 | 5.0 | 21.0 | 26.0 |
| 1991 | 678.0 | 28.1 | 71.9 | 6.7 | 17.0 | 23.7 |
| 1992 | 1049.2 | 17.8 | 82.2 | 5.3 | 24.7 | 30.0 |
| 1993* | 1303.5 | n.a. | n.a. | n.a. | n.a. | 34.2 |
| 1994* | 1233.8 | n.a. | n.a. | n.a. | n.a. | 29.4 |

*Preliminary.
*Sources*:
1. Data for column [1]: CBJ, *Monthly Statistical Bulletin*, (various issues).
2. Column [2]. Calculated by employing the data of Government GFCF in the IMF, *Government Statistics Yearbook* (1991a, 1992a, 1994a).
3. Column [3]= 100% – figures in column [2].
4. Columns [4] [5] and [6] are calculated by employing the GDP data in CBJ, *Monthly Statistical Bulletin*.

particularly before 1986. On average its share was 70 per cent during 1980–92. Yet, as short-term profit is a feature of private activity, or the economy in general, investment was mainly in the construction sector (buildings) and transport rather than capital equipment for industry (Central Bank of Jordan, 1995).

Secondly, government investment was limited on average to about 8 per cent of GDP. Most government investment is concentrated on two sectors, namely infrastructure (construction, transportation, telecommunications, energy and irrigation) and the social and services sectors (health, education, housing and government buildings) (Ministry of Planning, 1986; 1994).

According to the normative theory of public sector intervention, government intervention through public spending seems to be consistent with the policies advocated by the market proponents. The question is whether there is another role for the state which affects private activities more than is apparent from public spending measurements.

### 6.2.2 Government Regulations

The UNDP (1993, p. 52) has argued that private entrepreneurs in developing countries are less concerned about government spending than with government control. Thus, the role of the government in regulating the economy has a more vital impact because the institutional context of the state is reflected in its regulatory role.[2]

Although the government in Jordan pursues free-market policies, the economy is a market-based political economy (MBPE) (Reid, 1994). Decisions on imports (who? what? how much?) are made through centralized units. The government also determines the domestic prices at which goods can be imported or exported. In other words, it uses licensing as an effective means of favouring and rewarding special distributional interest groups. Moreover, the government indirectly decides who obtains bank credits because most financing is based on collateral rather than on risk assessment (Ghezawi, et al., 1989, p. 19). In other words, the rich can get access to loans, especially in the specialist financial institutions. Other protectionist policies, such as the competition with imported goods and the use of overvalued exchange rates (until 1988), are also decided by central government.

So, spending to establish, acquire or maintain a government-granted monopoly or secure an otherwise privileged position is widespread. In this context, the effect of government regulation is more excessive than the figures shown by the government spending ratio. The problem with this role however, is that it cannot be quantified or measured although its effect could be assessed by employing the institutional approach.

The Jordanian state is a mercantile state. In a mercantile state, consumers are not allowed to decide what should be produced, in the sense of demand and supply; instead the state reserves to itself the right to single out and promote certain economic activities. In Jordan the Ministry of Industry and Trade, and the Ministry of Supply, were the major players in deciding who and what was to be supplied and consumed in the market.

De Soto (1989) contended that there are major differences between a market economy and a mercantile economy.

Competition prevails in the first while privileges and the employment of the law to one's own advantage is a feature of the latter as regulation is the determinant factor of the economy. Under the standard perfect competition model, selfish behaviour by small independent economic players, such as utility maximization by consumers and profit and wealth maximization by producers, results in a situation which is also desirable in the sense that the value of output, at prevailing market prices, cannot be increased, and which is, moreover, Pareto optimal. However, as Buchanan (1980, p. 4) argued, once 'institutions have moved away from ordered markets toward the near chaos of direct political allocation', DUP activities will arise. Therefore, market economies tend to serve consumers efficiently, while in mercantilism, bureaucrats serve at the cost of society.

Entrepreneurs in market economies tend to satisfy customer requirements of quality, price and sustainable supply, while in a mercantile society entrepreneurs seek to satisfy the state so as to win privileges through its policies. Hence, corruption is often a feature of a mercantile state and this is Jordan's major illness as parliamentary debates reveal (Susser, 1992, p. 462).

Further, in a mercantile economy, entrepreneurs and workers spend an increasing amount of time complaining, flattering and negotiating. Competition for the profits connected with political influence become the concern of entrepreneurs. The aim is to obtain economic monopoly positions as the political domain becomes subordinated to economic self-interest. The consequences are that resources are spent obtaining a larger share of a given stake rather than on increasing the size of the stake itself. So the government, as in Jordan, has to employ more bureaucrats to meet the demands of special interest groups. In Jordan half the workforce is employed by the government, mainly in its services sector. Such bureaucrats are not the same as genuine workers. They increase neither production nor investment by their efforts. However, they do increase the complexity of state regulation by their daily intervention in the economic life of small producers and the general population.

In Jordan access to the market is restricted. Special licences are required for almost everything. This creates a constant need for assistance from privileged private groups or authorities who control or guard the administrative gates. Thus rent-seeking becomes the norm, while large numbers of working papers are needed to gain access to markets.

In brief the attributes of the state regulatory role in Jordan are: centralization of economic decision-making within a small elite; special interest legislation; the non-existence of or only very weak public accountability; and the non-involvement of basic local institutions or smaller business groups (as the small producers) in the economic process. Its features also include favouritism and the promotion of monopoly powers. So it can be concluded that the regulatory role of the state in Jordan is more important in its effect than government spending because it restricts the market and the initiatives of ordinary private entrepreneurs who lack access to the decision-making body.

### 6.2.3 Government Ownership

In Jordan, there was no nationalization or centralized planned economy, as was the case in the majority of developing countries, particularly after their independence. This is because of the ideological belief of the state in market-oriented policies and in the effectiveness of the free-enterprise model as a path for development. Although it has carried out indicative planning, the state officially pursues a *laissez-faire* approach based on individual initiative and adjustment to market demand and supply (Ministry of Planning, 1986).

Historically, government ownership in Jordan passed through three different phases. The first was between 1921 and 1950 when there was neither the place for government ownership nor the funds to build the economy. The state's main priority was to establish its authority and legitimacy while responding to private sector demands through regulation; an example was the relinquishing of income tax declarations.

The second phase lasted from the official formation of the Kingdom until 1972 when the private sector was the leader, initiator and main engine of investment. The only exception was the establishment of a state cement industry in 1951 because the size of the investment was beyond the financial capabilities of the private sector. Thus, a joint venture, in which the state owned 51 per cent of the cement industry, was the first form of government ownership. In other cases the government participated with fewer than the majority shares and in order to overcome the shortages of funds in private projects. Given the relatively limited external and internal sources for financing the government budget at the time and the limited demand in the economy, the allocative role of the state was restricted to 'helping' the private sector (Sha'sha, 1991).

In 1973 the role of the state entered its third phase as an owner of major projects. Two main factors were responsible for this phase, which is the more relevant for the privatization discourse. The first was the increase in government revenues, which created a new and immense capacity for the government to intervene through the means of production. The second was the need to build services, an infrastructure and a modern industrial base in a country lacking many of the natural resources owned by its neighbours. As a result, the Jordanian state participates directly in the production sector for three reasons. The first is the substantial capital required for capital-intensive projects, particularly in mineral projects which the private sector cannot afford. The second is the high risk surrounding investment in some projects, and the final reason is related to the two above, namely control of the commanding height industries, which the state is keen to be involved in, in order to generate revenue and foreign exchange (i.e. mineral-based industry) (Kanovsky, 1990, p. 338).

The small size of the Jordanian market will naturally lead one to the conclusion that most government participation in ownership implies a high probability of a monopolistic position and indeed this is often the case. The share of value added generated by the central government (pure state sector) during the period 1970–94 averaged 21 per cent. This includes all government services such as defence, public administration, education, health, etc. Thus, it is obvious that the state sectoral contribution is highly limited. On the public sector level it was estimated that in mid-1986 it produced about 40 per cent of the country's GNP, possessed nearly 50 per cent of capital formation and employed nearly half the country's workforce (Fank (1986) as cited in Brand (1992, p. 170).

*Notions of State-Owned Enterprises (SOEs)*
There are three kinds of SOEs in Jordan and according to the International Monetary Fund, there were 19 non-financial SOEs in 1987 (Table 6.5), as there were in 1995.

a. *Pure State Sector Departments:* Some such departments are involved in commercial activities and are fully owned by the central government. Their funding is derived from the government budget and they are staffed by civil servants. Examples are the Civil Employees Consumption Corporation and the Free Zones Corporation. Their relative importance derives from the spending power of the central government. In the five-year development plan (1981–85) 27 per cent of the resources allocated for development expenditure were to be used by the central government departments.

b. *Autonomous State Institutions*: These institutions arise through a gradual transformation of government departments or similar administrative structures. They are owned by government but are at the same time legally, financially and administratively independent. In spite of this apparent autonomy the board is generally appointed by the cabinet and central government continues to exercise administrative and

*Table* 6.5  Non-financial state-owned enterprises in Jordan

| Non-financial SOEs | Non-financial SOEs |
|---|---|
| 1  Aqaba Railway Corp. | 11  Water Authority |
| 2  Civil Aviation Authority | 12  Jordan Electricity Authority |
| 3  Civil employees Consumption Corp. | 13  Jordan Hijaz Railway |
| 4  Free Zones Corp. | 14  Jordan Hotels and Tourism Co. |
| 5  General Transportation Corp. | 15  Ports Corp. |
| 6  Himmeh Hot Springs Co. | 16  Jordan Phosphate Mines Co. and Subsidiary: Jordan Fertilizer Co. |
| 7  Holy Lands Hotel Corp. | 17  Royal Jordanian Airlines |
| 8  Hotels Corp. | 18  Posts and Telecommunication |
| 9  Housing Corp. | 19  Jordan Cement Co. |
| 10  Jordan Broadcasting & Television | |

*Source*: IMF (1987, p 67).

financial control. Examples are the Public Transportation Corporation, the Water Authority, Jordan Electricity Authority and Royal Jordanian Airlines. Their share of development expenditure was estimated to be 34 per cent of the total allocated in the 1981–85 development plan.[3]

c. *Mixed Enterprises*: These are shareholding companies in which the central government or autonomous state institutions have equity participation. Government representation on the board of directors in such enterprises is linked to its share in the company's paid-up capital. Their total number in 1985 was about 90. Examples are the Arab Potash Company (the largest in Jordan, with a government share of 53 per cent) and the Jordan Phosphate Mines Company (government share 69 per cent) (Khalaf, 1989, pp. 236–7).

*The Role of SOEs on the Sectoral Level*
*Pure Domination.*  The government operates as a monopolist in the water sector, which is the domain of an autonomous public institution (the Water Authority); in telecommunication activity, represented by the Telecommunication Corporation, which operates as an integral part of the central

government; and finally in electricity generation through the Jordan Electricity Authority, which accounted for 92 per cent of the total electricity output in 1994. The remainder of electricity is generated by the industrial companies (e.g. Refinery, Cement Factory, Potash Company, and the Fertilizer Company) for their own use (Jordan Electricity Authority, 1995, Table no. 5, p. 18).

*Equity Sharing*
a. *Mining*: In this sector, the state holds its largest share. The country is the world's fifth biggest producer of phosphates rock and the third biggest exporter after Morocco and the USA. The government possesses 38.4 per cent of the equity of the Phosphate Mines Company, and in potash it holds 53 per cent of the Arab Potash Company. Total state investment amounts to about 50 per cent of the capital of mining companies and represents almost half of the total state shareholding in all Jordanian corporations (Anani and Khalaf, 1989, p. 216).
b. *Manufacturing*: The total equity share of government in this sector amounts to about 23.2 per cent of the whole capital of the manufacturing shareholding companies in Jordan. The state's participation ranges from less than 1 per cent in the Arab Aluminium Industry and Arab Food and Medical Appliances to 49.7 per cent in the Jordan Glass Industries. In actual terms, 87 per cent of state equity sharing in this sector is held in the four largest companies: the Jordan Cement Factories, the Jordanian Petroleum Refinery, the Glass Industries and the Engineering Industries. The share of capital in these four companies represents 56 per cent of all the capital of the 48 manufacturing companies in Jordan (ibid.).

*Mixed Sectors.* There are two mixed activities where the state operates to some extent with the private sector. The first is transportation where the state contributed about two-thirds of the value added during 1970–88. However, the only competition between the private sector and the state is in land transportation. Air transportation is a monopoly, and rail transportation (Aqaba Railway and the Hijaz Railway) is an oligopoly. The ports are run by an autonomous state institution (The Ports Authority) (Khalaf, 1989, pp. 240–1). The second is electricity distribution. In this activity there are two shareholding companies (the Jordan Electricity Company and Irbid Electricity Company) which distributed 62 per cent of the electricity power generated by Jordan Electricity Authority in 1994 (50 and 12 per cent respectively) (JEA, 1994, Table no. 12, p. 25). However, the state possesses shares in both of them (13.6 and 55 per cent respectively) and they are regulated by the government.

Therefore, the absolute private sector can be found operating in agriculture and quarrying while the Jordanian state possesses a limited allocative effectiveness through direct ownership and production. In this, it appears to be on the same side as the advocates of the market approach. However, privatization in Jordan started to become visible on the government agenda during the mid-1980s.

## 6.3 OBJECTIVES AND REASONS FOR PRIVATIZATION OF SOEs

Privatization as a new economic policy in Jordan was initiated in 1985 after a new government took office in April. The new prime minister, Al-Rafai was a major advocate of reform policies in Jordan. Privatization was part of a larger reform package and was announced in a paper entitled *The Role of the Private Sector in Development* presented to the Jordan Development Conference held from 8 to 10 November 1986.[4] The main goal of the conference was a review of the 1986–90 five-year plan. The government established a special permanent privatization committee at ministerial level to study the most suitable techniques for implementing the proposed privatization policies. The objectives set out in the paper and reported by Al-Quaryoty (1989, p. 170) provide a clear view of the government's objectives and privatization measures:

First, promoting the private sector in its traditional domain through the following measures:
1. Minimizing market distortions by allowing market forces to determine the prices of factors of production as well as the price of final output of industries.

2. Providing support for research to enhance the efficiency of private sector operations and to have pre-feasibility studies made available to private investors at a minimal cost.
3. Devising policies and incentives to encourage private investors.
4. Pledging consistent and uniform application of government policies to reduce disparities in the treatment of foreign and domestic firms.
5. Providing a supportive legal environment to property rights and contractual obligations and having a commercial law for the settlement of disputes.

Second, transferring public control of PEs to the private sector. This strategy envisages the following measures:
1. Sale of state-owned shares in mixed enterprises to the private sector.
2. Transferring ownership of autonomous PEs to the private sector.
3. Authorizing the establishment of private universities.
4. Leasing state-owned agricultural land to the private sector.

The conclusion is that privatization in Jordan does not reflect any shift in economic or political ideologies and one must therefore ask why privatization was initiated at this time.[5]

### 1. Economic Recession and Deterioration in Living Standards

Jordan's economic development after 1973 was mainly linked to the increases in oil prices which led to demands for its labour force in the oil-rich Gulf states, and to the grants given by those countries in the boom years of the 1970s and early 1980s. Therefore, the recession in the economies of the oil-rich Gulf states after the decline in oil prices had an immense effect on Jordan. When oil prices declined sharply in 1985 and 1986, government external revenues declined from JD350.2 million in 1985 to JD303 million and JD190 million in 1986 and 1987 respectively (Central Bank of Jordan, 1989, pp. 45–6). This was combined with a sharp decline in workers' remittances from JD414 million in 1986 to JD317.7 million in 1987 (ibid., pp. 26–9). GDP real growth rates started a decline from 9 per cent in 1986 to only 2.5 per cent in 1987 and entered negative growth during 1988–90 (see Figure 6.1).

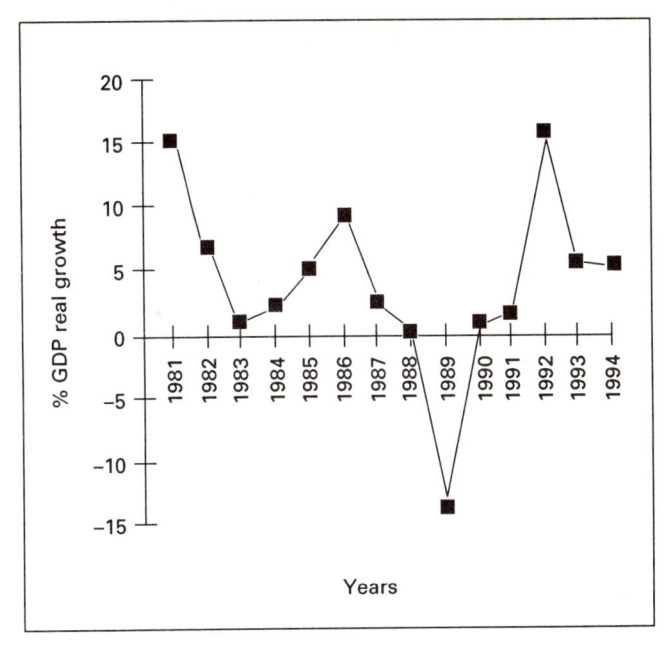

*Figure* 6.1  Real GDP growth rates in Jordan (1985=100), 1981–94
*Source*: Central Bank of Jordan, *Monthly Statistical Bulletin* (various issues).

In a country where the annual average population growth rate is 3.5 per cent, GDP growth rates need to be at least 5 per cent in order to maintain the people's standard of living. While the reduction in Arab aid and workers' remittances may be attributed to economic factors of recession in the Gulf states, the decision of the Kingdom in July 1988 to disengage from its administrative role in the West Bank revealed the political vulnerability of the country. Palestinians working abroad stopped transferring money back to Jordan while those inside the country transferred their funds out. As a result the government was forced to devalue the Jordanian currency (dinar) in 1988 and 1989. From an exchange rate of $3 during the 1970s, the Jordanian dinar in 1989 lost about half its value (1 JD = $1.74). With the recession deepening, real per capita income regressed from JD742.6 ($2227.8) in 1981 to JD653 ($1959) in 1987 and to a low JD374.7 ($652) in 1989 (Figure 6.2).

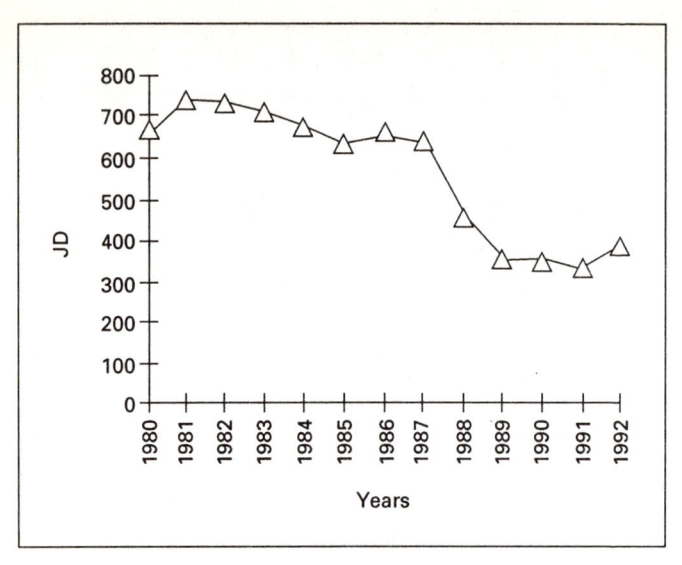

*Figure* 6.2  Real annual per capita income in Jordan (1985=100), 1980–92
*Source*: Calculated by using the national income data from the IMF *International Financial Statistics* (various issues), and the gross domestic product deflator in Central Bank of Jordan, *Monthly Statistical Bulletin* (various issues).

Unemployment rates doubled from only 4 per cent in 1981 to 8 per cent in 1986 and continued to grow, particularly after the 1990–91 Gulf War, to reach about 20 per cent (Khasawneh *et al.*, 1993, p. 13). Within the above context, there were many ideas for reducing the role of the state and giving the private sector the first initiative on the grounds, though without solid evidence, that the Jordanian private sector would be far more efficient than the state sector, and could therefore lift the economy from its recession. The privatization discourse started in 1986 but the deterioration in the economic conditions at the end of the 1980s gave further cause for policy-makers to consider privatization as a cure to the problems.

*2. Growing Budgetary Deficit*
A second reason for considering privatization was the Jordanian central government's growing budgetary deficit.

*Table* 6.6  Overall deficit in the Jordanian central government budget, 1980–94

| Year | Deficit (MJDs) | Year | Deficit (MJDs) |
|---|---|---|---|
| 1980 | 109.9 | 1988 | 204.6 |
| 1981 | 115.9 | 1989 | 137.1 |
| 1982 | 128.2 | 1990 | 95.1 |
| 1983 | 108.5 | 1991 | 5.94 |
| 1984 | 139.7 | 1992 | 144.2 |
| 1985 | 153.1 | 1993 | 26.4 |
| 1986 | 130.0 | 1994 | 55.1 |
| 1987 | 247.8 | | |

*Sources*:
1. Data for 1980–88 from the IMF (1991b), *International Financial Statistics*.
2. Data for 1988–94 from the IMF (1995), *International Financial Statistics*.

The deficit rose more than twofold from JD109.9 million in 1980 to JD247.8 million in 1987 (Table 6.6). As Satloff (1992) argued, Jordanian decision-makers, after feeling the crisis in the economy during the mid-1980s, chose not to respond with a tight fiscal policy but instead 'to ignore the glaring structural weaknesses in the economy, to hide them under the rug of further borrowing at commercial rates, or to exacerbate them with expansionary policies that only shrank the Kingdom's finite foreign currency reserves' (1992, p. 132). A further option was considering the sale of SOEs to raise money in order to reduce the budgetary deficit.

## 3. The Debt Crisis

The debt crisis has had an immense impact upon Jordan's economy. During the period 1984–88 external debt rose sharply from $3508 million to $5733 million (Table 6.7). The main factors behind the uncontrolled expansion in foreign debt were first, the uncontrolled pattern of merchandise imports, which increased from JD108.2 million in 1973 to JD1074.4 million in 1985 while merchandise exports only increased from JD19 million in 1973 to JD310 million in 1985, leaving the country with a trade deficit equal to JD763.5 million in 1985 or 39.3 per cent of the GDP. Second, total consumption

*Table* 6.7  Jordan's external debt, 1984–93 (US$ millions)

| Items / Years | Total external debt [1] | Public disbursed debt [2] | Total debt service [3] | [1]/ GDP (%) [4] | [3]/Total Exports of goods and services (%) [5] |
|---|---|---|---|---|---|
| 1984 | 3508 | 2832 | 452 | 71.3 | 25.8 |
| 1988 | 5733 | 5352 | 1025 | 95.2 | 37.7 |
| 1989 | 6467 | 6222 | 1160 | 156.7 | 49.0 |
| 1990 | 7276 | 7023 | 690 | 180.5 | 38.5 |
| 1991 | 7787 | 7447 | 659 | 185.5 | 26.4 |
| 1992 | 7184 | 6914 | 442 | 140.0 | 16.5 |
| 1993 | 6972 | 6825 | 205 | 127.0 | 7.3 |

*Sources*:
1. Debt data from World Bank, *World Debt Tables* (1990 and 1995).
2. Columns [4] and [5] calculated using the GDP and exports figures in Central Bank of Jordan, *Monthly Statistical Bulletin*, (various issues).

inflated over a ten-year period (1973–83). As a percentage of the GDP it increased from 97 per cent to more than the productive capacity of the economy during the second half of the 1980s (Central Bank of Jordan, 1989 and 1995).

With such structural problems, Jordan approached the eurodollar financial markets and other international aid agencies for more financial support in the second half of the 1980s. In April 1989 Jordan concluded a five-year structural adjustment package with the IMF. Because of the Gulf crisis, however, a second agreement between the two sides was concluded in October 1991 and will last for seven years.

A privatization plan was essential for the government in approaching the IMF, and the World Bank in particular, because it dressed the government in a reformist outfit and matched the demands of the international agencies (Dessouki and Aboul Kheir, 1991, p. 221). As a result the government secured credits worth $262 million from the IMF during the period 1985–88, and $107 million worth of loans from the World Bank in 1987–88.[6] Part of the World Bank's loans was allocated to the consultancy service costs required to study the feasibility of privatizing the Telecommunication Corporation (TCC).

### 4. Attracting Foreign Investment

Another reason for seeing privatization as a viable solution to the economic problems in Jordan was the need to increase the flow of foreign investment to the country. As Table 6.4 shows, there was a real need to substitute the shortages of investment in the country. While in 1981 the investment ratio (total investment to the GDP) was about 39 per cent, it declined to only around 20 per cent in 1986. Although historically Jordan was not an attractive destination for private investment, as Table 6.8 proves, the declining share of investment in the GDP forced the Jordanian decision-makers to rethink their policies, particularly as there was little prospect of increasing Arab aid.

Privatization in the context of deregulation and new incentives for foreign ownership were ways of increasing investment in the country as well as the efficiency of that investment because foreign investors will not invest their capital in unviable projects. For example, the idea of privatizing Royal Jordanian Airlines (RJ) originated from the need for new investment to replace its ageing fleet of aircraft and expand its services to new destinations. In the case of the Telecommunication Corporation (TCC) about 70 per cent of the investment projects with estimated costs of JD91 million during 1986–90 had to be financed by hard currency, particularly as the bulk of the technical equipment for the projects had to be imported. Reliance on foreign consultants as technical staff imposed further constraints on the financial capacity of the corporation. Similar arguments can be found in the purchase of new buses for the Public Transport Corporation (PTC) in

*Table* 6.8  Net private foreign investment in Jordan, 1979–89 (selected years)

| Years | Net private foreign investment ($ million) | Years | Net private foreign investment ($ million) |
|---|---|---|---|
| 1979 | 26 | 1986 | 21 |
| 1981 | 143 | 1987 | 33 |
| 1983 | 30 | 1988 | 0 |
| 1984 | 71 | 1989 | 0 |
| 1985 | 23 | | |

*Source:* Joffe (1993, Table no. 7.1, p. 134).

Amman (Ministry of Planning, 1986, pp. 421–65). It was believed that higher foreign investment and greater efficiency of the economy would be essential ingredients for the achievement of respectable GDP growth.

Given the marginal role of foreign investment in Jordan, the other benefit from the liberalization policies, of which privatization constitutes but one cornerstone, is 'to show some concurrence with the perceptions of the IMF and the World Bank' on the openness for such investment (Joffe, 1993, p. 139).

*5. The Imitation Factor*
Another reason is the imitation of the western idea of privatization, particularly that of the new conservatives in the USA and Britain. Since most of the government is composed of professionals educated in those two countries, any new academic or western image has been emulated to give the country a modern face. The preference for foreign experts, foreign models, and foreign standards is a consequence of Jordan's imitative modernism. Also, the economic crisis gave an edge to a coalition of technocrats who believed that domestic crisis can be overcome by international prescriptions.

All the above factors indicate there was no deep-seated commitment on the part of Jordan's decision-makers to follow the path of privatization, but the government's freedom to continue the management of the economy as they had done before the economic crisis in the mid-1980s was limited by several factors. The recession and the pressure from international financial institutions to cut public expenditure, the lack of investment funds as well as the modern image of the country in an integrated international environment all played a significant role in the consideration of privatization proposals.

6.4 PERFORMANCE OF SOEs

**6.4.1 The Economic Performance**

*The General Economic Performance*
There are no comparative studies of the economic performance of public versus private sector enterprises in Jordan.

There has been a difficulty finding like-with-like efficiency comparisons between different enterprises. This stems from the advantages of economies of scale in a small market, which provide most public enterprises in Jordan with the basis for a monopolistic position. However, three commentators have referred to the comparative efficiency between public and private ownership in Jordan.

Robins (1986, p. 52) claimed that the rate of return on public investment is roughly half the rate achieved by the private sector, a conclusion not based on any conclusive evidence or methodological empirical studies.

A second study by two senior Jordanian economists, Anani and Khalaf (1989), stated that

> Although there is a complaint that government-owned enterprises are not as efficiently run as those in the private sector, there is no clear-cut empirical evidence to support such a statement in the case of Jordan. While there are clear indications that testify to better management in privately owned and managed organizations, evidence to the contrary is also available (p. 212).

The study also pointed out that an inadequate rate of return could be found in government shares in the shareholding companies. Where the opportunity cost of maintaining such shares exceeded 7 per cent, the rate of return on average was less than 3 per cent (ibid., p. 212).

Al-Quaryoty (1989, p. 177) asserted that the efficiency of the Jordan Electric Company, which is a private franchise, is not much better than that of the Jordan Electricity Authority, which is a state enterprise. He dismissed the option of franchising SOEs in Jordan because of the limited number of contractors willing and able to provide such services.

*Jordan Electricity Authority (JEA)*
Table 6.9 displays the performance indicators of one Jordanian state enterprise, the Jordan Electricity Authority (JEA), during the period 1987–94.

JEA produced more than 91 per cent of the total electricity generated in the Kingdom during this period. There was an increasing trend in employee productivity during the period 1990–94. Nevertheless, the figure for 1992 (1973

Table 6.9 Performance indicators of Jordan Electricity Authority, 1987–94

| Years<br>Indicators | 1987 | 1988 | 1989 | 1990 | 1991 | 1992 | 1993 | 1994 |
|---|---|---|---|---|---|---|---|---|
| **Workforce indicators** | | | | | | | | |
| 1. Annual productivity (MWH/employee) | 1730[a] | 1530 | 1627 | 1623 | 1641 | 1973[a] | 2119[a] | 2190 |
| 2. Generating capacity (MW/employee) | 0.5 | 0.5 | 0.5 | 0.46 | 0.46 | 0.46 | 0.43 | 0.43 |
| 3. Number of customers (customer/employee) | 103 | 107 | 107 | 109 | 112 | 112 | 116 | 120 |
| **Technical indicators** | | | | | | | | |
| 1. Thermal efficiency for generating stations (%) | 33.5 | 33.8 | 34.6 | 34.3 | 33.8 | 33.3 | 32.9 | 32.0 |
| 2. Average cut in power for consumers (hour/year) | 8.4 | 6.8 | 7.0 | 6.0 | 5.5 | 17.0 | 5.5 | 6.0 |
| 3. Total Percentage of electricity loss (%) | 10.1 | 10.2 | 10.1 | 10.3 | 10.2 | 9.9 | 9.6 | 9.3 |
| **Rate of return on fixed assets** | 4.4 | 3.2 | −1.8 | 6.4 | 4.04 | 5.99 | 10.5 | 10.8 |

a. In 1987, 1992 and 1993 the figure includes electricity exports.
MWH: Megawatt per hour.
MW: Megawatt.
Source: JEA (1993) and (1994).

MWH/employee) reflects the increase in production for export (to Syria), which constituted 1.7 per cent of the total electricity generated by JEA in 1992. This in itself represented a new way of utilizing the enterprise's capacity. The increase in employee productivity in 1994 was 35 per cent in comparison with 1990.

In terms of technical efficiency, the indicator for the thermal efficiency of generating stations revealed a slight decline in 1994 when compared with 1990. Nevertheless, in comparison with the total sector in the Kingdom, the efficiency of JEA was 0.2 per cent higher (JEA, 1994, p. 14). Another important measure of quality for the services provided by the JEA is the average time spent without electricity by consumers in the Kingdom. Apart from 1992, in which snow storms affected the provision of services, there was an improvement in the quality of services provided by the corporation. The average time without electricity supply declined from 7.9 hours/year in 1987 to less than 6 hours/year in 1991, 1993 and 1994.

The percentage loss in electricity, which is one of the technical features in the electricity industry, was much less than for that in the whole sector. While it was 14.7 per cent for the latter, it was only 9.3 per cent in JEA during 1994 (JEA, 1994, p. 14).

The rate of return on fixed assets shows a positive trend. The nearly 7 per cent increase in the rate of return, from 4 to 6, and 10.8 per cent, between 1991, 1992 and 1994 according to JEA reports, was a result of hard budget policy and strict monitoring of corporate expenditure, particularly investment in new projects. This reduced the opportunistic behaviour of the corporation's employees, which reduced the agency costs. This is consistent with Vickers and Yarrow's (1991) argument regarding the positive effect of tightened state budgets on limiting managerial discretion and increasing efficiency.

The above figures suggest that the economic efficiency of the JEA was better in comparison with the indicators for the total electricity sector. Furthermore, there is evidence that the quality of services reached higher standards during the eight years 1987–94, and there was a positive rate of return on the

JEA's fixed assets. These increased by 80 per cent between 1992 and 1994.

From the empirical studies review, and the case study of the JEA, there is no clear-cut evidence of superior economic performance within the private sector in Jordan as opposed to the state-owned sector, or that SOEs are necessarily linked with economic inefficiency. This is consistent with the empirical evidence provided in Chapter 4 on the comparative efficiency of public versus private ownership in developing countries.

### 6.4.2 The Financial Performance

One of the problems facing Jordanian SOEs is the low profitability if not the large losses incurred by them. The reasons for such poor financial performance vary from one enterprise to another and in any case, economically efficient does not necessarily mean financially profitable, especially in decreasing-cost industries. However, other factors such as equity considerations also play a major role in determining the profitability of a state enterprise.

*Jordan Electricity Authority (JEA)*
Despite a trend of increasing productivity and a positive rate of return on fixed assets JEA suffered large losses between 1987 and 1991, particularly during 1989 and 1990 (JD19.1 million and JD14.5 million respectively). Table 6.10 reveals that the problem of profitability lies mainly with three factors.

The first is the government pricing policy. This imposed a tariff rate on the corporation which did not reflect the marginal costs of the electricity unit supplied to the customer and resulted in losses from the sale of each unit of electricity at the rate of −0.04, −0.96, −6.74, −4.97 and −2.51 fils during 1987–91.

The second factor relates to investment. Many of the proposed projects required a high proportion of external finance. The policy of external borrowing to finance questionable projects, such as the unification of electricity grids with neighbouring Arab states, led to a long-term debt burden which affected the profitability of the JEA.

Table 6.10  The financial performance of Jordan Electricity Authority, 1987–94 (thousand JDs)

| Years<br>Indicators | 1987 | 1988 | 1989 | 1990 | 1991 | 1992 | 1993 | 1994 |
|---|---|---|---|---|---|---|---|---|
| 1. Electricity sale net profits | (88) | (3637) | (19161) | (14514) | (7525) | 2415 | 10301 | 9015 |
| 2. Unit cost (F. per KWH)* | 20.74 | 22.98 | 27.76 | 27.23 | 27.38 | 24.38 | 25.18 | 26.98 |
| 3. Unit revenue (F. per KWH) | 20.7 | 22.02 | 21.02 | 22.28 | 24.87 | 25.04 | 27.78 | 29.1 |
| 4. Net profit per unit sold (F. per KWH) | (0.07) | (0.96) | (6.74) | (4.97) | (2.51) | 0.88 | 2.6 | 3.2 |
| 5. Annual capital investment | 11760 | 27452 | 12658 | 2454 | 8826 | 4820 | 10020 | 46456 |
| 6. External contents of (5) (%) | 100 | 68 | 55 | 14.3 | 9.5 | 10.0 | 100.0 | 27.5 |
| 7. Net working capital | 3974 | (18894) | (26697) | (33527) | (35830) | (37640) | (41395) | 7191 |
| 8. Debt payment and service as % of total revenue | 41 | 54.4 | 57.4 | 89.7 | 70.2 | 43.1 | 33.8 | 30.1 |
| 9. Self finance (%) | 15 | (–) | (–) | (–) | (–) | (–) | 10.4 | 23.83 |

*Unit cost measurement in Fils per Kilowatt hour.
Each 1 JD is equal to 1000 fils.
Sources:
1. Indicators no. 2, 3, 5 and 9 adopted from JEA (1993, p. 52; 1994, p. 52).
2. Indicators 1, 4, 6, 7 and 8 calculated by employing the data in JEA (1993; 1994).

The debt payment and its servicing constituted about 60 per cent of the total revenue generated from electricity sales during 1987–92. Also, the outturn costs of foreign borrowing crucially depended upon movement in relative exchange rates completely outside the control of JEA. For example, a major conflict between the Finance Ministry and the JEA arose over the rouble exchange rate for the repayment of a Russian loan to the JEA. While the Ministry insisted upon an exchange rate of $1.65 to the rouble, the JEA said that the rate should be equal to the rate at the date of borrowing. Following the same argument, the devaluation of the Jordanian dinar in 1988 and 1989 imposed heavy losses on the Authority during 1989 and 1990. As a result, the net working capital of the JEA was negative until 1993, which made it impossible for the enterprise to finance any proportion of its projects. The last factor, related to the previous two, is the management of the enterprise. The policy of increasing accountability and responsibility, started in 1992, bore fruit by converting JD7.5 million losses from 1991 into JD2.4 million profits in 1992. Imposing restrictions on current expenditure was among the major factors behind the successes of 1993 and 1994. For example, general and administrative expenses reduced from JD4.35 million in 1993 to JD3.9 million in 1994. However, the main factor behind the transfer of JEA from loss-maker to profitable enterprise is the increase in the tariffs imposed on different consumer groups to reflect the marginal costs of electricity production and supply. For example, between 1991 and 1994 the bulk supply tariff for electricity companies increased on average by 35 per cent while it increased by 15 per cent for large industries.[7] So, pricing policies transferred losses into profits, and as a result, in 1994 the Authority achieved for the first time a positive net working capital and 23.8 per cent self-finance.

In summary, the financial performance of JEA during the period 1987–91 was poor because of a number of factors not exclusive to its ownership. Increasing accountability, tighter budget control, and correct pricing policy lay behind increasing profitability during 1993 and 1994. However, the debt and investment problems in JEA are part of the structural problems stemming from poor management of the economy as a whole rather than a result of the geometry of ownership.

*The General Financial Performance of SOEs*
According to the available data the financial performance of many SOEs seems to be poor. The total external debt of the non-financial SOEs in Jordan was $1517.2 million (about JD871.8 million) in 1989 (see Table 6.11). This debt constituted 36.7 per cent of the country's GDP. In 1990, however, there was an estimated decline in the external debt for these enterprises of $194.5 million, which is a much healthier sign in comparison with previous years.

*Table* 6.11  Jordanian non-financial SOEs' external debt, 1970–90 ($ million)

| Year | External debt | Year | External debt |
|------|---------------|------|---------------|
| 1970 | 5.0 | 1981 | 705.8 |
| 1971 | 21.2 | 1982 | 906.3 |
| 1972 | 21.2 | 1983 | 891.7 |
| 1973 | 21.4 | 1984 | 976.4 |
| 1974 | 43.8 | 1985 | 1060.1 |
| 1975 | 61.1 | 1986 | 1220.5 |
| 1976 | 61.8 | 1987 | 1423.1 |
| 1977 | 167.9 | 1988 | 1345.2 |
| 1978 | 227.0 | 1989 | 1517.2 |
| 1979 | 299.2 | 1990 | 1322.7 |
| 1980 | 430.0 | | |

*Sources*: World Bank, *World Bank Tables* (1991 and 1992).

The external debt began its increase in 1970. From $5 million in 1970 it reached $430 million in 1980. This reflects the poor overall management of the economy, particularly its dependence on external sources of finance, and the poor financial performance of Jordanian SOEs. As long as loans, foreign aid and grants were able to maximize government revenues and minimize transaction costs, particularly monitoring costs, the government relied on them rather than on reforming its monitoring system.

Another remarkable phenomenon of SOEs is the poor financial performance of the public shareholding companies in which government participates through its paid capital. In 1985, about 22 per cent of the 90 shareholding companies suffered losses, more than 60 per cent of them in the industrial or mining activities (Brand, 1992, p. 171). More recent figures for the financial return on government investment in shareholding companies are presented in Table 6.12.

State investment is mainly directed through the Jordan Investment Corporation (JIC): the government investment arm established in 1988 as a substitute for the Pension Fund. At the beginning of 1995, JIC owns parts of 75 public shareholding companies with an estimated market value between JD300 million ($432.25 million) and JD500 million

*Table* 6.12  The financial returns of government investment in shareholding companies, 1989–91

| Year | Number of companies | Value of investment (MJDs) | Total profits (MJDs) | Rate of return (%) |
|---|---|---|---|---|
| 1989 | 70 | 150.3 | 15.89 | 10.5 |
| 1990 | 70 | 149.9 | 3.1 | 2.1 |
| 1991 | 67 | 116.1 | 10.3 | 8.8 |

*Source*: Ministry of Finance (1992, pp. 127–39).

($720.46 million). The rate of return on state investment fluctuated sharply between 1989 and 1990 because of the 1990s Gulf War. However, even in 1991, only 16 out of 36 companies in the industrial and mining sectors produced profits while the remaining 20 did not distribute any profits to their shareholders (Ministry of Finance, 1992, pp. 129–130).

Losses are a very serious problem because these companies were set up to operate in an essentially commercial environment. No one could argue that the companies were established with non-commercial objectives, the argument always employed by the state to defend its position in the case of poor performance of its enterprises.

There are many reasons for the poor financial performance of both shareholding companies and purely state-owned enterprises. One is that companies whose products are mainly for export, such as the Arab Potash Company (APC) and the Jordan Phosphate Mines Company (JPMC), suffered from unfavourable terms of trade; for example, the declining prices of their products on world markets during the 1980s. The Arab Potash Company, which recorded its first profit of JD39.6 million, began commercial operations in 1983 (Fisher, 1993, p. 568). Declining prices for phosphates during 1986, 1987 and 1988 brought the unit value of their export prices (1985=100) to 87.4, 76.8 and 92.0 during 1986, 1987 and 1988 respectively (IMF, 1992b, p. 316). After the boost in world phosphate prices in 1989 and the devaluation of the dinar in 1988 and 1989, the Phosphate Mines Company enjoyed profits totalling JD107 million and JD41.4 million in 1989 and 1990 respectively (Fisher, 1993, p. 568). The decline or losses in such companies depend upon international demand and their competitiveness on the world market. Although both are shareholding companies, they are primarily financed through state funding and backed by state-sector institutions because they represent an important part of the commanding heights industries in Jordan.

Losses may also result from inadequacy of feasibility studies. One example is the South Cement Company, which was established on the basis of an inadequate feasibility study conducted in the 1970s. This company faced difficulties in marketing even in its initial levels of output and the result was a merger with the Jordan Cement Factories company in September 1985 (Al-Quaryoty, 1989). Another example is Jordan's Fertilizer Industries Company (JFIC). It was estimated that the cost of the project would be about $300 million but actual costs reached $410 million. In addition, as a result of a slump in world fertilizer prices, JFIC lost about JD13 million in 1984, its first year of trading; and in 1986, the JPMC bought the corporation, which by the end of 1985 had accumulated losses of $40 million, for only JD60 million (Fisher, 1986, p. 516).

Poor financial performance can also be the result of uncompetitive prices when compared with imported products. The Jordan Glass Industry Company (JGIC) faced a problem in marketing its inefficiently produced glass. Continuous government injection of capital into the company failed to transform its losses into profits. Government protectionist policies, completely banning the import of white glass, as well as other cost control measures undertaken by the company, only succeeded in cutting losses by a third in 1986 (Brand, 1992, p. 171). These two companies (fertilizer and glass) are clear examples of inappropriate government policies of import-substitution industrialization.

The lack of appropriate incentive and monitoring systems also has a profound effect on performance. The Public Transport Corporation, for example, which carries about 20 per cent of public transport passengers in and around greater Amman, faces strong competition from buses and taxicabs in the private sector. Since its establishment in 1975 it has made an annual loss of JD0.5 million (Khalaf, 1989, p. 246). Weak institutional management and an ill-functioning incentive and monitoring structure are the main reasons.

In SOEs such as the Electricity Authority, or institutions such as the Water Authority, government pricing at a level below the marginal unit cost of production has led to planned losses (see Table 6.9, indicator 4). This is because of social criteria implicit in government decisions to subsidize such basic goods for the population. Other companies, however, produced poor financial performances because of inefficiency in their operations. It is questionable whether they should ever have been established in the first place.

Corruption in some public enterprises also contributed significantly to their poor financial results. One of the state departments spent $350 million on a communications system which could have been purchased at much lower cost on the world market (*Guardian*, 28 April 1989, p. 15). Another scandal concerned Royal Jordanian Airlines. In 1989, the company was found to have debts amounting to about $192 million although all of this debt is believed to have been repaid the same year from the sale of its fleet of aircraft. Other cases of corruption can be found throughout the different institutions (*Guardian*, 25 April 1989, p. 14; *Guardian*, 21 April 1989, p. 10).

Another factor which seems to affect the economy as well as public enterprises is regional political spillover. For example, the Gulf War caused Royal Jordanian Airlines losses estimated to be around $100 million (Fisher, 1991, p. 586). Another example is the effect of UN sanctions on Iraq on business in Jordan's Ports Corporation. The cost of UN inspections was estimated at $30 million in 1992 and was expected to go up by 10 per cent by the end of 1993 (*Arab News*, 17 November 1993), while the amount of goods to the port of Aqaba declined by 43 per cent, from 18.7 million tonnes in 1989 to 10.6 million tonnes in 1994. Such factors demonstrate the extent to which regional politics affect the financial performance of some SOEs.

Anani and Khalaf (1989) in their study of privatization in Jordan listed six reasons for the inefficiency of SOEs: (1) overstaffing and recruitment policies, particularly in the autonomous state enterprises; (2) government pricing regulations; (3) weak systems of control where they existed; (4) weak incentive systems with some enterprises giving a bonus equal to two months' salary every year to every employee; (5) inadequate accounting systems leading to further misallocation of future investments; and (6) the absence of systematic monitoring since government representatives on the board of directors in many shareholding companies are appointed for political rather than technical reasons (ibid., 1989, pp. 217–18).

From the previous analyses it appears that the problem in the state-owned sector was not *exclusively* a result of government ownership *per se*. Most of the companies with government participation, which were formed to operate according to commercial criteria, were performing inefficiently while at the same time there were some SOEs performing as efficiently as the private operators. Despite poor financial performance and frequent announcements recorded on privatization by different government officials, there is no case of divestiture recorded in the country, apart from the JIC sale of 62.3 per cent of its shareholding in a hotel, the Intercontinental Jordan, to a group of Arab and Jordanian investors in February 1995. The following section provides a record of privatization plans and actions by different public corporations.

## 6.5 PRIVATIZATION PROGRESS TO DATE

Only three of the objectives listed in the development conference paper of November 1986 had been implemented by the end of 1995. The first was the establishment of five private universities and as Whittington (1992, p. 10) reported; 'students are presently accepted on the basis of being able to afford the fees rather than academic ability, ... therefore the private universities are for those students with wealthy parents'.

The second was the leasing of unused state-owned land at a rent of one Jordanian dinar per dunum in November 1990. This decision should be understood in the context of agricultural output deterioration. In the oft-quoted words of Fisher (1991): it was 'a crisis-induced move to increase domestic agricultural production, ... *particularly*, to increase cereal output, on the basis of guaranteed prices for farmers' (Fisher, 1991, p. 584, italics added).

The third, and the most important step, is the enactment of the investment promotion law in December 1995, but it is yet to be seen whether this law can attract investors. Other factors may play the decisive role in attracting foreign investment, such as geo-political stability and particularly a comprehensive peace settlement in the Middle East.

According to the World Bank three enterprises, all in the transport and communication sector, were initially included in the government's privatization plan (Candoy-Sekse, 1988, p. 35). The main candidates were Royal Jordanian Airlines (RJ), the Public Transport Corporation (PTC), and the Telecommunication Corporation (TCC). However, there have been several announcements and comments on privatization by government officials and others between 1986 and 1995.[8]

*March 1986*: Jordan's Minister of Communications, Muhyi Eddeen Huseini, who is also the chairman of the Wire and Wireless Communication Establishment (WWCE), announced that it had been decided to convert WWCE from a state-owned enterprise into a public shareholding company (*Al-Ra'i*, 20 March 1986).

*November 1986*: In an interview with *Al-Tadamun* weekly in London, the PM Zaid Al-Rafai confirmed his government's policy of backing the private sector-role in the economy and the need to deter public-sector firms from doing what the private sector could do. On the privatization of public firms, he explained that the government would continue to hold part of the equities; the balance, however, was to be offered for private-sector subscription (*Al-Ra'i*, 1 November 1986).

*February 1987*: the Jordanian cabinet decided to convert the state-owned Jordanian Company for Marketing and Processing of Agricultural Products to a private shareholding where the government would acquire JD7 million of the capital (70 per cent), the Pension Fund and the Social Security Fund would subscribe 12.5 per cent each, while the remaining 5 per cent would be acquired by the Agricultural Credit Corporation (*Al-Ra'i*, 20 February 1987).

*July 1987*: The government announced its decision to privatize the Public Transport Corporation (PTC). An inter-departmental committee was also formed to evaluate the market value of the corporation (Khalaf, 1989, p. 247).

*December 1987*: Ali Ghandour, the chairman of Royal Jordanian Airlines (RJ), said that RJ had signed a $165 million deal with a consortium of Arab and foreign banks to sell and lease back five of its eight Lockhead Tristar jets. Negotiations were in progress for the sale of two other Tristars. Earlier in the year RJ had sold a Boeing 747 to British Caledonian Airways for $64 million. These moves were made in order to repay debts worth $305 million. The RJ chairman said that the corporation would submit a final report on privatization in January 1988 including the legal aspects. He estimated the preliminary value of RJ to be around JD85 million–JD87 million ($259 million–$269 million). However, he confirmed that under the plan agreed with the government RJ would become a shareholding company with the government holding all the shares (*Al-Khaleej*, 18 December 1987).

*December 1988*: The chairman of RJ said that the state-owned airline was set for partial privatization the following year. The airline's 5000 employees would take 10 per cent of the equity and foreign ownership would be limited to 35 per cent. The government would not necessarily retain a controlling share. It was also suggested that the company would offer shares to Jordanian frequent fliers and travel agents who sold tickets worth more than 100 thousand JDs ($200 thousand) in 1988. Ghandour said aircraft sales and leaseback deals had enabled the company to pay off all its debts on aircraft, including $276 million repaid in 1988 (*Al-Ra'i*, 21 December 1988).

*April 1989*: Jawad Anani, a former Jordanian Minister of Labour, Trade and Industry, said in a lecture during a week of Jordanian activities in Abu Dhabi in UAE, that the financial crisis in Jordan would force the government to cut public-sector jobs, raise tax revenues and privatize firms. Privatization according to him was a viable solution despite the rising figure of unemployment in the Kingdom (*Khaleej Times*, 4 April 1989).

*August 1989*: King Hussein of Jordan removed the chairman of RJ, Ali Ghandour, due to the discovery of fraud and embezzlement in the company after a financial scandal in Jordan's second largest commercial bank, Petra Bank, which affected more than 37 companies in Jordan. The new management, under the chairman Abu Ghazaleh, started to sell most of RJ's fleet of aircraft, cut some of its unprofitable routes, and imposed a recruitment freeze to repay a debt of $192 million (EIU, 1992b, p. 26; Fisher, 1991, pp. 579–80).

*September 1991*: In an interview with *Interavia*, an air transport journal, Abu Ghazaleh, chairman of RJ, said that as a result of the Gulf War the corporation had started a 'slimming down strategy' in which it had reduced its staff by 400 people, or 6 per cent, which allowed it to save from 13 to 15 per cent on salaries particularly through 'the reduction in higher-salaried overseas staff'. RJ is still committed to privatization and the process is well on the way according to Ghassam Ali, executive vice-president of corporate planning. There is also a plan to sell up to 49 per cent of shares to interests outside Jordan (Endres, 1991, p. 29).

*September 1991*: The Jordan Telecommunication Corporation (TCC) started to revive its plans for expansion after their cancellation in 1989 as part of government measures to cut public expenditure by encouraging local and foreign private-sector involvement on a build–operate basis. This move was seen by observers as the first concrete form of the government's privatization plan. The new scheme encouraged potential investors to plan, finance, build, operate and maintain projects on a shared-revenue basis. The TCC identified the governorates of Mafraq and Ma'an as the most suitable for the implementation because their existing networks and facilities required almost total replacement (*MEED*, 20 September 1991).

*September 1991*: The Jordan Investment Corporation (JIC) announced its intention to sell its shares in hotels, newspapers (15 per cent in *Al-Ra'i* and 15 per cent in *Ad-Dustour* dailies) and a number of hotel projects. Its total equity holding in hotels was valued at between JD8 million and JD8.5 million ($11.8 million–$12.6 million). The move was described by the JIC's acting general manager as a way of concentrating efforts to help new projects rather than hold the shares of well-established ones (*MEED*, 20 September 1991).

*August 1992*: On 3 August, a government official in Amman said that the Council of Ministers had endorsed the principle of transforming the Royal Jordanian corporation into a public corporation whose shares were fully owned by the government and running it on a commercial basis as a first step towards its privatization. In the last two weeks of July a government committee evaluating RJ's assets and liabilities met twice. The committee was also responsible for preparing the new company's founding charter bylaws and defining its capital before its registration as a public company. The external British auditor (Arthur Anderson) advised the Jordanian government to increase RJ's capital from $20 million to $100 million in order to attract foreign interest in the corporation (*Arab Times*, 4 August 1992; *MEED*, 14 August 1992).

*March 1993*: The committee set to supervise the structural overhaul of RJ opted for full privatization rather than a limited form of commercialization. The Deputy Prime Minister and Transport Minister, who is the committee chairman, revealed that eight British consultancy firms had been invited to bid to pilot the privatization process. The task of the winner would be to evaluate RJ and to provide technical assistance for the privatization programme. The debt service for the company is now estimated to be around $40 million a year (*MEED*, 2 April 1993).

*July 1993*: The Jordanian Telecommunication Corporation (TCC) announced a planned investment of $300 million during its five-year plan 1993–97. The finance has World Bank approval. The TCC director-general said that the basic policy would be for TCC to be responsible for the provision of the basic telephone network throughout the country; all other services would be the task of the private sector. Local companies contended that the main problem with this approach to privatization was the regulation of services and the price mechanism employed and regulated by the TCC. They expressed their doubts about the TCC's ability to succeed in such a big task (*MEED*, 23 July 1993).

*November 1993*: On 16 November, the director-general of Jordan Ports Corporation revealed a preliminary plan to privatize the state-owned corporation. In this plan the private sector would be given investment opportunities in Aqaba in 1994 because the government did not want to keep full control over port activities in the future. He pointed out that an export port would be constructed and managed by the private sector and as a first step the private sector could share the port management with the government (*Arab News*, 17 November 1993).

*December 1993*: It was announced in Amman that the RJ airlines were likely to start a privatization programme in April 1994. The RJ signed a contract with a British company (Peat Management Consultants) to conduct a detailed study of the financial and managerial position of the corporation and to evaluate its assets and liabilities as a first step toward privatization. It was also revealed that RJ had a heavy external and internal debt of $270 million at the end of 1992. About 40 per cent of the debt ($108 million) was held by local companies (i.e. Jordan Petroleum Refinery and Social Security Corporation), while 60 per cent ($162 million) was with foreign institutions and corporations (*Arab News*, 9 December 1993).

*May 1994*: The Jordanian government increased the capital of RJ airlines from JD21 million ($30 million) to JD56 million ($79 million) in April so that it could help the company to reschedule part of its debt and improve its performance prior to privatization (*MEED*, 2 May 1994).

*October 1994*: In order to pave the way for privatizing Jordan Electricity Authority (JEA), a UK consultancy firm is preparing the balance sheet so the government can register JEA as a company totally owned by the state by January 1995. However, the shares of the company will be open for trade by 1997 (*MEED*, 31 October 1994).

*January 1995*: JIC has called for bids from local and international investors for its 87 per cent stake (3.2 million shares) in the Jordan Hotel and Tourism Company, owners of the Intercontinental Hotel in Amman. The funds from the sale will be used by JIC to develop new projects with the private sector where the latter will have the majority shares (*MEED*, 13 January 1995).

*January 1995*: For the first time, the chairman of RJ, Basel Jardaneh, emphasized that there was no need to rush the privatization of RJ; a commercialization policy may be more beneficial. However, acting on recommendations made, in a study by a UK consultancy firm, to develop part of the RJ activities as independent profit centres, plans have been drawn up for a partial sale of the Alia Gateway Hotel and the Queen Alia duty-free shopping facilities at Amman airport to JIC and the Social Security Corporation (SCC) (*MEED*, 20 January 1995).

*February 1995*: In its first step to implement Jordan's policy of selling its stakes in listed companies, JIC has accepted the highest bid to sell 54 per cent of its holdings (87 per cent) in the Jordan Hotels and Tourism Company. The buyer is the largest local private tourist company in Jordan (Zara

Investment Company). The general manager of JIC said that they were studying the sale of other stakes in its other tourism ventures, such as in the Arab International Hotels, which owns Jordan's Marriot (Reuter, 20 February 1995).

*April 1995*: In an interview with *MEED*, the Jordanian Finance Minister said that 'our main challenge is to be a leader in the region in deregulation and the liberalisation of the economy ... we want to create a business environment conducive to investment and to making private inflows a major activity in the economy'. A major reason for liberalizing the economy is to accelerate the pace of privatization and commercialization 'to convince the international community that Jordan's is a liberal economy' (*MEED*, 21 April 1995).

*May 1995*: According to the general manager of JIC, the government arm of investment has plans to reduce its stakes in all shareholding companies within two years, but also it will continue to hold a majority of shares in strategic industries which can provide a good rate of return, such as phosphate, potash and cement. He said that JIC cannot sell all its holdings in one major operation and is currently planning for a second privatization of Jordan's Marriot. The growing demand from private investors, following the peace agreement with Israel in October 1994, is the reason for the sale in the tourism sector. Also he reported that the government had started plans to transfer the ownership of public corporations into government-owned public shareholding companies, as a step towards later privatization (*Al-Ra'i*, 19 May 1995).

*June 1995*: Jordan's cabinet approved a draft law that transforms TCC into a state-owned commercially-run company as a first step to privatization after the approval of the Parliament (*Ad-Dustour*, 27 June 1995).

*August 1995*: The lower house of Parliament passed a new telecommunications law that sets up a regulatory body and transforms TCC into a commercially-run company (Reuter, 21 August 1995).

*December 1995*: Parliament approved the new investment promotion law (no. 16), which includes measures to relax the previous regulations for foreign companies wanting to invest in local stocks and shares. The law provides tax exemptions and facilities to projects in industry, agriculture, hotels, hospitals, maritime transport and railways, and any other sectors or its branches which the cabinet decides to add according to a recommendation by the Council for Investment Promotion formed under this law. Non-Jordanian investors shall have the right to invest in Jordan by whole ownership or by partnership or by sharing, and shall be treated in the same way as Jordanian investors. It is expected that the law will attract $5 billion of Jordanian capital abroad (*MBC News*, 24 December 1995).

Such statements reveal that the implementation stage of privatization, although a required commitment from the government, should not be rushed into until every aspect of the divestiture mechanism has been considered.

## 6.6  OBSTACLES TO PRIVATIZATION

Two sets of factors delayed the implementation of the privatization programme in Jordan; the first are economic factors and the second non-economic and influenced by the notion of the state–society relationship.

### 6.6.1  Economic Factors

*The Process of Valuation*
One of the key problems for the privatization of Jordanian enterprises is the time and resources needed for the valuation of assets, liabilities, and market value. Taking the Jordanian national airline (RJ) as an example we can observe that from 1986 more than three committees were formed to determine an accurate valuation of the airline's assets and liabilities. As the corporation records reveal, many foreign, as well as local, consultancy companies were invited to conduct this very important task, the first and most vital stage in privatization. The cost of the studies totalled $640 thousand by the end of 1995. These extra transaction costs have to be added to the total costs of the corporation, which ultimately increases doubts about its already doubtful solvency. Moreover, with the lack of appropriate accounting records, particularly in the case of foreign debt and debt service, the delay in reaching a decision about privatization means another round of valuation

is required. This vicious circle delayed the privatization of many establishments planned for divestiture in Jordan.

*Restructuring and Rehabilitation*
Many firms targeted in the privatization programme are characterized by financial difficulties which make them unattractive to private buyers (local and foreign). In the case of TCC, for example, the corporation has to change much of the existing telephone network in a number of Jordan's governorates before being able to proceed with privatization. Because of this the TCC has contracted different foreign companies to modernize the old equipment. It is planned to add 280 000 lines to the local network by 1997. In addition to the cost of £3.852 million, granted by the British government to finance the consultancy services for restructuring, the restructuring is planned to cost more than $300 million during the period 1993–7.[9] Such an investment means that the total market value of the corporation will go up, making it more difficult for it to be sold to a local buyer.

Restructuring may be physical and lead to the fragmentation of the enterprise, as is the case with TCC, or it may be financial as in the case of the national airline (RJ). RJ has to capitalize its $270 million debt, which means that foreign ownership will exceed 49 per cent and thereby contradict the Jordanian companies' rules and regulations, prior to December 1995. To solve this problem the consultancy company studying the case for privatization proposed an increase in the airline's capital of nearly $80 million so that the new capital would be consistent with the size of the company's operations, and to encourage foreign investors to buy into its equity. However, by April 1995, the government had injected only $49 million into RJ.

The physical and financial conditions of the targeted enterprises are, therefore, serious factors behind the delay in the implementation of privatization. However, in the case of the Public Transport Corporation (PTC), the privatization proposal was intended to include the restructuring of the whole transport sector rather than the corporation alone (Candoy-Sekse, 1988, p. 35). Thus, the task of enterprise restructuring and rehabilitation may go beyond the boundary of the enterprise because of problems in the sector concerned.

### The Lack of Regulatory Capacity

Jordan, as is the case in many developing countries, lacks the capacity to regulate a privatized utility such as those in the transport or the telecommunication sectors. Most of the corporations targeted for privatization in Jordan possess a heavy economic and political weight which may shift the parameters of regulation towards benefiting the company rather than the consumer.

Despite the advanced regulatory institutions available in developed countries, regulating privatized utilities has proved to be a difficult task. In the United Kingdom, for example, regulatory bodies such as OFTEL, OFGAS, and OFWAT are often in conflict with the privatized utilities when trying to regulate their monopolistic behaviour. The question is whether the bureaucratic establishment in Jordan possesses similar capacity and competence to that which exists in the developed countries.

One reason for delaying privatization is the need to devise a regulatory framework which suits the economic sector's concerns. In the case of TCC, the Jordanian private local companies doubted the ability of TCC's bureaucrats to provide a suitable mechanism for regulation (*MEED*, 23 July 1993).

It may be argued that the lack of an appropriate regulatory design may be solved by copying or amending regulatory models based on the experience of developed countries such as the UK, but the main problem lies at the implementation stage where differences in bureaucratic efficiency, competence and energy are of vital importance to the end results. Even the design cannot be imitated in the majority of cases because it was based on a particular policy design derived from the specific sectoral features of the country.

The interest attached to regulation could stem from our analysis of the principal–agent theory in Chapter 3. In the absence of an effective regulatory mechanism, the asymmetry of information between the regulator and the enterprise will reintroduce the information asymmetry problem which dominated the relationship between the principal (government) and agent (manager) in the case of state ownership. The difference would lie only in the distribution of benefits from the state to the private monopoly and ultimately the shareholders.

In the absence of real competition or contestability the privatization of a monopolized industry may create more problems than privatization was intended to solve. Thus, designing the appropriate regulatory framework for a telecommunications or airline corporation may take a long time before the mature stage of implementation is reached.

The reason why the Jordanian government does not have the opportunity to correct policy errors related to inefficient regulation is that the size of their corporations and their numbers are not similar to those in Europe; for example, where the experience gained from one privatization case can be transferred to many more cases. Where foreign ownership is introduced, the bureaucratic capacity and ability to rectify policy errors may prove more costly for the Jordanian government than for a developed country's government. Part of the difference derives from their different bargaining positions in the privatization process and part from the abilities of their bureaucrats. All these factors have proved to be obstacles to smooth privatization in Jordan.

Another dimension of regulation derives from property rights literature. As a developing country Jordan has the problem of defining property rights and all its subsequent entitlements. In western industrial countries, on the other hand, privatization does not require an entirely new legal framework to deal with such a situation because their societies as well as their economies have had two centuries of gradual adjustments and now function according to a relatively well defined and advanced legal framework of property rights.

The objective of (a) providing a supportive legal environment for property rights and contractual obligations and (b) developing a commercial law for the settlement of disputes is yet to be formulated and tested in Jordan although it was one of the main requirements for privatization. This reflects the weak capacity of the country's regulatory body where, as North (1991) contended, an efficient system of property rights might offend the interests of the interest groups. Both dimensions, the regulation of enterprise operations and the introduction of an efficient system of property rights, required an institutional building process rather than a privatization decree. Their absence in Jordan presented an obstacle to the implementation of privatization.

*Inefficient Capital Market*

In Jordan there is a capital market which was established before the idea of privatization emerged in the country. The Amman Financial Market (AFM) is an independent public institution established in 1976 under special law no. 31. The establishment of the market was seen as a device to attract investors and traders who had been conducting their businesses in Beirut but left after the start of the civil war in 1975. The AFM is considered an emerging market by international fund managers, despite the fact that access to it has been problematic. In 1994, the AFM had a market capitalization of $4.4 billion, a price/earning ratio of 19.5, a dividend yield ratio of 2.38 per cent, and a price/book ratio of 2.1 (AFM, 1995). However, all these positive statistical indicators for the Jordanian financial market do not necessarily mean that it provides efficient and helpful support for privatization.

There are questions which have to be asked in relation to privatization. Is there sufficient capital available, particularly for the purchase of enterprises in the transportation and telecommunication sector planned for privatization? Is this market able to reflect the performance of management and increase their X-efficiency as happens in the industrial nations?

In any developing country the major question is the availability of capital to buy the public enterprises targeted for privatization. In the case of Jordan there are three possible sources; local capital, Arab investment or foreign capital.

The first possibility, the raising of local capital, does not seem to be promising since the banking and financial institutions in Jordan, although the most expanding in the economy, still suffer from many deficiencies: the narrowness of the money markets and the narrowness of the secondary market for money instruments as well as the inadequacy of the short-term instruments in use (Ministry of Planning, 1986, p. 74). Moreover, the Jordanian public is sceptical and wary of management practices within financial institutions as many financial scandals have occurred in the country. The Petra Bank scandal in 1989/90, for example, put the bank into liquidation. Another factor is the lack of long-term interest in productive activities shown by the holders of local capital. In 1994, a flotation by the Arab Potash Company met with poor market response although there are good long-term prospects

for this company. The search for fast-earning activities, particularly during the economic recession, and the relative concentration of local capital in Palestinian hands may have impeded the government in privatizing its enterprises. In general terms, capital restrictions as well as the risk of *crowding out* private investment in the case of privatizing big enterprises played a major part in delaying the privatization programme.

Without any doubt, the Arab alternative depends strongly on regional political spillover. Historically, Arab countries and Arab investors have had little interest in investing in other Arab countries. Thus, it is less likely that Arab investors, particularly from the rich states, would be attracted to buy shares in such enterprises. However, the strong effect of the institutional factor on the running of the Jordanian economy may prove otherwise if new political and economic relationships between Jordan and the rich Gulf states emerge in the near future.

The third and the last scenario is foreign ownership of the targeted enterprises. The difficulty of this approach to privatization comes from two dimensions. The first is the instability of the country's socio-political environment, particularly between 1989 and 1991, which causes foreign buyers to shy away from any major investment in Jordan. Also, until the end of 1995, the regulations regarding foreign investors restricted majority foreign ownership in the country. It is also the case that complex socio-political and economic reasons make it difficult for the government to sell important segments of the economy, concentrated in the transportation and telecommunication sector, to foreign companies. Young argued that the widespread foreign ownership of enterprises greatly contributed to the initial wave of nationalization in developing countries; thus privatization will inevitably invite charges of recolonization (Young, 1986, as cited in Hanke and Walters, 1990, p. 105). This should be understood with the new wave of Islamicization in the country, and the region in general.

The second dimension for the capital market is related to its ability to transform the information necessary to increase the pressure on managers which subsequently increases the efficiency of the firms. This is the most strongly declared objective of privatization. AFM, as is the case in most other developing countries, is not as efficient as markets in developed countries. Civelek (1991) conducted an empirical study to examine the efficiency of the Amman stock exchange and asked the most important question regarding the success or failure of privatization, namely whether capital-market prices can be relied upon to provide accurate signals about the optimal allocation of capital in the economy. By examining the information effect on market prices for 15 industrial companies listed on the market the scholar found that the market was thin and discontinuity in trading constituted one of its major features. Regulations governing the market prohibited any major movements in share prices; consequently, the 'stock prices established in the Amman Stock Exchange (ASE) do not appear to have any significant policy relevance' (Civelek, 1991, p. 30).

This conclusion is consistent with our perception of the market. As the market is small, there are two problems which seem to characterize it. The first is volatility whereby the small size of the capital market makes share prices and transactions in general subject to intense fluctuation which could be a result of manipulation by certain parties in the market. For example, although the government currently holds 48 per cent of the shares, their sale will lead to the manipulation of specific interests which might affect the stability of the economy. Another reason for volatility is the effect of regional politics. For example, in the third week of January 1994 transactions in the Amman stock market shrank by 55 per cent because of the Security Council's decision to extend sanctions against Iraq. Another influence was related to obstacles in the peace negotiations between Palestinians and Israelis about the control of trading routes between the West Bank and Jordan (*MBC News*, 24 January 1994).

The second problem emerging from the small size of the Amman capital market is that of short-termism. In its report on Jordan the EIU said that

> the Amman Financial Market, although resistant to anything but more tangible investments, such as those in bricks and mortar, still exists among the bulk of the population. Even among business people and financiers, the attractions of trade outweigh the uncertain promise of only long-term profits on industrial investment (EIU, 1992a, p. 25).

The problem facing the Jordanian government is precisely a result of this factor. It was short-termism and the merchant tradition of activities which led the government to undertake big projects and enhance its activities by owning the means of production. More than half of the turnover of the AFM is in the financial, insurance and service sectors.

All the above clearly demonstrates the limited room for manoeuvre available to the Jordanian government in its privatization programme.

### 6.6.2 The Non-Economic Factors

Although it may seem that the Jordanian government lacks the will to implement the privatization programme, the explanation may actually lie within the package of choices the government possesses. Apart from the economic reasons there are other socio-political or so called *systemic factors* which have also impeded the implementation of reform policies, including privatization, in Jordan. Bery (1990) pointed out that

> what is seen from the outside as 'lack of will' or commitment may in fact be the wisest course of action given such systemic factors. Outsiders are obliged to appreciate these systemic factors before exerting undue pressure and provoking failure (Bery, 1990, p. 1125).

What are these factors? The crisis of unemployment and the increasing number of people living below the poverty line prevented the government from proceeding with the privatization of its public enterprises during the period before the Gulf War, and brought privatization completely to a halt from the end of the war until 1993. Since public sector employment represents about one-half of total employment in Jordan, the implementation of privatization will be seen as a state retreat from its historical responsibility and a breach by the state of the social contract agreed between its leaders and the people, particularly in the absence of any unemployment benefits or effective social security system. Although the government has attempted to balance differential social advantages and disadvantages, severe inequalities inevitably accompany privatization. An increase in the number of job seekers is linked with an unavoidable increase in the concentration of wealth and income.

In a socio-political environment similar to that in Jordan decision-makers have historically been characterized by a vulnerability to internal and external events. The patron–client relationship and the distributive responsibility of the state stemming from its heavy dependence on external resources led the state to be the employer of last resort. This means that large numbers of people became totally dependent on the state for their income. Such people, particularly the East Jordanians, are politically significant for the country's stability because of their loyalty and support, which is based on their economic dependence on the state. In other words, there is a contract of shared benefits. So privatization means a great gamble for politicians unless there is a careful policy design and a gradual mechanism for implementation.

The state in Jordan, although supportive of private initiatives, plays and will continue to play a key role in the process of economic and social development. Limited and carefully designed privatization is a rational political strategy for successive Jordanian governments and bureaucrats. The case in Jordan suggests that systemic factors based on state–society relationships may prove to be constraints on the choices of policy and policy implementation available to decision-makers.

## 6.7 FUTURE PROSPECTS

Legislation and restrictions on market forces form an integral part of the daily management of the Jordanian economy. Thus, although the state believes in free enterprise and private initiative, markets in Jordan are not free. In the absence of free access to resources a transfer in the status of ownership will not necessarily mean greater freedom of choice for consumers and producers. The state will still retain its power to influence private activities in the same way as in the public sector.

Privatization in Jordan was proposed in 1986 as part of the reform programme initiated by the government of Al-Rafai. Five factors played a major role in the consideration of privatization as a viable alternative; recession and regressing living standards, a growing deficit in the central government budget, the huge burden of external debt, the need to attract foreign investment and finally the influence of western-oriented bureaucrats on the decision-makers. By 1991, privatization had become a commitment on the Jordanian government within the package of the structural adjustment programme agreed with the IMF.

In 1996, after ten years, the Jordanian decision-makers realized that the constraints and the consequences of privatization were complex. Therefore, they shifted the policy design from changing ownership through divestiture to the 'commercialization' of SOEs. The private sector, which is characterized by short-termism and the search for quick and secure returns on investment, cannot in Jordan take over the role of the state at least in providing employment opportunities for the large army of unemployed. However, it was expected that instead of high-profile privatizations that might draw political and financial objections, the new government of Al-Kabariti, formed in February 1996, would sell part of its shares in the shareholding companies with fewer interests, particularly when the JIC owned more than 10–12 per cent of the Amman financial market's total market $4.4 billion capitalization.

The peace with Israel may also bring new opportunities for future capital inflows to Jordan. The sale of part of government stakes in the tourism sector is a reflection of the demand generated by the peace.

At the macro-level, a durable peace may over time enable a reduction in military expenditure, freeing up resources for use in productive purposes. Also, projects in the form of joint ventures between Jordan, Israel, and other countries in and outside the region are expected to stimulate more investment.

The Middle East and North Africa Economic Summit held in Amman between 29 and 31 October 1995 brought new hopes for regional cooperation. For the first time in the history of the Middle East a new bank will be established in Cairo to promote economic cooperation and finance development projects in the Middle East and North African countries.

In the short term, enterprises such as RJ airlines benefited from the peace when they gained the rights to overfly Israel from March 1995. RJ will save $4–$5 million in fuel and maintenance costs and an average of 17 minutes in flight time. This will help the company to increase its solvency.

However, competition with mature Israeli enterprises may also bring the risk of bankruptcy to many Jordanian economic activities. The government, therefore, should understand the balance between economic efficiency and the strategic economic goals of sustainable development.

The current five-year plan (1993–97) emphasizes that the government should provide investment information, cut red tape to simplify the complexity of regulation, enhance competition in the marketplace, and increase investment in infrastructure, particularly for the agricultural sector and for health, education and human development. Therefore, privatization will provide new opportunities for private entrepreneurs through government support and incentives. The plan envisages that the total gross fixed capital formation in the country will be JD5.132 billion during 1993–97, 63.5 per cent to be supplied by the private sector and 36.5 per cent by the public sector. It is expected that the private sector will be allowed to participate in the implementation and management of infrastructure, such as water distribution and the collection of water fees. Cooperation between the private sector and the Telecommunication Corporation (TCC) will give the former increased participation in the construction of the corporation's projects and the provision of some selected services.

There is an obligation on the government to conduct a careful and detailed study of privatization in the country. The main objective should be to develop a clear conception of which public sector activities are suitable for privatization; the strategic activities in which the state would continue its current role, but with additional emphasis on their costs and benefits; and public activities which need to be run on commercial grounds as a first step toward their full privatization.

In his appointment of the new government on 4 February 1996, King Hussein has given the new Prime Minister (Al-Kabariti) a green light for a comprehensive economic and political transformation:

> My hope is that the new government will go with all its energy and capacity towards full and comprehensive change ... in a revolution that does not reject what the older generation has done but one that builds on what they have built (*MEED*, 16 February 1996, p. 5).

In such an environment privatization itself will be more related to creating the institutions necessary for better government. This implies a need for privatization in Jordan to be looked at in a wider context of participation and decentralization.

# 7 Privatization, Decentralization, Participation and Development in Jordan

## 7.1 INTRODUCTION

Chapter 5 concluded with the statement that development may mean decentralization and the latter certainly does mean participation, but privatization does not invariably lead to participation. It depends on how it is designed and implemented. This chapter will study this argument within the context of decentralization and participation, and hence development in Jordan. However, as there is no actual experience of privatization, the conclusions will be hypothetical, except for that of leasing state lands.

Sections 7.2, 7.3 and 7.4 analyse government objectives on decentralization and participation, the policies pursued to achieve this, and whether they were successful or not. Section 7.5 measures the degree of financial decentralization and the changes in the decentralization indicators between the period 1980–84 and 1988, to assess whether the decentralization objectives of the government, in the 1986–90 development plan, were achieved or not and why. Part of the investigation will focus also on the effect of privatization policies on participation in agriculture by small farmers (Section 7.6).

Democracy and free-market policies are two important components of participation. Yet their introduction in Jordan since 1989 has been forced by pressure from below but in practice has been used not as an instrument to increase popular participation but as a new means of controlling decision-making on the one hand and of speeding up the delayed process of economic reform, including privatization, on the other (Sections 7.7 and 7.8). Finally, Section 7.9 provides the evidence regarding the clear shift from participation and empowerment, in the five-year development plan 1993–97 – a shift consistent with the confirmed relationship between privatization, decentralization, participation, and development.

## 7.2 THE OBJECTIVES OF DECENTRALIZATION AND PARTICIPATION

Jordan's approach to development has been top-down mainly because:

1. Colonial rule influenced the administrative structure from one side while the historical and religious power of the leaders led also to extensive centralization. Such power rests on the patron–client relationship *vis-à-vis* the country's traditional tribal leaders and other notables who constitute the 'ruling elite' (Owen, 1992).
2. The Arab–Israeli conflict and the complex effect of the Palestinian question on the state–society relationship increased the tendency to centralize the decision-making process.
3. A major reason for centralization is the sources financing the government budget, which lead to dependence on either domestic (pressure for participation) or external sources (state insulation) (Dessouki and Aboul Kheir, 1991). Dependency on exogenous sources of finance in Jordan led to reduced pressure on the government for participation in decision-making because in many countries, particularly in the developed world, increased taxation means an increase in pressure from below for participation. In the case of Jordan the state, instead of taxing to raise revenue, became a patron which distributed benefits on society, in particular by employing half the workforce. Furthermore, the drive to build the nation and its industrial base contributed to a more top-down approach towards development. Nevertheless, this factor represents the most powerful one because, in the face of economic crisis, pressure on government for participation through decentralization starts to mount and the voice option, using Hirshman's concept, starts to activate. This is what happened following the decline in government revenue in 1982. By the mid-1980s revenue had declined

because of the fall in oil prices and the negative effects of this are denoted by the decline in external revenue. Inflation, unemployment and poverty increased as recession hit the economy. As a result, there was a tendency for the government to bring about more participation in the decision-making process. It was at this time that the idea of privatization was born.

Decentralization was viewed as a way to combine regional with sectoral planning, and preparation of the 1986–90 development plan was conducted within such a context. The Jordanian Ministry of Planning worked with the United States Agency for International Development (USAID) and adopted USAID's Rural Development Strategy framed by Rondinelli (1984 as cited in Honey and Abu Kharmeh, 1989) and entitled, *Urban Functions in Rural Development Strategy*[1] (Honey and Abu Kharmeh, 1989, p. 80). This provided positive evidence for the simultaneous imitation of both policies, privatization and decentralization, by Jordanian decision-makers and planners. This is fully consistent with the frame set by the World Bank, USAID, and other advocates of their line of thought.

While planning before 1986 was sectoral in both base and goals,[2] the fifth development plan (1986–90) was regarded as the first phase of establishing a system for regional planning in Jordan. It represented a departure from the old system of sectoral planning which had characterized previous national plans.

Two main principles in this plan revealed the decision-makers' and planners' vision of decentralization and participation. The first is *social justice*. This argues that territorial decentralization contributes to the achievement of a more balanced distribution of the fruits of development, particularly in circumstances where the landowners, the trading and the business communities have benefited substantially more than rural people. Planners, therefore, saw territorial decentralization as increasing the base for people-participation in the initiation, formulation, implementation and monitoring of the projects. This would lead to greater efficiency in the distribution of services and to increased social equality. In the words of the plan document:

> Realizing social justice in all regions of the Kingdom and ensuring a balanced geographical distribution of social and

economic services through regional development, promotion of popular participation in the formulation, implementation and follow-up of overall development programs and adoption of regional planning methods to direct future development at the national, regional and local levels (Ministry of Planning, 1986, p. 78).

The second concept referred to *people as the means and objects of development.* Thus it called for popular participation as a way to increase human capabilities and choices. The plan stated popular participation to be

> The enhancement and expansion of popular participation in the various phases of the planning process as well as in decision-making, determining of priorities and monitoring the implementation of development projects and programs. The emphasis on popular participation stems from the concept that man is the means and object of development. He is the means by participating in the planning process, contributing as much effort as he could, and he is the object because he reaps the achievements of development in the form of employment opportunities and appropriate income (ibid., p. 114).

A second vision of decentralization and participation is available from an interview with Crown Prince Hassan of Jordan. In reply to a question in August 1988 about his opinion on decentralization in Jordan he stated that

> There has to be an effort made to move people out of high population areas – hence the importance of regional planning. I still feel that greater participation is essential on the part of the local elected bodies. [The problem] is what is available in terms of finance.... One of my major disappointments ... is the inability to monitor the (planning) process in the regions (Interview with Crown Prince Hassan, 1988, p. 7).

Concerning the future of the decentralization his reply was:

> I hope the government will take the necessary decision on this all-important subject to allocate a decentralised budget more effectively to regional councils and provide the necessary staffing to assist those councils (Interview with Crown Prince Hassan, 1988, p. 7).

Both answers revealed that there was a vision of decentralization, on the state side, which may not necessarily lead to empowerment, firstly because financial constraints do not mean that priorities at the local level cannot be selected by the local people despite the funding shortages (Cernea, 1991, pp. 9–10). Secondly, the wish to continue monitoring the planning process even at the local level provides limited support for decentralization, if not continuous central intervention. What is needed in a 'bottom-up' development is empowerment, not a programme conducted from above and evaluated from above. This requires a real spatial reversal to the 'local scale' in village councils. The question, therefore, is whether failure is caused by the design or the implementation.

## 7.3 THE DESIGN OF DECENTRALIZATION AND PARTICIPATION

There were four levels in the hierarchical top-down system established to coordinate the plan (Honey and Abu Kharmeh, 1988; Honey and Abu Kharmeh, 1989).

At the national level there was the Ministry of Planning with officials and experts who held the upper hand in the ultimate decision-making processes. The Ministry developed a geographical information system (including a locational network with all settlements) which depended on field-level surveys as well as information provided by other ministries.

The second level was in the governorates. There are eight of these, considered to be regional planning agencies. Their main task was to update data for the Ministry of Planning files. The governorate structure possessed only a modest planning staff, but they were still important as a territorial division to provide state services for the regions.

The third tier in the system was the subdivision of the governorates, nominated as development sub-regions. Each one had a 'development council' consisting of public and private leaders. These were new territorial units. The selection of these was based on two principles, physiography (valley, highlands or desert) and spatial linkages. There were, according to those two principles, 37 sub-regions, as illustrated in Table 7.1. However, in theory, the councils were expected

*Table* 7.1  Regional planning units in Jordan's development plan (1986–90)

| Governorate | Sub-regions | Number of development units | Number of villages |
|---|---|---|---|
| **Amman** | Amman | 1 | 52 |
| | Ma'adaba | 8 | 143 |
| | Na'our | 4 | 38 |
| | Sahab-Muwaqqar | 2 | 25 |
| Sub-total | 4 | 15 | 258 |
| **Zarqa** | Zarqa | 5 | 36 |
| | Dulail | 1 | 7 |
| | Azraq | 1 | 6 |
| Sub-total | 3 | 7 | 49 |
| **Irbid** | Irbid First | 5 | 28 |
| | Irbid Second | 6 | 42 |
| | Ramtha | 2 | 6 |
| | Bani Kananah | 3 | 21 |
| | North Ghors | 4 | 4 |
| | Koura | 4 | 31 |
| | Ajloun | 6 | 53 |
| | Jerash | 8 | 55 |
| Sub-total | 8 | 38 | 283 |
| **Mafraq** | Mafraq | 6 | 76 |
| | North desert | 8 | 73 |
| Sub-total | 2 | 14 | 149 |
| **Balqa** | Balqa Ghor | 7 | 25 |
| | Balqa Middle | 7 | 40 |
| | Balqa'a Basin | 4 | 17 |
| Sub-total | 3 | 18 | 82 |
| **Karak** | Karak | 1 | 38 |
| | Qasr | 3 | 22 |
| | South Mazar | 3 | 41 |
| | Ay | 1 | 6 |
| | Safi | 2 | 10 |
| | Desert | 1 | 5 |
| Sub-total | 6 | 11 | 122 |
| **Tafila** | Tafila | 3 | 23 |
| | Bsairah | 2 | 10 |
| | Hassa | 1 | 3 |
| Sub-total | 3 | 6 | 36 |
| **Ma'an** | Ma'an | 3 | 17 |
| | Al-Husseinial | 1 | 6 |
| | Al-Shoubak | 1 | 21 |
| | Wadi Mousa | 2 | 18 |
| | Desert | | 13 |
| | Aqaba | 1 | 14 |
| | Quwairah | 1 | 6 |
| | Wadi Araba | 3 | 9 |
| Sub-total | 8 | 15 | 104 |
| **Grand Total** | 37 | 124 | 1083 |

*Source*: Honey and Abu Kharmeh (1988, p. 279).

to identify development plans for their respective territories mainly to enhance employment opportunities and increase income. At the same time, they had to work with the governorates and the Ministry of Planning to find financial support (domestic and foreign) for the implementation of the plans.

The last level in the hierarchy was the development cluster of villages, known as 'development units'. Each unit had a representative on the respective development council. This level was seen chiefly as an information line rather than one of any executive power.

Therefore, from the design point of view it could be said that the plan would have provided the appropriate structure as well as a solid base for territorial decentralized development if the assumption had matched the intentions of the bureaucrats. However, this was not the case, as the implementation process revealed.

## 7.4 DECENTRALIZATION IN PRACTICE

The inclusion of a proposed activity in any development plan is not a guarantee of its implementation. The Jordanian 1986–90 development plan although sound in its design, could be judged as a successful failure from the implementation aspects. In Jreisats words;

> Once more, the proposed projects and measures in the plan are devoid of empirical content, reasoned justification, or assessment of expected outcomes at any level of tentativeness. The general approach is basically of the traditional, legal genre of prescriptions that lack an action oriented, conceptual sophistication, or substantive relevance; hence, they are old remedies of proven inadequacy (Jreisat, 1989, p. 97).

The failure to achieve decentralization and participation could stem from the field studies conducted in Jordan during the period 1989–91. These emphasized the lack of power at the local level to alleviate the problems facing people in villages, such as the lack of social services and other important infrastructural requirements such as roads (Al-Edwan *et al.*, 1990; Sadik and Al-Khasawneh, 1990; Al-Ahmed *et al.*, 1989;

Al-Ahmed *et al.*, 1991a; Al-Ahmed *et al.*, 1991b). All the studies pointed out the powerless status of local authorities and institutions from their establishment to their budget and plans.

1. The establishment of the village council requires a request from at least 2500 people in the area to the municipalities' minister through the governor of the village. The minister then establishes a committee, which advises him on the case. Later the minister makes a recommendation to the cabinet, which then decides whether to establish the council or not. After a positive decision the municipality minister sets up a two-year administration for the village; an election is then held to choose the administration. However, the minister still possesses the right to approve or reject the elected council. In addition, there are two members on the village council who are appointed by the minister himself but are subject to the national regulations governing the civil service.
2. The municipalities ministry controls all the municipalities in Jordan. The staff of the municipalities are appointed by the ministry.
3. The Ministry of Interior relates with rural Jordan through the administration governors. In addition to maintaining the rule of law, the governors control the civil servants in the municipality. Most importantly the head of the municipality cannot initiate any project costing more than JD5000 without the approval of the governor. The governor is also responsible for the relationship with the municipalities ministry on project funding. The role of the governors in the southern regions is more important than in the northern regions (Sadik and Al-Khasawneh, 1990, p. 53). That explains, at least partially, the relationship between greater poverty in the south and excessive centralization.
4. Although the municipalities proposed the projects and explained their advantages to the rural people in the area, the municipalities ministry often altered the proposed budgets in order to be more consistent with the national plan. The Ministry issued their final plan for implementation. However, even with such excessive centralization 94 per cent of the heads of the municipalities believed that

this method was a decentralized approach while the 6 per cent who did refer to excessive centralization were in the municipalities of Amman, Irbid and Mafraq (ibid., 1990, p. 57). This explains the consistency in the objectives of the ruling elite whether at the central or local level.

In brief, government in Jordan below the national level is not local government as is the case in western countries; it is much rather a local administration composed of bureaucrats executing government policies from the centre. Thus, the goals of the plan in initiating, planning, implementing and monitoring did not find any place in practice.

## 7.5 MEASURING DECENTRALIZATION AND PARTICIPATION

The UNDP (1993) in its Human Development Report (HDR) listed a number of indicators to measure financial decentralization in local government. However, the HDR referred to the scarcity of information regarding local government in developing countries as is the case in Jordan. This section provides statistics of financial decentralization in local government for the period 1980–84. More detailed local data for 1988 is then calculated for the national level using the data provided by Sadik and Al-Khasawneh (1990) in their study of 50 Jordanian municipalities.[3] We will also examine whether or not funds granted to local governments are directed towards the provision of basic needs such as health, education, sanitation and clean water. The emphasis on basic needs derives from their link with participation and our concept of bottom-up development.

### 7.5.1 Decentralization Indicators

We will employ five indicators to measure the degree of financial decentralization.

1. The expenditure decentralization ratio (EDR) = local government expenditure (LGE) ÷ total government expenditure (TGE).

2. The modified expenditure decentralization ratio (MEDR) = local government expenditure (LGE) ÷ modified total government expenditure (TGE − defence and debt servicing expenditure).
3. The revenue decentralization ratio (RDR) = local government revenue (LGR) ÷ total government revenue (TGR).
4. Financial autonomy ratio (FAR) = local government revenue (LGR) ÷ local government expenditure (LGE).
5. Proportion of total expenditure controlled by local government (PTECLG) = (FAR) × (EDR).

### 7.5.2 Decentralization Ratios (1980–84)

As many aspects of the relationship between the centre and the local level in Jordan cannot be quantified, Table 7.2 sets out the proportion of expenditure spent by local government to that spent by central government. There are two kinds of ratios. The first is the EDR, and the second is the MEDR. EDR does not discriminate between central government expenditure that cannot be decentralized, such as military expenditure and debt-servicing payments, or that could be decentralized, such as health, education, and development projects. Thus, EDR has to be modified in order to take the military and debt-servicing expenditure out of the central government total spending. MEDR, therefore, is more appropriate for assessing the real proportion of finance that the centre can allow the local level to assume responsibility for spending.

Table 7.2 shows that in Jordan EDR is very low, not even reaching 7 per cent during 1980–84. Even when debt-servicing payments and military expenditure are deducted, the MEDR figures show that spending in Jordan is highly centralized. The average MEDR for 1980–84 was only 8.3 per cent. Thus, the decentralization of public expenditure in Jordan is extremely limited. A summary of the main reasons for this was set out in Section 7.2, but it is important to mention that the increase in transaction costs, when spending is decentralized, has to be taken into account. In other words, decentralization policies go against the rule of the game (maximize revenue and minimize transaction costs).[4]

Likewise, the revenue decentralization ratio (RDR), which measures the importance of local government revenue to that

*Table* 7.2  Expenditure decentralization ratios in Jordan, 1980–84 (MJDs)

| Years<br>Details | 1980 | 1981 | 1982 | 1983 | 1984 |
|---|---|---|---|---|---|
| Amman | 15.7 | 21.1 | 20.6 | 22.8 | 24.1 |
| Zarqa | 1.7 | 2.1 | 3.4 | 3.1 | 3.3 |
| Irbid | 4.0 | 5.9 | 8.3 | 10.1 | 10.1 |
| Mafraq | 0.7 | 0.9 | 1.0 | 1.2 | 1.2 |
| Balqa | 1.6 | 1.1 | 1.5 | 2.0 | 1.5 |
| Karak | 0.9 | 0.9 | 1.2 | 1.7 | 1.5 |
| Tafila | 0.3 | 0.4 | 0.8 | 0.4 | 0.7 |
| Ma'an | 0.6 | 1.0 | 1.5 | 0.9 | 1.8 |
| [1] LGE (MJDs) | 25.5 | 33.4 | 38.3 | 42.2 | 44.2 |
| [2] TGE (MJDs) | 487.9 | 546.2 | 632.0 | 656.3 | 720.8 |
| [3] MTGE (MJDs) | 352.7 | 408.0 | 470.2 | 488.2 | 520.6 |
| [4] EDR (%) | 5.2 | 6.1 | 6.1 | 6.4 | 6.1 |
| [5] MEDR (%) | 7.2 | 8.2 | 8.1 | 8.6 | 8.5 |

*Sources*:
[1] LGE figures from Ministry of Planning (1986, Table no. 6, p. 398).
[2] TGE from Table 6.1, this volume.
[3] MTGE figures calculated after deducting debt-sevicing payments and defence expenditure from (TGE).
[4] & [5] EDR and MEDR are calculated by the author.

of central government provides further evidence (Table 7.3) for the argument that Jordan's high dependency on external sources of finance increased the tendency towards centralization. The RDR average was only 5.7 per cent during 1980–84. Another indicator shown in Table 7.3, the financial autonomy ratio (FAR), measures the degree of local government control on local spending. It appears that Jordanian municipalities are highly autonomous in their spending as the FAR was 98.7 per cent during the period 1980–84. Two important factors have to be pointed out: the first is that this ratio (FAR) is high because local government spending was very low when compared with central government spending, and the second is that the figures for local government revenue imply revenue transferred by central government to the local level.

Table 7.3  Revenue decentralization ratios in Jordan, 1980–84 (MJDs)

| Years<br>Details | 1980 | 1981 | 1982 | 1983 | 1984 |
|---|---|---|---|---|---|
| Amman | 13.6 | 15.5 | 21.2 | 21.9 | 29.2 |
| Zarqa | 1.7 | 2.3 | 3.0 | 3.1 | 3.1 |
| Irbid | 3.6 | 5.8 | 6.9 | 9.5 | 9.0 |
| Mafraq | 0.6 | 1.3 | 1.0 | 1.1 | 1.2 |
| Balqa | 0.8 | 0.9 | 1.5 | 1.5 | 1.3 |
| Karak | 0.7 | 0.8 | 1.0 | 2.0 | 1.4 |
| Tafila | 0.3 | 0.5 | 0.7 | 0.4 | 0.6 |
| Ma'an | 0.6 | 1.3 | 1.4 | 1.7 | 1.8 |
| [1] LGR (MJDs) | 21.9 | 28.4 | 36.7 | 41.2 | 47.6 |
| [2] TGR (MJDs) | 507.0 | 591.2 | 627.1 | 674.4 | 643.3 |
| [3] RDR (%) | 4.3 | 4.8 | 5.9 | 6.1 | 7.4 |
| [4] FAR (%) | 85.9 | 85.0 | 94.6 | 120.5 | 107.7 |

*Sources*:
[1] LGR figures from Ministry of Planning (1986, Table no. 4, p. 396).
[2] TGR figures from Central Bank of Jordan (1989, Tables 37 and 38, pp. 45–6).
[3] & [4] RDR and FAR are calculated by the author.

This is why more detailed data is needed to show the percentage of local government revenue (collected by the local government itself) against total revenue, which includes transfers from other sources. Another indicator which shows the proportion of total expenditure controlled by local governments is (PTECLG). This reveals ratios of 4.5, 5.2, 5.8, 7.7 and 7.4 per cent during the period 1980–84.

All the above indicators of decentralization indicate very limited financial powers for local governments in public spending and revenue collection during the period 1980–84.

### 7.5.3 Estimated Decentralization Ratios for 1988

The unavailability of published figures for the expenditure and revenue of local government necessitates estimation of data relying on information collected by Sadik and

Al-Khasawneh (1990) from a sample of 50 municipalities constituting 29.1 per cent of the total municipality councils in Jordan and about 10 per cent of the 516 municipality and village councils existing in 1988.

*The Methodology of Estimation*
Sadik and Al-Khasawneh calculated their figures directly from local authority budgets. They distributed the councils in the sample between the eight Jordanian governorates. To estimate data for 1988 the per capita expenditure and revenue for each municipal and village council included in the sample is calculated. Then the figures for per capita expenditure and revenue are multiplied by their counterparts at the governorate level. All the expenditure and revenue ratios as well as the shares for each kind of expenditure and revenue source are also calculated so that they can be related to the governorate in the sample. By totalling the data for the eight governorates we produced the figures to be used in measuring the different decentralization ratios at the national level for 1988.

*Expenditure Decentralization Ratios*
One of the important indicators derived from the expenditure figure and the number of councils in Table 7.4 is that per capita council spending varied widely between the eight governorates. In Amman governorate, average council spending was the highest in Jordan (98.7 thousand JDs), while in Zarqa, an industrial governorate, the spending was only 26.9 thousand JDs. Another important indicator from the table is that related to the notion of expenditure. On average, the current expenditure share of the local authorities' total expenditure amounted to about 47 per cent while that spent on development projects was only about 22 per cent.

If all development expenditure was allocated to social priority projects such as health and education, which is not true in practice, then Jordan's local government social allocation ratio (social expenditure ÷ total expenditure) would be similar to those of Kenya and Malawi in 1989 and 1984 but less than those in Chile in 1988 (31 per cent) and Zimbabwe in 1986 (34 per cent) (UNDP, 1993, Table no. 4.4, p. 71). In comparison with the industrial countries, the social allocation ratio in Jordan was about half that in Germany (47 per cent in 1988)

Table 7.4  Estimated municipal councils' expenditure according to Jordan's governorates for 1988 (thousand JDs)

| Governorate<br>Details | Amman | Zarqa | Irbid | Mafraq | Balqa | Karak | Tafila | Ma'an |
|---|---|---|---|---|---|---|---|---|
| No. of councils | 85 | 19 | 161 | 73 | 54 | 66 | 16 | 42 |
| Total local expenditure | 8389.5 | 511.1 | 8082.2 | 4547.9 | 4438.8 | 3471.2 | 1004.8 | 1625.4 |
| Average council expenditure | 98.7 | 26.9 | 50.2 | 62.3 | 82.2 | 52.6 | 62.8 | 38.7 |
| *Expenditure share* (%) | | | | | | | | |
| Current | 42.9 | 54.1 | 45.0 | 39.4 | 44.6 | 38.6 | 34.1 | 46.9 |
| Capital | 5.4 | 26.8 | 3.5 | 2.5 | 5.7 | 7.4 | 1.5 | 0.7 |
| Development | 19.4 | 2.0 | 24.2 | 18.6 | 20.0 | 28.7 | 16.7 | 28.3 |
| Others | 32.3 | 17.1 | 27.3 | 39.5 | 29.7 | 25.3 | 47.7 | 24.1 |
| Total (%) | 100.0 | 100.0 | 100.0 | 100.0 | 100.0 | 100.0 | 100.0 | 100.0 |

and the United Kingdom (43 per cent in 1989) (ibid.). Measurement of the EDR revealed that the percentage of local government spending to that of total government was small at 3 per cent, which is about half that for 1984.

In comparison with other developing countries the EDR in Jordan was lower than in the majority of developing countries (14 out of 17) listed by the UNDP (1993, Table no. 4.2, p. 69). Even after deducting debt-servicing payments and military expenditure from total government spending in 1988, the MEDR for Jordan was only 4.4 per cent, which is the lowest among the seven developing countries listed in the HDR of 1993. The explanation for such a low ratio is that the reduction in local government expenditure was enforced by central government because of the financial crisis which developed in the country after the mid-1980s.

*Revenue Decentralization Ratios*

A number of interesting observations can be derived from Table 7.5. The first is that total local authority revenue in Jordan was JD33.3 million in 1988. This means the RDR was only 4.1 per cent, which is also less than it was in 1984.

*Table* 7.5   Estimated municipal councils' revenue in Jordan according to source of revenue in each governorate for 1988 (thousand JDs)

| Governorate<br>Revenue source | Amman | Zarqa | Irbid | Mafraq | Balqa | Karak | Tafila | Ma'an |
|---|---|---|---|---|---|---|---|---|
| Total revenue | 8381 | 484.5 | 10061.9 | 4555.2 | 3681.2 | 3367.8 | 1190.4 | 1579.6 |
| of which | | | | | | | | |
| Government | 4097 | 383.8 | 5957 | 2963.8 | 2516.4 | 2516.4 | 680.0 | 1142.4 |
| % of total | 49 | 79.2 | 59.2 | 65.0 | 68.3 | 68.3 | 57.1 | 72.33 |
| Municipality | 2023 | 66.5 | 1360.5 | 562.1 | 804.6 | 402.6 | 92.8 | 193.2 |
| % of total | 24.1 | 13.7 | 13.5 | 12.3 | 21.4 | 12.0 | 7.8 | 12.33 |
| Extraordinary* | 2261 | 34.2 | 2744.4 | 1029.3 | 360.2 | 448.8 | 417.6 | 244 |
| % of total | 26.9 | 7.1 | 27.3 | 22.7 | 10.3 | 19.7 | 35.1 | 15.34 |
| Total share | 100.0 | 100.0 | 100.0 | 100.0 | 100.0 | 100.0 | 100.0 | 100.0 |

* Extraordinary revenue includes: projects revenue; interests, grants and aid; and loans.

In comparison with other developing countries Jordan's RDR was less than that of South Korea (31 per cent), Zimbabwe (17 per cent), Algeria (16 per cent), Bangladesh (8 per cent), while more than that of Brazil (1 per cent), Ghana (2 per cent) and Costa Rica (3 per cent). However, the most important observation is related to the structure of revenue sources for local councils.

All local councils in Jordan were highly dependent on central government to provide them with revenue because they had no powers to collect taxes. About 59 per cent of local council revenue came from government while only 15 per cent was collected by the local authorities. In the extraordinary revenue category, revenue from capital projects did not account for even 1 per cent of total local revenue while the other main source was loans, which constituted about 19 per cent of total municipality and village council revenue. Thus, the financial autonomy ratio (FAR) calculated for Jordan during the period 1980–84 is highly misleading because local council revenue does not equal local council revenue *raised by local taxation*. The first produces an FAR equal to 104 per cent while the second gives an FAR of only 15.5 per cent.[5]

### 7.5.4 The Allocation of Projects at the Local Level and the Issue of Participation and Development

In the HDR of 1993 the UNDP stated that investment at the local level, particularly through borrowing, may lead central government to lose 'control over the national creation of credit- and macroeconomic management' (UNDP, 1993, p. 74). The report suggested that special funds for investment such as the one in Jordan called 'Cities and Villages Development Bank' might provide an alternative means of financing investment at the local level. The report went on to assess the results of this development bank in the following oft-quoted words: 'this has helped finance improvements throughout the country, bringing roads, schools, clinics and water supplies to even the smallest and most remote communities' (UNDP, 1993, p. 74).

In order to examine the extent of the success referred to by the United Nations in the Cities and Villages Development Bank of Jordan, Table 7.6 provides detailed data on the kind of projects invested in by the Bank.

The argument of this chapter as well as the entire book is that providing basic needs, such as medical centres, schools,

*Table* 7.6  Allocation notion of the loans given by Cities and Villages Development Bank to Jordan's municipalities (thousand JDs)

| Municipalities<br>Project notion | Amman | Zarqa | Irbid | Mafraq | Balqa | Karak | Tafila | Ma'an |
|---|---|---|---|---|---|---|---|---|
| Roads | 269 | 135 | 960 | 848 | 477 | 103 | 35 | 20 |
| Electricity | 67 | 16 | 0 | 0 | 24 | 0 | 0 | 0 |
| Water | 0 | 0 | 0 | 0 | 0 | 0 | 0 | 0 |
| General Buildings | 0 | 0 | 42 | 50 | 0 | 12 | 0 | 0 |
| Sanitation | 0 | 0 | 0 | 0 | 0 | 0 | 0 | 0 |
| Schools | 0 | 0 | 12 | 0 | 7 | 14 | 0 | 0 |
| Medical Centres | 0 | 0 | 0 | 0 | 0 | 0 | 0 | 0 |
| Productive | 550 | 0 | 589 | 247 | 50 | 0 | 100 | 0 |
| Others | 229 | 100 | 1506 | 159 | 68 | 303 | 0 | 75 |
| Total (%) | 1115 | 251 | 3109 | 1304 | 626 | 432 | 135 | 95 |

*Source:* Cities and Villages Development Bank (1987, Table no. 9, p. 26).

clean water, electricity and sanitation as well as roads and other infrastructures, is the most important step towards enhancing the capabilities, capacities and choices of the people. From Table 7.6, it is clear that loans allocated for investment in roads constituted about 40 per cent of the total. Such investment is essential for local people in rural areas. However, loans allocated for *investment in basic needs* were 1.5 per cent in electricity, 0.5 per cent in schools. There was no investment in water, sanitation or the construction of medical centres. It seems, therefore, that investment in human development at the local level is weak in Jordan. Instead the central government provides such investment directly. As a result of this top-down approach, many field studies in Jordan's rural areas pointed out that shortages in the provision of basic needs at the local level led to internal migration to the urban centres (Al-Lawze *et al.*, 1989; Al-Tayeb *et al.*, 1990).

Therefore, the success of Jordan's approach in allocating projects to the rural areas has been overestimated by UNDP (1993). The problem for this bank as for other specialist development banks in Jordan is that the centre determines the projects to be implemented with the priorities set by planners and other decision-makers at the national level. For example, investment in productive projects, which constituted about 21.7 per cent of the total loans allocated by the bank in 1987, is usually based on an allocation suggested by the development plan. Thus, there is no participation at the local level either in the initiation, implementation and monitoring or in the evaluation of success or failure. All phases of the project are discussed and agreed by bureaucrats at both levels, central and local. This is because local councils and municipalities are not local government but local bureaucrats. They form part of the central government's apparatus for centralization rather than for decentralization. Thus, the UNDP assessment of the role of the bank in providing basic needs was not completely accurate.

Another criticism of the Cities and Villages Development Bank in Jordan stems from the highly distorted and unequal distribution of loans among the governorates. In the southern governorates, Karak, Tafila and Ma'an together received less than 9.5 per cent of the total loans allocated. Given the level of poverty and the low level of development in the southern region there is no reason why a greater proportion of investment should not take place there. The only reason we can give is the effect of powerful interest groups in the centre on loan allocation decisions. Such a conclusion is consistent with the history of centralization and the features of administration in Jordan.

## 7.6 PRIVATIZATION AND SMALL FARMERS

The consistency between privatization or market-oriented policies and functional decentralization as proposed by the World Bank and its advocates has had a negative effect on small farmers in rural Jordan.[6]

One of the major factors determining the degree of efficiency in the agriculture sector is land tenure. Prior to 1956, the tenure of much but not all state land, which constituted 31 per cent of the total land (called *miri* land), was on the *musha'a* system. In other words, the land was held in common and individual rights were based on shares of the total, not in particular parcels. In fact every two to nine years there was a redistribution of land. Thus, there was security in tenure but no continuity on the same piece of land. In 1957, the government embarked on a programme called 'Land Settlement' in order to determine and register traditional rights (IBRD, 1957, p. 126). However, the programme was not introduced to establish communities on land or to achieve land reform. Rather, because ownership rights are important for traditional social values, its purpose was to reduce conflicts between the tribes as well as to attract settlement by the nomads in the south for security reasons. Thus, there was no economic significance or purpose behind the programme. On the contrary, the failure in the design of the programme, due to the inability of the government to bear the transaction costs required to design and establish an effective system of property rights, resulted in a system where most of the land users were not the traditional owners. This privatization of state land has led to a rapid transference of the land to speculators on the one hand and to its unequal distribution on the other.

The leasing of government lands to capitalist farmers in the irrigated areas in particular, led to a more unequal distribution of land-holding and thereafter of wealth and income in the country. The UNDP (1993, Table no. 2.2, p. 29) placed Jordan among the countries with high inequality in the distribution of land-holding, 0.57 on the Gini coefficient measurement.[7] Therefore, the recent policy of privatization through the leasing of unused state land is not an alternative to a land reform programme. However, Lipton (1993, p. 644) believes that land privatization (i.e. leasing) can be classified as land reform 'only if it is invoked at the option of small farmers'. This was not the case in Jordan where land privatization led to a greater deterioration of the incentives to small farmers.

Two important negative consequences were the result: the first is that, while many Jordanian small farmers have abandoned farming because they cannot afford the debt forced on them by the middlemen and merchants in the rural areas, there were 150 thousand foreign workers working mainly as wage farmers. Crown Prince Hassan admitted the negative impact of the problem.

> With 150,000 workers from abroad largely in agriculture, I feel that something is tragically wrong. The incentives are obviously not viable for Jordanian farmers. This is something that has to be looked at (Interview with Crown Prince Hassan, 1988, p. 8).

The second negative consequence is that commercialization has led to an emphasis on more efficient, profitable, modern (technically), high-yield crops. As a result government loans have been directed toward the capitalist farmer elite. This trend has led farmers to move from self-sufficiency and semi-subsistence farming to a dependence on commercial farming. The latter includes all the risks arising from new crops as well as the need to engage in marketing. Such developments lead to the breakdown of personal exchange and its most important effect is the 'breakdown of communities of common ideologies and of a common set of rules in which all believe' (North, 1989, p. 1321). Both spelled disaster for small farmers. In the case of marketing, dependence on the State Marketing Board led to groups lobbying to gain early access to the market when prices are high. Even after the dismantling of the

State Marketing Board in 1989, capitalist farmers remained powerful groups in the agricultural sector. It should be explained that it is not ownership *per se*, but government centralized policies, which favour capitalist farmers. The latter lobby to secure access to government loans as well as to secure the marketing of their products (in particular at the beginning of the cultivation season) at home and abroad. This has left small farmers in an unequal position and is consistent with what North (1989, p. 1321) said, 'the rise of impersonal rules and contracts means the rise of the state, and with it unequal distribution of coercive power'.

Participation in the context of privatizing or leasing state land (the free-choice principle of participation) failed because the policy was not complemented by territorial decentralization, through which local organizations of small farmers can be active enough to achieve free choices for their members. This problem might be overcome if leasing were based on decisions by local bodies governed by an efficient system of checks and balances (Nugent, 1993).

Another problem unsolved by privatization is the government food pricing policy, which contributed to the shift from subsistence to commercial farming. Cheap food for the urban sector led the country to increase its share of food imports. The policy of food aid from countries such as the USA to Jordan also contributed to the transfer from subsistence to commercial farming. Wheat production has declined to the extent that the country could only provide 14 per cent of its actual consumption during the period 1981–85 while for barley the ratio of self-sufficiency was only 18 per cent. For other field crops (including corn and soyabeans) the ratio of self-sufficiency for the same period was only 6 per cent (Ministry of Planning, 1986, p. 536).

Supporters of the commercialization of agriculture such as the experts in the Jordanian Ministry of Agriculture have come to believe that farms with an area of less than 4 ha. are inefficient and unprofitable (Honey and Abu Kharmeh, 1988, p. 76). In reality more than half the farms in Jordan fall below this level and there is an obvious contradiction between what the experts believe, using their modern knowledge, and what the poor need. The latter basically need to enhance their capacity to use traditional experience and knowledge. However, this problem has also been identified by the Crown Prince of Jordan.

> More work is needed to develop a policy which is relevant to the bulk of small producers – mainly subsistence farmers who cannot afford the outlays necessary for modern production (Interview with Crown Prince Hassan, 1988, p. 9).

It is the Jordanian decision-makers, planners and experts who have proved unable to work out an approach which is committed in reality to a *spatial reversal*. They continuously regarded modernization as the subject, and people as the object. There is need for a shift in real policies to put people first rather than modernization, a manipulative technology, and a deficient centralization. As Uphoff (1993, p. 619) has stated, the goal should be to achieve a positive-sum outcome, which government programmes and the working of market forces alone cannot do.

The use of market forces as a way of increasing participation does not work because the existence of product surpluses and deficits within centralized policies for the benefit of the rich in itself distorts the market forces. As long as there is a lack of healthy local organizations and institutions, and territorial decentralization is weak or does not exist, the universal solution of 'getting the price right' will fail to achieve a sustainable level of development particularly in rural areas. Small Jordanian farmers are the main losers from the privatization of land.

## 7.7 DISSATISFACTION AND THE INSTITUTIONAL ROLE

The enforcement of western models of development in Jordan has eroded traditional values and undermined the people's confidence in themselves and their cultural heritage. They have had their values and norms denied to them by western attitudes of cultural superiority reinforced through an alien system of institutions and material welfare. Particularly in rural areas, there is a 'power of belief' in Islamic values. These values do not operate in a similar way to those modelled by rational choice theory or the context of individualism inherent in public choice theory.

Institutionalists emphasize the importance of studying the characteristics of social institutions in order to understand the evolution of society and its institutional change. There are three characteristics which could be considered basic to the concept of a social institution. The first is the rule and constraint nature of institutions; the second is the ability of institutions to govern relations among individuals and groups as well as being applicable in social relations, and the third is their predictability where the rules and constraints have to be understood, at least in principle, to be applicable in repeated and future situations (Nabli and Nugent, 1989, p. 1335).

In rural Jordanian communities social responsibility and accountability exist. Individuals voluntarily curtail their own freedom in order to maximize collective freedom. Participation in this sense will not be valued individually but collectively. The head of the family is still respected and is able to enforce his decisions on family members because denying recognition to the father of the family means denying recognition to the other members of the family. There is a feeling of security in belonging to a family and community. In Jordan these needs cannot be enhanced and worked to their full capacity when alien values and models of development are introduced. In these communities there are rules and norms which from a western point of view work irrationally. For example, in a field study of the socio-economic conditions in Tafila governorate in the south conducted in 1989 Al-Ahmed and his colleagues found that only 33.5 per cent of the total households in the sample covered by the study (1147 households) took loans and most of these were working in military service. This was because most of the *families did not believe in paying interest on loans for religious reasons* as Islam prohibits transactions based on financial interest (Al-Ahmed *et al.*, 1989, p. 76). Other field studies of rural areas in Jordan reached the same conclusion (Al-Ahmed *et al.*, 1991a; Al-Ahmed *et al.*, 1991b; Sadik and Al-Khasawneh, 1990). This does not mean that the Islamic religion is an obstacle to development but that it is a way of life which has to be taken into account.

The above view is shared by a growing number of scholars who believe that traditional values are not inefficient values, particularly in the Islamic context (Reilly and Zangeneh, 1990; Banuri, 1990a, 1990b; Slater, 1989; Choudhury, 1990; Said, 1989). This cannot be recognized without combining the space factor in any analysis of a development strategy. It is introducing the place factor, as Barnes and Sheppard (1992) argued, which can explain the rationality of human actions because the latter 'varies systematically and unpredictably according to the context in which the action occurs'(p. 18). So, the question is whether or not international organizations such as the World Bank and the IMF take such factors into account when they put forward their policy proposals.

The Jordanian government started its economic reform programme in 1988 by freezing expenditure and subsidies while increasing revenue through new taxes and duties. However, the measures of 1988 failed to bring about a significant reduction in the budgetary deficit. In 1989, the Jordanian government concluded a structural adjustment package with the IMF. The agreement itself represented the first admission by the government that it had mismanaged the economy.

A first condition of the agreement was a cut in government subsidies on fuels and foods in order to reduce the budget deficit (excluding grants) from 23.7 per cent of GDP in 1988 to 19.6 per cent in 1989. This meant that the measures, although economically sound, were also directed against the interests of the poor. On 16 April 1989, the government implemented price increases on a wide variety of goods such as petroleum products (11–33 per cent), alcoholic beverages (40–50 per cent), and detergents (25 per cent). Water charges in the Jordan Valley were also doubled. Moreover, the government, on IMF advice, agreed to reduce its subsidies on essential goods such as powdered milk, barley, bran and olive oil by increasing their retail prices (Satloff, 1992). As the price burden fell too heavily on low-waged Jordanian workers and small farmers, who had benefited least from the country's boom years in the late 1970s and early 1980s, riots spread from the southern region of the country, which is also the poorest, within hours of the price increases being announced (*Guardian*, 21 April 1989, p. 10). This shows that neither the authorities nor the IMF had given thought to the effects of such measures on the poor.

The demands of the people during their collective action (riots) provided a clear voice against the government's economic reform policies on the one hand and the centralization of decision-making on the other. In relation to Hirschman's (1970) concepts of exit and voice the riots represented the activation of voice when the exit option had achieved its limit. The first demand of the rioters was for the dismantling of the measures towards cuts in price subsidies; the second was support for small farmers; the third, while pledging loyalty to the King, was a demand for the end of economic inequalities and corruption and greater political freedom and participation (Brynen, 1992, p. 90).

Although it is not possible to find a direct causal linkage between privatization and the riots, because no privatization took place, the people's dissatisfaction with the economic reform policies can be understood as a *no vote* against privatization as well. This is because the state is the major employer, and a severe cut in its expenditure meant cuts in jobs and a resulting increase in uncertainty, unemployment and poverty. In such an environment privatization and policies of 'getting the price right' and 'functional decentralization' cannot secure choices and participation for the people within the context of decentralization as a strategy for development. It simply makes the rich richer and the poor poorer.

Crown Prince Hassan, when asked for his view on the IMF measures after the riots, said 'these measures will be more than we can bear unless we can secure Arab aid' (Interview with Crown Prince Hassan, 23 April 1989). However, Satloff (1992) contended that the riots were a result of the lack of consideration given by Jordan's decision-makers to the effect of such measures on the poor, especially since the Jordanian team postponed discussions with the IMF on specific policies in order to protect the poor from the above measures. However, a failure to anticipate the outcome of government policies is a feature of Jordan's economic management.

The resulting riots were an opportunity for the people to show the authorities their degree of dissatisfaction with the political and economic management, which left them struggling with the country's severe economic crisis.

The reaction of the monarch was to appoint a new PM critical of his predecessor's policies. The riots represented for some commentators the turning point in the drive towards political liberalization and participation in Jordan. The question, however, is what kind of relationship developed between democracy, participation and privatization (functional decentralization).

## 7.8 DEMOCRACY, PARTICIPATION AND PRIVATIZATION

The riots led the monarch to appreciate that political reform was important in order to temper the repercussions of the IMF adjustment Plan (Robins, 1990). Thus, from the preceding discourse, the two main factors which determined the introduction, form and nature of the democratic process were the short- and long-term objectives of political stability and the economic reform programme, which includes privatization. Both have led to greater political freedoms and new political controls. In such an environment participation through democracy and pluralism cannot be equal to popular participation through territorial decentralization because the 'spatial reversal' factor is absent from the first mechanism of participation.

Democracy has been introduced to enable the same economic reform programme to be implemented with parliamentary approval. Even if opposition to economic reform is mounted, Parliament will have no alternative but to accept the reforms because that is the only way to ensure that Jordan's debt can be rescheduled and the economy will receive additional funds from international aid agencies and western countries.

The democratization process started in November 1989 with the election of the Chamber of Deputies, but since then the process has been manipulated by the authorities in a way consistent with their general aim of political stability and the approval of economic reforms. The aim of starting the democratic process early could be seen as a way of pre-empting any further violence or rioting in the country.

In April 1990 King Hussein appointed a Royal Commission (RC) to draw up a National Charter (NC) governing the democratization process in the country (Susser, 1993, p. 498). Rather than relying on the National Assembly to draft the Charter the leader, through his assignment to the RC of this very important task determining the future and the form of popular participation in Jordan, proved that the process of political liberalization or democratization would be subject to direction from above. This is consistent with the objective of 'keeping in control' because the authority saw that the NC was essential to Jordan's democratic experiment (i.e. to define the legal and ideological framework). It also ensured that 'the process of liberalization would not get out of hand and endanger the regime' (Susser, 1992, p. 468). It could be said that it was also a way to escape the danger of the Islamic movement having an influence on the shaping of the NC.

The Prime Minister, Badran, in 1990 declared that political liberalization in Jordan 'was the "real safety valve" for a country in prolonged economic crisis' (ibid.). Similarly, the King's adviser, Adnan Abu Awda, noted that the National Assembly should 'serve to complement [i.e. not oppose] the state in carrying out its duties' (ibid.).

The three quotations above show that the authorities believed they were best placed to define the rules of the game. One result was that ratification of the NC on 9 June 1991 was carried out by a specially summoned national conference (Susser, 1993, p. 501).

The Charter was composed of eight sections dealing with different dimensions (e.g., the rationale and aims, the law-abiding state and political pluralism, the economy, society). However, three of them provide an important linkage between democracy, participation and privatization. The first principle of the NC reserved the right of forming and designing policy:

> The system of government in the Hashemite Kingdom of Jordan is Parliamentary, monarchic and hereditary. Adherence by all to legitimacy and to respect of the letter and spirit of the Constitution shall enhance the union between the people and their leadership (Ministry of Information, 1991, p. 14).

In the section dealing with the principles and limitations governing the political parties the NC withdrew the right to use demonstration and violence, thus depoliticizing the issue of economic reforms.

> Jordanians enjoy the right to establish and belong to political parties and grouping provided that their objectives are legitimate, their methods are peaceful and their statutes do not violate the provisions of the Constitution (ibid., p. 21).

Also, in Chapter 1, the citizens have a right

> to change their circumstances and improve their lot by legal means, express their views, and resort to whatever they deem necessary for the benefits of the whole by legitimate methods, and participate in the decision-making process (ibid., p. 13).

Control of the democratization process was necessary but not in itself sufficient to absorb the dissatisfaction with economic management and economic reforms. Therefore, cooptation was another goal for democracy. In other words, it was an avenue for the political leaders to bring key opposition figures under control (Pool, 1993, p. 51). The opposition's acceptance of the rules of the game in itself denoted a major victory for the leaders because it secured the goal of political stability while putting them on line to share responsibility for managing the economic crisis and the economic reform programme. Any criticism from the people of the government's economic management implies criticism of Parliament. However, that does not mean Parliament will in practice have the upper hand in managing economic policy.

In summary, a measure of popular participation in difficult decisions about resource allocation was necessary since the authorities had no intention of lifting either the economic reform programme or the austerity measures it implied. In fact, between 1991 and 1992, state subsidies were reduced from JD120 million to only JD40 million.

Chapter 5 of the NC explained that the future relationship between the state and the private sector should be based on encouraging private ownership. However, the state would retain control over strategic industries as well as regulating the economy.

> The Jordanian economy must be based on respect for private ownership and encouragement of private enterprise. On the other hand, natural resources and strategic projects must be the property of the state, with a full right to their management and supervision in the public interest. The state must also retain the prerogative of regulating the economy and allocating resources in accordance with national priorities (Ministry of Information, 1991, pp. 26–7).

Thus, the relationship between democracy, participation and economic reforms including privatization was formed in order to serve political stability rather than popular participation. By 1992 democracy in Jordan, as Amawi (1992, p. 29) argued, had become limited to the Parliament, parties and the press, and therefore it had to include socio-economic rights, such as the right to form grassroots organizations (GROs). But such high expectation of democracy may be inappropriate in a country where policies are usually designed to serve certain goals.

In his speech to Parliament on 2 December 1995 the King said 'democracy does not mean anarchy ... or harming national unity, or denigrating every accomplishment and smearing the good reputation of our country' (*The Economist*, 16 December 1995, p. 68). It is therefore understandable that measures and policies may be formulated from above in order to contain the threat which voices of discontent might have on achieving the state's goals of democracy. Although political freedom is an essential element of human development, it is important that it is understood within its particular applications, objectives and limits.

Political participation may be secured through democracy, but the latter cannot secure social and cultural participation. Likewise, economic participation through economic reforms and privatization cannot assure social and cultural participation unless privatization measures and implementation techniques are well designed.

Economic reforms, on the other hand, go beyond the issue of privatization or public versus private since they belong to the centralization/decentralization sphere of policy formation. Both processes, democratization and economic reform including privatization, are state-induced and relatively the state retains a considerable degree of management over them in spite of the fact that 'democracy has to be valued and sought for itself, not for its economic rewards' (Harik, 1992, p. 22).

## 7.9 THE SHIFT FROM DECENTRALIZATION AND PARTICIPATION

Decentralization is often associated with democratization, but the political and developmental impact of devolving decision-making, from the state point of view, might act as a constraint rather than an advantage for proceeding with economic reforms.

A measure of the authority's achievement in democratization is its success in passing the budget and economic reform programme for 1992 through Parliament with a comfortable majority (EIU, 1992b, p. 16). The Parliament elected in November 1993 also supported implementation of IMF policies for structural adjustment. Nevertheless, the most important evidence of increased centralization is the shift in planners' and decision-makers' orientation and thought from participation and empowerment within the context of decentralization and development (i.e. devolution), similar to that in the 1986–90 development plan, to a more functional decentralization (i.e. deconcentration, delegation and privatization) in the latest five-year development plan (1993–97).

The word 'decentralization' appears only three times in the new 211-page development plan document, published in 1994. The first objective of decentralization is to increase the efficiency of government administration by reducing intervention and duplication of responsibility between different government departments (Ministry of Planning, 1994, p. 104). The second occasion where the word decentralization appears is in the context of conducting studies of government agencies and departments outside the capital in order that some of the centre's responsibilities can be delegated (ibid., p. 189). The third and last occasion in which decentralization emerges is in the context of increasing the financial and economic efficiency of SOEs. The decentralization of power to branches of SOEs in the governorates will increase their flexibility and autonomy so that they can increase their degree of responsiveness according to location (ibid., p. 189).

In more than one case, the emphasis on privatization as a way of decentralizing decision-making to the marketplace was based on the argument of inefficient and highly centralized SOEs. However, the plan revealed that the state will continue to control strategic activities within the economy.

In summary, the 1993–97 development plan represents a clear shift from participation and empowerment (i.e., to territorial units) towards sectoral planning in which the emphasis is mainly concentrated on the limited delegation of power and responsibility within government departments. In this plan there is not even one mention of municipality and village councils. That is to say, the relationship between decentralization and development in Jordan is based on development from above in which the central authority determines to what extent participation and empowerment shall be allowed. Unless, therefore, privatization can increase participation (i.e. increase employee participation in decision-making, increase the number of lower-income shareholders) it cannot achieve a higher level of human development.

The danger comes when IMF policies and privatization programmes deliver no significant outcomes in terms of growth and efficiency, and lead to a deterioration in living standards because of increasing unemployment and poverty. An assessment of the social impact of the structural adjustment programme gives clear warning to the Jordanian decision-makers. In the words of Khasawneh (1995), 'the adjustment programme on its own may increase poverty and unemployment in Jordan, where the main group affected negatively ... are public sector employees' (p. 46). If privatization is in future to include health, education and other basic-needs sectors of the economy, then the human development achievements of Jordan during the last four decades will be thrown away. As Table 7.7 asserts, Jordan's success in human development is visible. The human development index rose from 0.428 in

*Table* 7.7   Comparison between trends of human development in Jordan and those of developing countries

| Trends in human development | Jordan | Developing countries |
|---|---|---|
| • Life expectancy at birth (years) 1960–90 | 46.9 to 66.9 years | 46.2 to 62.8 years |
| • Under-five mortality rate (per 1000 live births) 1960–90 | 217 to 52 child | 233 to 112 child |
| • Daily calorie supply (as % of requirements) 1965–88 | 93 to 118% of requirements | 90 to 109% of requirements |
| • Adult literacy rate (%) 1970–90 | 47 to 80% | 46 to 64% |
| • Real GDP per capita (PPP$) 1960–89 | 1120 to 2415 PPP$ | 784 to 2296 PPP$ |
| • Human development index (HDI) 1970–90 | 0.428 to 0.586 | N.A. |
| • The difference between GNP rank and HDI rank (1989–90) | –13* | N.A. |

*Shows that the GNP rank is higher than the HDI rank.
*Source*: UNDP (1992, Table no. 1, pp. 128–9, and Table no. 4, pp. 134–5).

1970 to 0.586 in 1990, which put the country among the leading nations in terms of human development.

The country's position according to the 1992 HDR is 14 out of 110 developing and developed countries listed (UNDP, 1992, Table no. 1.3, p. 94). However, the high investment in basic needs, particularly health and education, during the 1970s and the beginning of the 1980s was related to increasing external revenues, as was the increase in per capita income. Thus, the achievements should be understood within the context of a semi-rentier economy in which dependence on external factors determines policy direction.

If the Jordanian government is forced to cut expenditure in the future, as a result of IMF and World Bank conditions, the targets will be the softest items such as health and education.

This represents a risk particularly if the decision-makers continue to exercise a top-down approach towards development. Therefore, the final chapter will outline a policy framework for the Jordanian government to increase efficiency and accountability, and encourage participation by the informal sector.

# 8 Policy Framework: Necessary Ingredients for Successful Reforms

## 8.1 INTRODUCTION

Privatization in Jordan, as is often the case in other developing countries, lacks four basic ingredients in the relationship between privatization, decentralization, participation, and development. These are: reforming SOEs, bureaucratic reforms, crowding in the informal sector, and legal decentralization.

Given that privatization will take a gradual rather than a revolutionary approach in Jordan, this concluding chapter will highlight the importance of reforming the state through policies directed to increase the activation of the 'voice' rather than the 'exit' option alone. However, these policies are not exclusive to the Jordanian context but are also relevant to decision-makers in other developing countries because reforming the public sector seems to be more challenging than privatizing it. Reforms become important because the state in the developing world will continue to play a crucial role. In fact its capacity to initiate and implement the right kind of reforms might be of crucial importance to the achievement of sustainable development.

## 8.2 REFORMING SOEs

One of the important factors to be taken into account is the reform of Jordan's SOEs because, according to the 1993–97 plan and the 1991 National Charter, many of them will continue to operate under state ownership.

1. Decentralization of authority: The first step is to decentralize the authority of such SOEs from the government to their managers so that they can operate with some

autonomy. Government intervention in the running of such enterprises has been one of the main constraints on their performance. Multiple objectives and political appointments to the boards of directors have allowed the state to divert these enterprises to non-economic objectives.

2. Performance evaluation system: Employing a system of performance evaluation linked with another system of incentives for managers and employees. This contrasts with the present system of routine bonuses for all managers and employees irrespective of performance. One of the major problems in Jordanian SOEs is the weak system of control, which raises the principal–agent problem. The difficulty is that 'the [SOE] manager plays a game without a score' (Jones, 1991, p. 6). Planned targets for the performance of every department over a certain period of time are important elements in distinguishing between 'efficient' and 'inefficient'. Such target achievement systems will, with efficient incentive schemes, offer better prospects for efficiency. This is a difficult task to implement. Moreover, such systems require continuous development of the performance indicators themselves. Therefore, Jordanian decision-makers may benefit from studying the experience of other countries, such as those in East Asia, where such systems proved their effectiveness.

3. Increasing accountability: Successful reform requires a new and competent system of accountability linked with an efficient accounting system. However, to design alternative accountability systems one needs to diagnose the real problems in holding managers accountable; first there is the nature of the information system, which in itself might not provide a clear and precise account of performance; second is the absence of parameters by which to judge results; third is the lack of an establishment competent to evaluate performance; fourth is the non-existence of procedures to follow up on the evaluation; and the fifth difficulty is how to measure the constraints on the managers that may affect performance.

Despite the above problems, it is very important for enterprise accounts to be monitored by an unbiased and competent third party. Thus, if decentralization proce-

dures are implemented, government could function as the third unbiased agent; it is unable to assume such a role when it is the suspect and the judiciary at the same time. However, this needs a specification of the enterprise's quantifiable objectives, commercial and non-commercial. Where the objectives cannot be quantified, qualitative measurements can be used with their effects weighted on a scale.

Managers should be held accountable for factors within their control, and they should know that their reward or punishment will be according to the behaviour of those variables; 'If autonomy is to be efficiently and permanently delegated to the enterprises, then accountability must be ensured by a signalling system which specifies and rewards socially desirable behaviour' (Jones, 1991, p. 9).

4. Performance information system: A performance information system is important for the dissemination of information. In any private company, such information is provided to the public or the shareholders so that they can assess the performance of the company. The same principle could be applied in SOEs. The corruption in many SOEs in Jordan would not have occurred if there had been a regular check on the information provided. The combination of these performance information and accountability systems can provide safeguards for the people.

5. Qualified appointments: Government representation on the board of directors should be for technical reasons only unless obvious objectives need to be considered and clear reasons can be given to justify the representation.

6. Checks on subsidies: Any subsidy should be accompanied by an evaluation of its reasons. Such subsidies need to be planned for over a period of time and the public kept informed about them. In Jordan, some subsidies have been necessary as the direct result of deficient government investments. A review of such enterprises and their prospects should be undertaken so that, through analysis of the different objectives, ways of improving performance can be agreed. Where the future prospects of such enterprises, from the social welfare point of view as well as from the micro- and macro-economic perspectives, are

severely restricted they should be liquidated or merged with other enterprises able to benefit from their output. Any subsidies because of deficiency in management performance, rather than specified exogenous factors outside management control, should be accounted for by the management team.

7. Double check: Elected members of outside organizations (private individuals, NGOs, public organizations, customer organizations and others) should participate in monitoring the quality of performance and report their findings and recommendations both to the enterprise and to the public. Employing the 'double check' principle can help overcome the difficulties of such enterprises. The ordinary people, or as Goulet (1989, p. 166) described them the 'non-expert populace', can often contribute positively to such evaluations because they are the customers affected by management performance. Evaluation from below as well as from above (experts) can coordinate efforts to improve the enterprise's performance. Open lines for customer complaints and recommendations should allow room for voices to be listened to rather than to be suppressed or avoided as has been the case in Jordanian SOEs.

8. Introducing the place factor: Evaluation of the provision of public enterprise services on a spatial scale by considering the balance of services provision for poorer local areas against urban areas and setting time–place targets. This could be achieved through discussion and the co-ordination of local people particularly in rural areas where participation is minimal.

9. Training programmes: Another problem facing SOEs in Jordan is overstaffing. In this case the government has to take the responsibility of introducing training programmes, which are in short supply, and redeploying workers, particularly the semi-technically skilled, towards these economic sectors with a shortage of employees.

10. Participation: Increasing employee participation in the initiation, planning, implementation and evaluation of different projects would give them an incentive to reduce shirking and opportunism. Participation will set new standards in the work place where every employee will be

considered an important member of the enterprise. Currently, shopfloor workers in Jordanian SOEs play no part in decisions about the operation of or the investment in their enterprises. This is because the socio-economic culture divides the workforce into managerial and manual workers, where the latter have no say.

## 8.3 BUREAUCRATIC REFORMS

Privatization does not take into account bureaucratic reform. As a centralized state in which bureaucrats constitute half of the total workforce, there is a need for Jordan to reform its administration. The fifth and the sixth development plans (1986–90 and 1993–97 respectively) describe the overcentralization of authority and its relevant problems as a weakness of commitment towards administrative development leading to a lack of confidence in efforts exerted in this direction.

- Too much centralization in certain agencies, where the agency head becomes the sole decision-maker on most issues, coupled with a responsibility span which is too broad for effective management.
- An indifferent attitude to public relations which takes the principle of reciprocity into account.
- Weakness of the administrative staff in local government organization, procedures, manpower and financial aspects, together with insufficient concern for their development.

Although bureaucratic reforms have been conducted since the 1960s, reform has been a slogan of every government rather than a genuine commitment. Ellayan (1987) conducted a survey by questioning the heads and permanent secretaries of 76 administration departments who in reality represented the bureaucratic elite: 56 per cent of the respondents admitted that their services did not meet people's expectations, and 52 per cent said that their departments lacked adequate information systems.

There is, therefore, a need to reform the bureaucratic structure by decentralizing the authority of the central agencies to the sub-regional and local levels. However, this should be accompanied by the introduction of an efficient accountability system (performance tables) to ensure that the people's views of the services provided by these departments are registered. Decentralization alone will not suffice without a change in the rules and legal structures which govern the bureaucratic environment. Training and accountability are important steps in changing the structure of bureaucratic practices. The promotion and stimulation of local initiatives as well as their vitalization will contribute significantly to this. It requires concrete commitment and change to the rules of the game, not a simple task. In his letter to the new Prime Minister Al-Kabariti, who took office in February 1996, King Hussein emphasized the necessity of making a white revolution (a clean sweep) in Jordan. A revolution against the old bureaucratic structure, the old practices, and the old elite; factors which caused Jordan its present economic crisis.

## 8.4 SUPPORTING THE INFORMAL SECTOR

While the concern of privatization is the transfer of ownership and/or control from the state to the private arena, its focus has been limited to one sector, namely the formal sector, where SOEs are operating.

The informal manufacturing sector represents 80 per cent of the total number of manufacturing establishments in Jordan. Thus, competition or contestability is the environment in which such micro-enterprises are operating. While sunk costs in such enterprises are negligible, their survival is determined by government regulations and policies. Privatization proposals in Jordan, as introduced in 1986, did not discuss the factors affecting the operation of this sector. Neither did the latest development plan (1993–97).

There is a need to support such micro-enterprises through a bottom-up approach. They are denied access to credit and financial assistance as well as the appropriate regulations to perform efficiently and thereby absorb the problems of unemployment and poverty in Jordan. This is because these enterprises are working on the fringes of the law. Most of them have been consistently discriminated against. They do not have legal protection and often rely on an informal structure and informal contacts with the formal system in order to survive.

While they rely on indigenous technology and innovations, which are the basic solutions for curing the illness of modernization, the decision-makers and Jordanian experts link them with inefficiency and traditionality which cannot bring about development.

Privatization is one of the policies that can diminish their contribution because privatization is associated with large enterprises and modern technology, which is capital-intensive. It might be argued that 'getting the price right' will enhance the possibility of bringing in labour-intensive technology because of the work of the relative prices mechanism. That probability is narrow because privatization is always associated with internal and external competition. Relying on distorted labour markets, with highly educated people as is the case in Jordan, makes the capital-intensive alternative more attractive to entrepreneurs. Profitability, efficiency and competition need economies of scale, that is modern technology, and often 'master key' projects in the case of Jordan. This relies on the assumption proposed by the proponents of 'development from above'. That is to say that such large enterprises are 'growth poles' to be integrated through linkages with other sectors in the economy. However, that is not the case in Jordan where weak linkages between and within the different economic sectors have been an integral character of the economy in the last three decades.

Privatization seems likely to reinforce the existing conditions (of formal and informal sectors) by focusing policy on the critical needs of the formal sector, which already has access to resources and information as well as the support of government. Supporting micro-enterprises which enhance self-employment is not a trade-off between profits and employment, but rather between private returns and social costs, or between short-term and long-term growth alternatives.

Thus, it could be said that promoting informal activities in Jordan would mean opening the administration gates so that firms can gain access to resources and reduce entry and participation costs. This is 'crowding in' the informal sector because markets are restricted in Jordan to the benefit of the large enterprises in the formal sector. Therefore, eliminating the restrictions (i.e. massive paperwork, ministerial approval, and so forth) would enhance the informal sector's capacity to produce and contribute rather than reduce its potential.

The second benefit from expanding the capacity of the informal activities is that they are naturally more responsive and flexible to people's needs and demands. They can reach everywhere whether in urban or rural areas. This could promote a mixture of the 'exit' and 'voice' options. Moreover, they usually rely on personal relations and community communication networks. This can reduce transaction costs within the community.

Many handicraft activities have been eliminated in Jordan because of their inability to compete and gain access to the markets. Two field studies in Jordan found that there would be a high potential for such small-scale industries in rural Jordan if they could have supportive policies (Sadik and Al-Khasawneh, 1990; Al-Ahmed *et al.*, 1989). The elimination of such traditional activities was also a result of the commercialization of the agriculture sector, the division of labour, and monetization of the economy whereby people devalued their traditional businesses in favour of new ones that could generate cash. Traditional products also faced unequal competition from similar imported goods from cheap origins such as Taiwan and Hong Kong. There is a need to reshape government policies so as to emphasize the importance of using *endogenous and appropriate technologies*, which people control rather than being controlled by them. The informal sector is solid ground for such a take-off point.

People have shared their knowledge and experience for generations. The efficiency of their technology might be unable from the point of view of technical standards to compete with the western technologies, but it is efficient enough to generate and express their values, balance, satisfaction, equity and respect. The latter can ensure their survival as a community rather than as individuals. Privatization and market-oriented policies eliminate such important factors.

## 8.5 LEGAL DECENTRALIZATION

In Jordan, there is an excessive centralization of judiciary, legislation and executive power in the hands of a few government agencies. Privatization does not eliminate or reduce such powers, which have been used discriminately for the benefit of particular interest groups. On the contrary, privatization increases their power, enabling the government to conduct its top-down market-oriented and privatization remedies. These powers should be transferred to decentralized units, vertically and horizontally, so that power can be shared rather than concentrated. This requires decentralization to the territorial units as well as within the bureaucratic structure itself. The strategy of development from below and within depends primarily on participation. This cannot take place if there is no decentralization of the legal system.

Many powers in Jordan are concentrated in the prime minister's and ministers' offices. Delays and inefficiency are features of the system. However, such transfers need a complementary policy of training to enhance the capability and capacity of the decentralized units to work efficiently on the one hand and to prevent them being manipulated by small interests on the other.

## 8.6 SUMMARY AND CONCLUSIONS

One can debate the strength and weaknesses of privatization as a policy in isolation, but where it is linked to development, the relationship becomes complex and multi-dimensional. In other words we believe that it is necessary to identify the institutional background in which privatization policies are adopted. Each society has a number of characteristics which may support or hinder the adoption of any institutional innovation such as privatization. Therefore, the argument is difficult to sustain that universal prescriptions such as privatization can work in every society and that it pays similar gains irrespective of the institutional background of the society.

Neither history nor economic theory provides a clear guide to the optimal pace and sequence of privatization measures. There is no 'master blueprint' for transforming a politically-based market economy, such as the one in Jordan, to a free-market economy. Instead, destroying the existing system without introducing the necessary institutional framework for the new free-market system may lead to counterproductive results particularly for the masses who cannot cope with the deterioration in their living standards. This stems from the immaturity of the representative associations in society and their inability to override narrow interests.

A major problem facing the policy of privatization is the real need for investment in the newly privatized companies. With shallow capital markets in developing countries, and with the reluctance of foreign investors to bring real investment, privatization may prove difficult to achieve unless the decision-makers have clear objectives in the first place. However, the imposition of some financial discipline on SOEs instead of the old soft-budget phenomenon should ease the pressure to privatize as quickly as is currently the case.

It must be recognized that privatization, if pursued within the wrong framework and without human development in mind, will fail to achieve the objective of development defined as increasing human well-being. Participation through privatization has to consider two facts, firstly the constraints imposed by government design and implementation policies for privatization (i.e. budgetary deficit) and secondly the need to make SOEs accountable to the people through the government as a competent third unbiased agent or through the people's representatives (i.e. democratic institutions). If we could activate the voice of the people, there would be a prospect of reforming SOEs and making them both more accountable and people-oriented.

The belief of most western advisers that a healthy and complete set of markets is sufficient for the achievement of an efficient allocation of resources and, conversely, that in most areas of economic life government intervention is harmful, may well be ill founded: they ignore externalities and they ignore issues to do with the division of labour between the state and the market. The state's role is important for the regulation of monopoly, the need for public supervision of trading processes, incompleteness of markets, the infrastructural requirement, and most important of all, providing human security. The state will undoubtedly continue to exert a significant influence on Third World economic development even after major reforms have taken place.

Unless we can pinpoint what the people's demands are it would be a great gamble to allow external advisers and donor agencies to determine the fate of millions. Increasing poverty and unemployment, and the disintegration of society, may become dangerous to the extent that the same people who revolt against the state for freedom and democracy may in the near future revolt against the market elite. The dilemma is that such a trade-off will be examined where the old state provided them with the essentials but took their freedom, while the market economy provided them with freedom but also took the essentials and with it their security as human beings.

Our aim as advisers, professionals, and practitioners should focus on increasing the capability of the people; the means and ends of development. Privatization should, at least, be given a human face as well as time to be compatible with the adaptive efficiency of the society. Unless it is well designed, and crisis-free, privatization will fail to generate sustainable development. Choices and freedom, on the other hand, can be improved if there is a commitment towards territorial decentralization, a commitment that few political leaders in the Third World appear capable of making.

# Notes

## 1 INTRODUCTION: PRIVATIZATION AND DEVELOPMENT FROM A HOLISTIC PERSPECTIVE

1. *Functional decentralization* means the decentralization of functions such as the functions of production or the provision of services from the monopolistic centralized bureaucracies to the market, while *territorial decentralization* means the decentralization of government decision-making to the sub-national levels such as local governments or authorities.
2. The large number of empirical studies was necessary because the book employed an institutional approach in which the analysis must be continuously monitored by reference to cases, observation, and examples.

## 2 THE ROLE OF THE STATE IN DEVELOPMENT

1. Recently, Taylor (1993) developed a three-gap model in which he added the fiscal limitation factor, i.e. public sector borrowing requirement (PSBR), as a further constraint on the economy.
2. This new style is what is called neoclassical political economy or the new institutional economics. The 'new' is different from the 'traditional neoclassical' school in four aspects. The first is that government in the NIE is at least partially endogenous and its policies are analogous to vested interests. Secondly, the invisible hand does not work in the NIE because individuals and groups use the political arena to secure or maintain rents. Thirdly, the NIE challenges the traditional neoclassical theory assumption of a stable perfectly competitive equilibrium because this means institutions will be passive in the analysis. Finally, the NIE believes that Pareto optimality will not be freely chosen by most societies because the incentive to achieve perfect equilibrium is often small and the potential rent from cartelization is large. However, both 'new' and 'traditional' believe in individual rationality and the assumption of utility maximizing behaviour (Colander, 1984, pp. 2–3).
3. The old institutionalists criticized the neoclassical school for its individualism and abstract models. For reading in the old institutionalist literature and its differences from other schools of thought see Kapp (1976), Wilber and Harrison (1978), Street and James (1982), Mayhew (1987), Radzicki (1988), Tilman (1990), Harvey and Katovich (1992).

4. Olson said that a selective incentive 'is one that applies selectively to the individuals depending on whether they do or do not contribute to the provision of the collective good' (Olson, 1982, p. 21).
5. For a more detailed analysis of the implications, review Olson (1982, pp. 36–74).
6. The studies are:
   Speder, J. and Smith, S., *The Development of Capitalism in Africa* (London and New York: Methuen, 1986).
   Lubeck, P. M. (ed.), *The African Bourgeoisie: Capitalist development in Nigeria, Kenya, and the Ivory Coast* (Boulder, Colorado: Lynne Rienner Publishers, 1987).
   Kennedy, P., *African Capitalism: The struggle for ascendancy* (Cambridge: Cambridge University Press, 1988).
7. For a review of the empirical estimates of the cost of rent-seeking, see Ampofo-Tuffuor *et al.* (1991).
8. The three dimensions of the transaction costs are related to three different literatures: economic organization, property rights, and institutional change. For more details, see Nabli and Nugent (1989).
9. Institutions are defined as 'rules, enforcement characteristics of rules, and norms of behaviour that structure repeated human interaction' (North, 1989, p. 1321).
10. The term has been used by Krugman (1993).
11. Similar argument is given by Taylor (1991, p. 109).
12. For further criticism of the theory of rent-seeking and DUP activities see Samuels and Mercuro (1984), McPherson (1984), and Miller (1992).

# 3 PUBLIC VS PRIVATE OWNERSHIP

1. For example, in the United State policy-makers tend to intervene through regulations, while in other countries, such as Britain, they tend to intervene through direct ownership.
2. The capital intensity ratio means the share of total capital employed, to the total value added or the total output of an economic activity.
3. Calculated by employing the data in Short (1984, pp. 116–22).
4. The figures are transferred to US dollars employing the exchange rate in the IMF (1992).
5. Sick = Companies with negative shareholders' fund.
   Weak = Loss-making companies with shareholders' funds <200% of paid-up capital.
   Satisfactory = Shareholders' funds <100%, but currently profitable.
   Good = Shareholders' funds >100% and profitable.
6. Hodgson argued that as the entrepreneur, in the traditional neoclassical theory, is an auctioneer, this will imply his gathering, processing and communicating a lot of information, particularly regarding the

formation of prices. Consequently, such knowledge needs to be centralized, which is '*against the spirit of the market system*' (Hodgson, 1992, p. 753). Thus, there is a contradiction within the neoclassical theory itself.

7. For critical examination, see Sah (1991).
8. *Bounded rationality* means that individuals have only limited information, and limited capability to process it without errors, which leads to such costs. *Opportunism* costs are the result of bounded rationality and self-interested behaviour while the costs from *information impactedness* arise from information asymmetry as some parties hold information which can be used in opportunistic ways so as to benefit them when contracting with other parties who lack such information.
9. For a methodological criticism of the theory, see Stigler (1976) and De Alessi (1983).
10. The essence of analysis for this theory is a mathematically oriented one. However, the intention is not to discuss the technicality of the approach but rather the main context in which the differences between private and public ownership are presented. For a sophisticated analysis of this literature within the context of privatization, read Vickers and Yarrow (1988) and Bös (1991). For a general mathematical treatment, see Rees (1985a and 1985b).
11. The 'adverse selection' *ex ante* costs arise from the inability of one party, such as the principal, to distinguish between true and false information provided by different contractual parties, which may lead to choices that increase the costs to the principal. The 'moral hazard' *ex post* costs arise in agreements in which at least one, the principal for example, relies on the behaviour of another party and information about that behaviour is costly.
12. Greenwald, Kohen and Stiglitz (1990) argued that financial market imperfection may negatively affect the productivity growth in large corporations.

# 4 REVIEW OF THE EMPIRICAL EVIDENCE ON PRIVATIZATION IN DEVELOPING COUNTRIES

1. Per capita GNP in 1993 for low-income countries ($695 or less), lower-middle income ($696–$2785), upper-middle income ($2786–$8625), and higher-income countries ($8626 or more) (World Bank, 1995).
2. More than US$50 000 in value.
3. TFP = (Weighted index of physical quantities of output)/(Total expenditure on inputs/Weighted index of input prices).
4. The countries were the Dominican Republic, The Philippines, Sri Lanka, Benin, Egypt, Morocco, Tanzania and Turkey.
5. The same argument is employed in this book.
6. More evidence will be provided in Chapter 5.

## 5 PRIVATIZATION, DECENTRALIZATION, PARTICIPATION AND DEVELOPMENT

1. One of the important empirical studies which established a strong relationship between development, democracy and growth is that of Pourgerami (1988).
2. Rondinelli and Nellis (1986, p. 5) argued that decentralization has a wide scope ranging from simply adjusting workloads within central government organizations to diverting all government responsibilities for performing a set of what were previously considered public-sector functions. In that they categorized decentralization into four types within developing countries' experience: deconcentration; delegation; devolution; and privatization. Such a classification reveals that the emphases are almost all on functional decentralization.
3. The evidence of successful local initiatives in Europe presented by Stohr (1990), in sub-Saharan Africa by Taylor and Mackenzie (1992) and in Latin America by Stephen (1991).
4. Rationality is considered in the context of the free-rider problem. 'Unless there is coercion or some other special device to make individuals act in their common interest, rational, self-interested individuals will not act to achieve their common or group interest' (Olson, 1965, p. 2).
5. For further evidence, see Martin (1993, pp. 128–36).

## 6 PRIVATIZATION IN JORDAN

1. For more details regarding the effect of social security schemes on income distribution in Jordan, see Musallam (1990).
2. For more detailed analysis, see Section 2.3.
3. The figures for the share of development expenditure in both pure and autonomous SOEs are adopted from Brand (1992, p. 170).
4. For a review of Jordan's reforms record (1985–89) see Brand (1992, pp. 173–9).
5. As the idea of privatization was first initiated at the end of 1986 and the begining of 1987, it is important to consider the changes that affected the Jordanian economy between 1981 and 1987. Therefore, healthier economic indicators after 1990 were a result of more external assistance to Jordan due to the Gulf War, higher workers' remittances in 1991, as a result of the return of 300 000 Jordanians to work in the Gulf states, and the government adoption of tight fiscal policy as a result of the structural adjustment programme agreed with the IMF in 1991.
6. The figure of $262 million was distributed between $63 mn, $70 mn, $81 mn, and $48 mn during 1985, 1986, 1987 and 1988 respectively (EIU, 1992c, p. 35).

7. This percentage change in tariffs is calculated from JEA (1993, 1994) on the basis of average increase in day and night energy-supply tariffs.
8. This record has been collected by the author from secondary sources, which include books, journals, newpapers and broadcasting agencies.
9. The restructuring plan is being financed by a $30 million loan from the European Investment Bank, a $20 million loan from the World Bank, a $23 million loan from the Export-Import Bank of Japan, and a $50 million World Bank guaranteed Eurobond issue. The rest of the finance will come from local resources.

# 7 PRIVATIZATION, DECENTRALIZATION, PARTICIPATION AND DEVELOPMENT IN JORDAN

1. The strategy calls for injecting investments in smaller towns of the rural regions as well as improving the communication, transportation and trade linkages (Honey and Abu Kharmeh, 1989).
2. Planning in Jordan started with 1963–67 economic and social development plan, later changed to the 1964–70 plan. Afterwards, five economic and social development plans were introduced: 1973–5, 1976–80, 1981–5, 1986–90, and 1993–7.
3. It is important to mention that there were no data available on the expenditure and revenue of municipality councils after 1984. Furthermore, even the new five-year development plan (1993–97) does not contain any information regarding municipality expenditure and revenue. Thus, the construction of the data for 1988 becomes important for two reasons. The first is for comparative purposes as many of the decentralization ratios asserted in UNDP (1993, Table 4.2, p. 69) were for 1988. The second reason is to assess whether the objectives of the 1986–90 development plan regarding decentralization were implemented, at least in financial matters, as it was a failure from the territorial side.
4. This argument is mainly derived from North (1989, 1991) and is explained in detail in Section 2.3.4.
5. In the first method: FAR = 33.3 MJDs (Local government revenues)/32.1 MJDs (local government consumption) = 104 per cent. In the second method: FAR = 33.3 × 0.15/ 32.1 = 15.5 per cent.
6. For more discussion on the differences between functional and territorial decentralization see Chapter 5.
7. The Gini coefficient measures the inequality in distribution. Its value ranges from 1 (highly unequal) to zero (exactly equal).

# References

Abu Shair, Osama J. Abdul Rahim, *Al-qitaa Assina'e Al-Khas: At-tattawer wa Al-itijahat* (The Private Industrial Sector: Growth and Directions), Economic Planning Commission, Study no. 573 (Baghdad: Ministry of Planning, 1988).

Adam, C., Cavendish, W., and Mistry, P. S., *Adjusting Privatization: Case Studies from Developing Countries* (London: James Currey, 1992).

Adda, W., 'Privatisation in Ghana', in Ramanadham, V. V. (ed.), *Privatisation in Developing Countries* (London and New York: Routledge, 1989), pp. 303–21.

*Ad-Dustor*, 'Transforming TCC into a Shareholding Company Owned by the Government' (27 June 1995), p. 30.

Adelman, Irma, 'Beyond Export-Led Growth', *World Development*, 12 (1984) 9–23.

Al-Ahmed, A. K., Al-Nabhani, N. M., Al-Khasawneh, M. M., and Al-Qutub, S. M., *Al-waqi'u Al-iqtisadi wa Al-ijtema'i Lemuhafadhat Atafila* (The Economic and Social Conditions in Tafila Governorate) (Amman: Royal Scientific Society, December 1989).

Al-Ahmed, A. K., Al-Khasawneh, M. M., Al-Nabhani, N. M., Al-Lawze, M. A., and Al-Rafai, A. A., *Al-waqi'u Al-iqtisadi wa Al-ijtema'i lemuhafadhat Ma'adaba* (The Economic and Social Conditions in Ma'adaba) (Amman: Royal Scientific Society, January 1991a).

Al-Ahmed, A. K., Al-Khasawneh, M. M., Al-Nabhani, N. M., Al-Lawze, M. A., Al-Kutub, S. M., and Al-Rafai, A. A., *Al-waqi'u Al-iqtisadi wa Al-ijtem'ai lemuhafadhat Ma'an* (The Economic and Social Conditions in Ma'an Governorate) (Amman: Royal Scientific Society, January 1991b).

Al-Edwan, Y., Al-Kutub, S. M., and Al-Rafai, A. A., *Al-waqi'u Al-iqtisadi wa Al-ijtem'ai lemuhafadhat Al-Mafraq* (The Economic and Social Conditions in Mafraq Governorate) (Amman: Royal Scientific Society, February 1990).

*Al-Khaleej*, 'Royal Jordanian Wiping Off Debts to Prepare for Privatization' (18 December 1987), p. 1.

Al-Lawze, M. A., Al-Majalee, K. and Al-Tayeb, S., *Al-waqi'u Al-iqtisadi wa Al-ijtema'i Li-sukaan Al-Mazar Aja-nubi* (The Economic and Social Condition of the South Mazar population') (Karak: Mu'tah University, 1989).

Al-Quaryoty, M. Q., 'Prospects for Privatization in Jordan', *Journal Of Arab Affairs*, 8 (1989) 159–190.

*Al-Ra'i*, 'Privatization of Wire, Wireless Communication Establishment' (20 March 1986), p. 1.

——, 'Rafai Confirms Backing Private Sector/30 000 Jordanians are Jobless' (1 November 1986), p. 1.

——, 'Privatization of Agricultural Marketing Firm' (20 February 1987), p. 1.

——, 'Ghandour Speaks on Royal Jordanian 1989 Plans Including Privatization' (21 December 1988), p. 8.

——, 'The Government Set a Goal to Sell its Stakes in Public Companies within Two Years' (19 May 1995), p. 8.

Al-Tayeb, S., Al-Lawze, S., Al-Jalode, J., and Al-Kutub, S. M., *Al-waqi'u Al-iqqtisadi wa Al-ijtema'i Lemuhafadhat Al-Karak* (The Economic and Social Conditions in Karak Governorate) (Karak: Mu'tah University, 1990).

Alchain, Armen, 'Some Economics of Property Rights', *Politico*, 30 (1965) 816–129.

Ali, M. R., Khaleque, A., and Hussain, M., 'Participative Management in a Developing Country: Attitudes and Perceived Barriers', *Journal of Managerial Psychology*, 7 (1992) 11–16.

Amawi, A., 'Democracy Dilemmas in Jordan', *Middle East Report*, 22 (1992) 26–9.

Amman Financial Market (AFM), *The Eighteenth Annual Report 1995* (Amman: Amman Financial Market, 1995).

Ampofo-Tuffuor, E., Jr, Delorme, C. D. and Kamerschen, David R., 'The Nature, Significance, and Cost of Rent Seeking in Ghana', *Kyklos*, 44 (1991) 537–59.

Amsden, A. H., 'Why Isn't the Whole World Experimenting with the East Asian Model to Develop?, Review of *The East Asian Miracle*', *World Development*, 22 (1994) 627–33.

Anani, J. and Khalaf, R., 'Privatization in Jordan', in El-Naggar, Said (ed.), *Privatization and Structural Adjustment in the Arab Countries* (Washington, DC: International Monetary Fund, 1989), pp. 210–25.

Andersson, T. and Brannas, K., *Nationalization and Investment Flows: A Panel Study*, Working Paper no. 330, 203 (Stockholm: The Industrial Institute for Economic and Social Research, 1992).

*Arab News*, 'Jordan Ports Corporation Faces Privatization' (17 November 1993), Arab News data bank.

——, 'Royal Jordanian Likely to be Privatized' (9 December 1993), Arab News data bank.

*Arab Times*, 'Jordan to Privatize Airline' (4 August 1992), p. 17.

Aylen, J., 'Privatization in Developing Countries', in Johnson, Christopher (ed.), *Privatization and Ownership*, Lloyds Bank Annual Review, Vol. 1 (London: Pinter Publishers Limited, 1988), pp. 124–38.

Balassa, Bela, *Public Enterprises in Developing Countries: Issues of Privatization*, World Bank Discussion Paper no. DRD292 (Washington, DC: World Bank, 1987).

——, 'The Lessons of East Asian Development: An Overview', *Economic Development and Cultural Change* (Supplement), 36 (1988) 273–90.

Banuri, T., 'Development and the Politics of Knowledge: A Critical Interpretation of the Social Role of Modernization', in Marglin, F. A. and

# References

Marglin, S. A. (eds), *Dominating Knowledge: Development, Culture, and Resistance* (Oxford: Clarendon Press, 1990a), pp. 29–72.

——, 'Modernization and its Discontents: A Cultural Perspective on Theories of Development', in Marglin, F. A. and Marglin, S. A. (eds), *Dominating Knowledge: Development, Culture, and Resistance* (Oxford: Clarendon Press, 1990b), pp. 73–101.

——, 'Introduction', in Banuri, T. (ed.), *Economic Liberalization: No Panacea; The Experience of Latin America and Asia* (Oxford: Clarendon Press, 1991), pp. 1–27.

Bardhan, Pranab, 'Symposium on the State and Economic Development', *Journal of Economic Perspectives*, 4 (1990) 3–7.

——, 'Analytic of the Institutions of Informal Cooperation in Rural Development', *World Development*, 21 (1993) 633–9.

Barnes, T. J. and Sheppard, E., 'Is There a Place for the Rational Actor? A Geographical Critique of the Rational Choice Paradigm', *Economic Geography*, 68 (1992) 1–21.

Bates, R. H., 'Governments and Agricultural Markets in Africa', in Bates, Robert (ed.), *Toward a Political Economy of Development: A Rational Choice Perspective* (Berkeley and London: University of California Press, 1988), pp. 331–58.

Baumol, W. J., 'Contestable Markets: An Uprising in the Theory of Industry Structure', *American Economic Review*, 72 (1982) 1–15.

Bery, S. K., 'Economic Policy Reform in Developing Countries: The Role and Management of Political Factors', *World Development*, 18 (1990) 1123–31.

Bhagwati, J. N. and Srinivasan, T. N., 'Revenue Seeking: A Generalization of the Theory of Tariffs', *Journal of Political Economy*, 88 (1980) 1069–87.

Bhagwati, J. N., 'Directly Unproductive, Profit-Seeking (DUP) Activities', *Journal of Political Economy*, 90 (1982) 98–1002.

——, 'Poverty and Public Policy', *World Development*, 16 (1988) 539–55.

Bhagwati, J. N., Brecher, R. A., and Srinivasan, T. N., 'DUP Activities and Economic Theory', in Colander (ed.), *Neoclassical Political Economy: The Analysis of Rent-Seeking and DUP Activities* (Cambridge and Massachusetts: Ballinger Publishing Company, 1984), Ch. 1.

Bhaskar, V. and Khan, M., 'Privatization and Employment: A Study of the Jute Industry in Bangladesh', *American Economic Review*, 85 (1995) 267–73.

Bienen, H. and Waterbury, J., 'The Political Economy of Privatization in Developing Countries', *World Development*, 17 (1989) 617–32.

Bishop, M. and Thompson, D., 'Privatization in the UK: Internal Organization and Productive Efficiency', *Annals of Public and Cooperative Economics*, 63 (1992) 171–88.

Blejer, M. I. and Khan, M. S., 'Private Investment in Developing Countries', *Finance & Development*, 21 (1984) 26–9.

Boardman, A. E. and Vining, A. R., 'Ownership and Performance in Competitive Environment: A Comparison of the Performance of Private, Mixed, and State-Owned Enterprises', *Journal of Law & Economics*, xxxi (1989) 1–33.

Bokhari, R., 'Privatisation in Pakistan', in Ramanadham, V. V. (ed.), *Privatisation in Developing Countries* (London and New York: Routledge, 1989), pp. 145–77.

Bös, Dieter, *Privatization: A Theoretical Treatment* (Oxford: Clarendon Press, 1991).

Bouin, O. and Michalet, Ch.-A., *Rebalancing the Public and Private Sectors: Developing Country Experience* (Paris: Development Centre for OECD, 1992).

Boycko, M., Shleifer, A., and Vishny, R. W., 'A Theory of Privatisation', *The Economic Journal*, 106 (1996) 309–19.

Brabant, J., 'On the Economics of Property Rights and Privatisation in Transitional Economies', in Cook, P. and Kirkpatrick, C. (eds), *Privatisation Policy and Performance: International Perspectives* (New York, London: Prentice-Hall/Harvester Wheatsheaf, 1995), pp. 48–83.

Brand, L. A., 'Economic and Political Liberalization in a Rentier Economy: The Case of the Hashemite Kingdom of Jordan', in Harik, Iliya and Sullivan, Denis J. (eds), *Privatization and Liberalization in the Middle East* (Bloomington and Indianapolis: Indiana University Press, 1992), pp. 167–88.

Brynen, R., 'Economic Crisis and Post-Rentier Democratization in the Arab World: The Case of Jordan', *Canadian Journal of Political Science*, xxv (1992) 69–97.

Buchanan, James, 'Toward Analysis of Closed Behavioural Systems', in Buchanan, J. and Tollison, R., *Theory of Public Choice, Political Applications of Economics* (Michigan: University of Michigan Press, 1972), Ch. 2.

——, 'Rent Seeking and Profit Seeking', in Buchanan, J., Tollison, R., and Tullock, G. (eds), *Toward a Theory of the Rent-Seeking Society* (College Stations: Texas A&M University Press, 1980), pp. 3–15.

——, *Liberty, Market and State: Political Economy in the 1980s* (New York: Harvester Press, 1986).

——, 'The Constitution of Economic Policy', *Science*, 236 (1987) 1433–6.

Buchanan, J. and Tollison, R., *The Theory of Public Choice*, Vol. 2 (Michigan: Ann Arbor, 1982).

Bulter, S. M., 'Privatizing Government Services', *Economic Impact*, 3 (1986) 21–5.

Cakmak, Erol and Zaim, Osman, 'Privatization and Comparative Efficiency of Public and Private Enterprises in Turkey: The Cement Industry', *Annals of Public and Cooperative Economics*, 63 (1992) 271–84.

Candoy-Sekse, Rebecca, *Techniques of Privatization of State-Owned Enterprises*, Vol. 3, World Bank Technical Paper no. 90 (Washington, DC: World Bank, 1988).

# References

Cardoso, Eliana, 'Private Investment in Latin America', *Economic Development and Cultural Change*, 41 (1993) 833–48.

Cardoso, Eliana and Iielwege, Ann, 'Below The Line: Poverty in Latin America', *World Development*, 20 (1992) 19–37.

Central Bank of Jordan, *Monthly Statistical Bulletin* (various issues).

Cernea, M., 'Knowledge from Social Science for Development Policies and Projects', in Cernea, M. (ed.), *Putting People First: Sociological Variables in Rural Development*, 2nd edn (New York: Oxford University Press for the World Bank, 1991), pp. 1–41.

Chambers, R., 'The State and Rural Development: Ideologies and an Agenda for the 1990s', in Colclough, C. and Manor, J. (eds), *States or Markets? Neo-liberalism and the Development Policy Debate* (Oxford: Clarendon Press, 1991), Ch. 12.

Cheema, G. S. and Rondinelli, Dennis A. (eds), *Decentralization and Development; Policy Implementation in Developing Countries* (Beverly Hills, London and New Delhi: Sage Publications, 1983).

Chenery, H. B. and Bruno, M., 'Development Alternatives in an Open Economy: The Case of Israel', *Economic Journal*, 72 (1962) 79–103.

Choudhury, M. A., 'Syllogistic Deductionism in Islamic Social Choice Theory', *International Journal of Social Economics*, 17 (1990) 4–20.

Cities and Villages Development Bank, *Annual Report* (Amman: Cities and Villages Development Bank, 1987).

Civelek, M. A., 'Stock Market Efficiency Revisited: Evidence from the Amman Stock Exchange', *The Middle East Business and Economic Review*, 3 (1991) 27–31.

*Civil Engineering*, 'Global Growth Spurt for Infrastructure Privatization', 65 (1995), p. 24.

Clark, J., 'The State, Popular Participation, and the Voluntary Sector', *World Development*, 23 (1995) 593–601.

Coase, R., 'The Nature of the Firm', *Economica* (1937) 386–405.

Cohen, J. M. and Uphoff, N. T., 'Participation's Place in Rural Development: Seeking Clarity through Specification', *World Development*, 8 (1980) 213–35.

Colander, D. C. (ed.), *Neoclassical Political Economy: The Analysis of Rent-Seeking and DUP Activities* (Cambridge, Massachusetts: Ballinger Publishing Company, 1984).

Conyers, D., 'Decentralization and Development: A Review of the Literature', *Public Administration and Development*, 4 (1984) 187–97.

Cook, P. and Kirkpatrick, C., 'Privatisation in Less Developed Countries: An Overview', in Cook, P. and Kirkpatrick, C. (eds), *Privatisation in Less Developed Countries* (Sussex: Wheatsheaf, 1988), pp. 3–44.

Datta-Chaudhuri, Mrinal, 'Market Failure and Government Failure', *Journal of Economic Perspectives*, 4 (1990) 25–39.

De Alessi, L., 'Property Rights, Transaction Costs, and X-Efficiency: An Essay in Economic Theory', *American Economic Review*, 73 (1983) 64–81.

Demsetz, H., 'Toward a Theory of Property Rights', *American Economic Review*, 57 (1967) 347–60.

——, 'The Market for Corporate Control: Corporate Control, Insider Trading, and Rates of Return', *American Economic Review*, 76 (1986) 313–16.

——, 'Exchange and Enforcement of Property Rights', in Cowen, Tyler (ed.), *The Theory of Market Failure: A Critical Examination* (Fairfax, Virginia: George Mason University Press, 1988), pp. 127–45 [Reprinted from *Journal of Economics and Law*, 7 (1964) 11–26].

De Soto, Hernando, *The Other Path: The Invisible Revolution in the Third World* (London: I. B. Tauris, 1989).

——, 'The missing ingredient', *The Economist*, Special Issue (11 September 1993) 8–10.

Dessing, M., *Support for Microenterprises: Lessons for Sub-Saharan Africa*, World Bank Technical Paper no. 122 (Washington, DC: World Bank, 1990).

Dessouki, A. E. and Aboul Kheir, K., 'The Politics of Vulnerability and Survival: The Foreign Policy of Jordan', in Korany, B. and Dessouki, A. E. (eds), *The Foreign Policies of Arab States: The Challenge of Change*, 2nd edn (Boulder, San Francisco and Oxford: Westview Press, 1991), pp. 216–35.

De Walle, N. Van, 'Privatization in Developing Countries: A Review of the Issues', *World Development*, 17 (1989) 601–15.

De Zevallos, M. and Ortiz, Felip, 'Privatisation in Peru', in Ramanadham, V. V. (ed.), *Privatisation in Developing Countries* (London and New York: Routledge, 1989), pp. 358–77.

Diamond, D. W. and Verrecchia, R. E., 'Optimal Managerial Contracts and Equilibrium Security Prices', *The Journal of Finance*, 37 (1982) 275–87.

Dollar, D., 'Economic Reform and Allocative Efficiency in China's State-Owned Industry', *Economic Development and Cultural Change*, 39 (1990) 89–105.

Domberger, S. and Piggott, J., 'Privatization Policies and Public Enterprise: A Survey', *Economic Record*, 62 (1986) 145–62.

Doner, R. F., 'Limits of State Strength: Toward an Institutional View of Economic Development', *World Politics*, 44 (1992) 398–431.

Echeverri-Gent, J., 'Public Participation and Poverty Alleviation: The Experience of Reform Communists in India's West Bengal', *World Development*, 20 (1992) 1401–22.

Economist Intelligence Unit (EIU), *Jordan: Country Profile 1991–92* (London: Business International, 1992a).

——, *Jordan: Country Report No. 1* (London: Business International, 1992b).

——, *Jordan: Country Profile 1992–93* (London: Business International, 1992c).

Ellayan, A., *Report: Conference on the Role of Higher Administrators in Administration Development* (Amman, Institute of Public Administration, 1987).

# References

Endres, G., 'Royal Jordanian Plots Rapid Revival', *Interavia*, 46 (1991) 29–31.

Evans, Garry, 'Africa Awaits a Response to Reform', *Euromoney* (May 1990) 103–4.

Fama, Eugene F. and Jensen, Michael C., 'Separation of Ownership and Control', *The Journal of Law & Economics*, xxvi (1983) 301–26.

Fisher, W. B., 'Jordan', *The Middle East and North Africa 1987*, 33rd edn (London: Europa Publications, 1986), pp. 504–31.

——, 'Jordan', *The Middle East and North Africa 1992*, 38th edn (London: Europa Publications, 1991), pp. 569–603.

——, 'Jordan', *The Middle East and North Africa 1993*, 39th edn (London: Europa Publications, 1993), pp. 551–85.

Fontaine, J.-M. and Geronimi, V., 'Private Investment and Privatisation in Sub-Saharan Africa', in Cook, P. and Kirkpatrick, C. (eds), *Privatisation Policy and Performance, International Perspectives* (New York, London: Prentice-Hall/Harvester Wheatsheaf, 1995), pp. 139–61.

Galal, Ahmed, *Public Enterprises Reform: Lessons from the Past and Issues for the Future*, World Bank Discussion Paper no. 119 (Washington, DC: World Bank, 1991).

——, *Welfare Consequences of Selling Public Enterprises: Case Studies from Chile* (Washington, DC: World Bank Conference on the welfare consequences of selling public enterprises, 11–12 June 1992).

Gaude, Jacques and Miller, Steve, 'Rural Development and Local Resource Intensity: A Case-Study Approach', in Griffin, K. and Knight, J. (eds), *Human Development and the International Development Strategies for the 1990s* (London: Macmillan, 1990), pp. 189–214.

Gerschenkron, Alexander, *Economic Backwardness in Historical Perspective* (Cambridge: Harvard University Press, 1962).

Ghai, Dharam, 'Participatory Development: Some Perspectives from Grass-Roots Experience', in Griffin, Keith and Knight, John (eds), *Human Development and the International Development Strategies for the 1990s* (London: Macmillan, 1990), pp. 215–46.

Ghezawi, A., Bakir, A., Qatarneh, A., Khasawneh, M. and Alluhaymaq, A., *Investment Project Profiles with Special Emphasis on Small and Medium Scale Enterprises* (Amman: Royal Scientific Society, December 1989).

Goulet, D., 'Participation in Development: New Avenues', *World Development*, 17 (1989) 165–78.

Greene, J. and Villanueva, D., 'Private Investment in Developing Countries: An Empirical Analysis', *IMF Staff Papers*, 38 (1991) 33–58.

Greenwald, B., Kohen, M. and Stiglitz, J., 'Financial Market Imperfections and Productivity Growth', *Journal of Economic Behavior and Organization*, 13 (1990) 321–45.

Griffin, K., 'Economic Development in a Changing World', *World Development*, 9 (1981) 19–34.

*Guardian*, 'Resentment Boils Over Among Poor' (21 April 1989), p. 15.

——, 'Jordanian PM Takes the Blame for Worsening Economic Crisis' (25 April 1989), p. 14.

——, 'Price Rises Deliver Jordan's Last Straw' (28 April 1989), p. 15.

Guerra, Silvio N. B., 'Post Privatisation Policy and Performance: International Dimensions; Brazil', unpublished paper presented at a Conference on 'Post Privatisation Policy and Performance: International Perspective', Bradford University, 1992.

Hanke, Steve H. and Walters, Stephen J. K., 'Privatization and Public Choice: Lessons for the LDCs', in Gayle, Dennis J. and Goodrich, Jonathan N. (eds), *Privatization and Deregulation in Global Perspective* (London: Pinter Publishers, 1990), pp. 97–108.

Harik, Iliya, 'Privatization: The Issue, the Prospects, and the Fears', in Harik, Iliya and Sullivan, Denis J. (eds), *Privatization and Liberalization in the Middle East* (Bloomington and Indianapolis: Indiana University Press, 1992), pp. 1–23.

Harvey, John and Katovich, Michael A., 'Symbolic Interactionism and Institutionalism: Common Roots', *Journal of Economic Issues*, xxvi (1992) 791–812.

Heller, P. S. and Tait, A. A., *Government Employment and Pay: Some International Comparisons* (Washington, DC: International Monetary Fund, 1983).

Hemming, R. and Mansoor, A., 'Is Privatization the Answer?', *Finance & Development*, 25 (1988) 31–3.

Herbst, J., 'The Structural Adjustment of Politics in Africa', *World Development*, 18 (1990) 949–58.

Higgins, B., 'Regional Development and Efficiency of the National Economy', in Higgins, B. and Savoie, D. J. (eds), *Regional Economic Development*, Essays in honour of Francois Perroux (Boston: Unwin Hyman, 1988), pp. 193–224.

Hirschman, A. O., *The Strategy of Economic Development* (New Haven: Yale University Press, 1958).

——, *Exit, Voice, and Loyalty, Responses to Decline in Firms, Organizations, and States* (Cambridge, Massachusetts and London: Harvard University Press, 1970).

——, *Shifting Involvements: Private Interest and Public Action* (Oxford: Basil Blackwell, 1982).

——, *Essays in Trespassing: Economics to Politics and Beyond*, 2nd edn (Cambridge: Cambridge University Press, 1984).

——, 'Exit, Voice, and the Fate of the German Democratic Republic: An Essay in Conceptual History', *World Politics*, 42 (1993) 173–202.

Hodgson, G. M., 'The Reconstruction of Economics: Is There Still a Place for Neoclassical Theory?', *Journal of Economic Issues*, xxvi (1992) 749–67.

Honey, R. and Abu Kharmeh, S., 'Organizing Space for Development Planning: The Case of Jordan', *Political Geography Quarterly*, 7 (1988) 271–81.

——, 'Rural Policy in Jordan's 1986–1990 Development Plan', *Journal of Rural Studies*, 5 (1989) 75–85.

Ikenberry, G. J., 'The International Spread of Privatization Policies: Inducement, Learning, and Policy Bandwagoning', in Suleiman, E. and Waterbury, J. (eds), *The Political Economy of Public Sector Reform and Privatization* (Boulder: Westview Press, 1990), pp. 88–110.

Ilokwu, J., *Privatization in Nigeria: An Assessment*, PhD dissertation (Dallas: University of Texas, 1991).

Ingham, B., 'The Meaning of Development: Interactions Between New and Old Ideas', *World Development*, 21 (1993) 1803–21.

Ingham, B. and Kalam, A. K., 'Decentralization and Development: Theory and Evidence from Bangladesh', *Public Administration and Development*, 12 (1992) 373–85.

International Bank for Reconstruction and Development (IBRD), *The Economic Development of Jordan* (Baltimore: Johns Hopkins Press, 1957).

Interview: Crown Prince Hassan, *MEED* (19 August 1988), pp. 7–10.

Interview: Crown Prince Hassan, *Al-Sharq al-awsat* (23 April 1989), p. 4.

IMF, *International Financial Statistics*, Supplement on public sector institutions (Washington, DC: International Monetary Fund, 1987).

IMF, *Government Finance Statistics Yearbook* (Washington, DC: International Monetary Fund, 1988a, 1989a, 1990a, 1991a, 1992a, 1993a, 1994a).

IMF, *International Financial Statistics* (Washington, DC: International Monetary Fund, 1986, 1988b, 1989b, 1990b, 1991b, 1992b, 1993b, 1994b and 1995).

James, E. Mahon, Jr, 'Was Latin America Too Rich to Prosper? Structural and Political Obstacles to Export-Led Industrial Growth', *Journal of Development Studies*, 28 (1992) 241–63.

James, J. (ed.), *The Technological Behaviour of Public Enterprises in Developing Countries* (London and New York: Routledge, 1989).

Jensen, M. C. and Meckling, W. H., 'Theory of the Firm: Managerial Behavior, Agency Costs and Ownership Structure', *Journal of Financial Economics*, 3 (1976) 305–60.

Joffe, G., 'Foreign Investment and Economic Liberalization in the Middle East', in Niblock, T. and Murphy, E. (eds), *Economic and Political Liberalization in the Middle East* (London and New York: British Academic Press, 1993), pp. 132–41.

Johnson, O. E., 'An Economic Analysis of Corrupt Government, with Special Application to Less Developed Countries', *Kyklos*, 28 (1975) 47–61.

Jones, L. P., *Performance Evaluation for Public Enterprises*, World Bank Discussion Paper no. 22 (Washington, DC: World Bank, 1991).

Jones, L. P. and Abbas, F. A., *Welfare Consequences of Selling Public Enterprises: Case Studies from Malaysia* (Washington, DC: The World Bank Conference on the welfare consequences of selling public enterprises, 11–12 June 1992).

Jordan Electricity Authority (JEA), *Annual Report* (Amman: Jordan Press Foundation for the JEA, 1993, 1994).

Jreisat, J. E., 'Bureaucracy and Development in Jordan', *Journal of Asian and African Studies*, 24 (1989) 94–105.

Kanovsky, E., 'Jordan's Economy: From Prosperity to Crisis', in Ayalon, A. and Shaked, H. (eds), *Middle East Contemporary Survey 1988*, xii (Boulder: Westview Press, 1990), pp. 333–83.

Kapp, K. W., 'The Nature and Significance of Institutional Economics', *Kyklos*, 29 (1976) 209–32.

Khalaf, R. M., 'Privatization in Jordan', in Ramanadham, V. V. (ed.), *Privatization in Developing Countries* (London and New York: Routledge, 1989), pp. 236–49.

*Khaleej Times*, 'Per Capita Income Down to $1,500, Unemployment Runs at 20%' (4 April 1989), p. 11.

Khan, M. S. and Reinhart, C. M., 'Private Investment and Economic Growth in Developing Countries', *World Development*, 18 (1990) 19–27.

Kharabsheh, A., 'Health Care Expenditure and Its Impact on Income Groups', in Abu-Jaber, K., Buhbe, M. and Smadi, M. (eds), *Income Distribution in Jordan* (Boulder: Westview Press, 1990), pp. 141–58.

Khasawneh, M., Nabhani, N., and Sadeq, F., *Unemployment in Jordan: Dimensions and Prospects* (Amman: Royal Scientific Society, 1993).

Khasawneh, M., *The Impact of Jordan's Structural Adjustment Programme on Employment and Poverty*, MA dissertation (Manchester: University of Manchester, 1995).

Kikeri, Sunita, Nellis, J., and Shirly, M., *Privatization: The Lessons of Experience* (Washington, DC: World Bank, 1992).

Kim, C., Kim, M.-K., and Boyer, W., 'Privatisation of South Korea's Public Enterprises', *Journal of Developing Areas*, 28 (1994) 157–66.

Kirkpatrick, C. H., 'The World Bank's View on State-Owned Enterprises in Less Developed Countries: A Critical Comment', *Rivista Internazionale di Scienze Economiche e Commerciali*, 33 (1986) 685–96.

Kone, T., 'Privatizing Health Care in the Ivory Coast: Searching for Efficiency Gains', in Gayle, D. J. and Goodrich, J. N. (eds), *Privatization and Deregulation in Global Perspective* (London: Pinter Publishers, 1990), pp. 264–76.

Koo, H. and Kim, E. M., 'The Developmental State and Capital Accumulation in South Korea', in Appelbaum, R. P. and Henderson, J. (eds), *States and Development in the Asian Pacific Rim* (Newbury Park, London and New Delhi: Sage Publications, 1992), pp. 121–49.

Koslowski, R., 'Market Institutions; East European Reform, and Economic Theory', *Journal of Economic Issues*, xxvi (1992) 673–705.

Krueger, A. O., 'The Political Economy of the Rent-Seeking Society', *American Economic Review*, 64 (1974) 291–303.

——, 'Government Failures in Development', *Journal of Economic Perspectives*, 4 (1990) 9–23.

Krugman, P., 'Increasing Returns and Economic Geography', *Journal of Political Economy*, 99 (1991) 483–509.

———, 'Toward a Counter-Counterrevolution in Development Theory', Annual Conference on Development Economics 1992, *Supplement to the World Bank Economic Review and the World Bank Research Observer* (1993) 15–38.

Kwon, J., 'The East Asia Challenge to Neoclassical Orthodoxy', *World Development*, 22 (1994) 635–44.

Lal, D., *The Poverty of Development Economics* (Cambridge, Massachusetts: Harvard University Press, 1983).

———, 'The Misconceptions of Development Economics', in Wilber, C. K. and Jameson, K. P. (eds), *The Political Economy of Development and Underdevelopment* (New York: Mcgraw-Hill, Inc., 1992), pp. 27–35.

Lall, S., '*The East Asian Miracle*: Does the Bell Toll for Industrial Strategy?', *World Development*, 22 (1994) 645–54.

Landau, D., 'Government Expenditure and Economic Growth: A Cross-Country Study', *Southern Economic Journal*, 49 (1983) 783–92.

Lee, B. W., *Should Employee Participation Be Part of Privatization?*, World Bank Working Paper, WPS 664 (Washington, DC: World Bank, 1991).

Lee, Chung H., 'The Government, Financial System, and Large Private Enterprises in the Economic Development of South Korea', *World Development*, 20 (1992) 187–97.

Leftwich, A., 'Bringing Politics Back In: Towards a Model of the Developmental State', *Journal of Development Studies*, 31 (1995) 400–27.

Leibenstein, H., 'Allocative Efficiency vs. X-Efficiency', *American Economic Review*, 56 (1966) 392–415.

———, 'On the Basic Proposition of X-Efficiency', *American Economic Review*, 68, No. 2 (1978) 328–34.

———, 'Organizational Economics and Institutions as Missing Elements in Economic Development Analysis', *World Development*, 17 (1989) 1361–73.

Levi, M., *Off Rules and Revenue* (Berkeley: University of California Press, 1988).

Levy, Victor, 'On Estimating Efficiency Differentials Between the Public and Private Sectors in a Developing Economy – Iraq', *Journal of Comparative Economics*, 5 (1981) 235–50.

Lipton, D. and Sachs, J., 'Privatization in Eastern Europe: The Case of Poland', in Sharma, S. (ed.), *Development Policy* (London: St Martin's Press, 1992), pp. 169–212.

Lipton, Michael, 'Agriculture, Real People, the State and the Surplus in Some Asian Countries: Thoughts on Some Implications of Three Recent Approaches in Social Science', *World Development*, 17 (1989) 1553–71.

———, 'Land Reform as Commenced Business: The Evidence Against Stopping', *World Development*, 21 (1993) 641–57.

Little, I., Scitovsky, T., and Scott, M., *Industry and Trade in Some Developing Countries: A Comparative Study* (London, New York and Toronto: Oxford University Press for the Development Centre of the OECD in Paris, 1970).

Low, L., 'Privatization Options and Issues in Singapore', in Galy, D. J. and Goodrich, J. N. (eds), *Privatization and Deregulation in Global Perspective* (London: Pinter Publishers, 1990), pp. 291–311.

Luders, R. J., 'The Success and Failure of State-Owned Enterprise Divestitures in a Developing Country: The Case of Chile', *Colombia Journal of World Business*, xxviii (1993) 98–121.

Luedde-Neurath, R., 'State Intervention and Export-Oriented Development in South Korea', in White, G. (ed.), *Developmental State in East Asia* (London: Macmillan, 1988), Ch. 3.

Madarassy, A., 'Private Investment in Developing Countries', *Finance & Development*, 27 (1990) 48.

Marglin, S. A., 'Towards the Decolonization of the Mind', in Marglin, F. A., and Marglin, S. A. (eds), *Dominating Knowledge: Development, Culture, and Resistance* (Oxford: Clarendon Press, 1990), pp. 1–28.

Marglin, F. A. and Marglin, S. A. (eds), *Dominating Knowledge: Development, Culture, and Resistance* (Oxford: Clarendon Press, 1990).

Marsden, K., *African Entrepreneurs: Pioneers of Development*, IFC Discussion Paper no. 9 (Washington, DC: World Bank, 1990).

Marsh, D., 'Privatization Under Mrs. Thatcher: A Review of the Literature', *Public Administration*, 69 (1991) 459–80.

Martin, B., *In the Public Interest: Privatization and Public Sector Reform* (London: Zed Books, 1993).

Mayhew, A., 'The Beginning of Institutionalism', *Journal of Economic Issues*, 22 (1987) 971–98.

McPherson, M., 'Limits on Self-Seeking: The Role of Morality in Economic Life', in Colander, D. (ed.), *Neoclassical Political Economy: The Analysis of Rent-Seeking and DUP Activities* (Cambridge: Massachusetts, 1984), Ch. 5.

*Middle East Broadcasting Centre (MBC)*, Special Report on Jordan's Economy, News Reports (24 January 1994).

——, 'Jordan: Special Report on Investment Promotion Law' (24 December 1995).

*Middle East Economic Digest (MEED)*, 'Private Sector Wooed for Telephone Schemes in Jordan' (20 September 1991), p. 15.

——, 'Jordan's Investment Corporation to Sell Hotel Shares' (20 September 1991), p. 16.

——, 'Airline Privatisation Moves Ahead' (14 August 1992), p. 19.

——, 'Committee Gives Go-Ahead to Privatise Airline' (2 April 1993), p. 29.

——, 'Private Sector Pressed into Bigger Role' (23 July 1993), p. 15.

——, 'Royal Jordanian Airlines Increases Capital to JD56 M' (2 May 1994) (from Reuter's Information Services).

# References

——, 'Ernst and Youngis Prepare Balance Sheet for Jordan Electricity Authority' (31 October 1994) (from Reuter's Information Services).

——, 'Jordan: Hotel Shares Offered to the Private Sector' (13 January 1995), pp. 24–5.

——, 'Jordan: Soft Steps on the Privatisation Road' (16 January 1995), p. 23.

——, 'MEED Special Report on Jordan, Interview: Finance Minister Basel Jardaneh' (21 April 1995), p. 21.

——, 'Kabariti Takes the Helm' (16 February 1996), p. 5.

Miller, B., 'Collective Action and Rational Choice: Place, Community, and the Limits to Individual Self-Interest', *Economic Geography*, 68 (1992) 22–42.

Millward, R., *Measured Sources of Inefficiency in the Performance of Private and Public Enterprises in LDCs*, Salford Economic Papers, Economic Department, University of Salford, Paper no. 1, 1987.

Millward, R. and Parker, D., 'Public and Private Enterprise: Comparative Behaviour and Relative Efficiency', in Millward, R. (ed.), *Public Sector Economics* (London: Longman, 1983), Ch. 5.

Ministry of Finance, *The First Annual Report 1991* (Amman: Ministry of Finance, 1992).

Ministry of Information, *National Charter* (Amman: Ministry of Information, 1991).

Ministry of Planning, *Five Year Plan for Economic and Social Development 1986–1990* (Amman: Ministry of Planning, 1986).

Ministry of Planning, *Five Year Plan for Economic and Social Development 1993–1997* (Amman: Ministry of Planning, 1994).

Mohamed, R., 'Performance of Public and Private Enterprises in Malaysia: An Empirical Analysis', *Singapore Economic Review*, 37 (1992) 35–47.

Montagu-Pollock, M., 'Privatisation: What Went Wrong', *Asian Business*, 26 (1990) 32–9.

Morris, C. T. and Adelman, I., 'Nineteenth-Century Development Experience and Lessons for Today', *World Development*, 17 (1989) 1417–32.

Mosley, P., 'Privatisation, Policy-Based Lending and World Bank Behaviour', in Cook, P. and Kirkpatrick, C. (eds), *Privatisation in Less Developed Countries* (Sussex: Wheatsheaf Books, 1988), pp. 125–40.

Mulji, S., 'Vision and Reality of Public Sector Management: The Indian Experience', in Scott, M. and Lal, D., (eds), *Public Policy and Economic Development: Essays in Honour of Ian Little* (Oxford: Clarendon Press, 1990), pp. 126–54.

Murphy, K. M., Shleifer, A., and Vishny, R. W., 'Industrialization and the Big Push', *Journal of Political Economy*, 97 (1989) 1003–26.

Musallam, G., 'Social Security Scheme and Income Distribution', in Abu Jaber, K., Buhbe, M. and Smadi, M. (eds), *Income Distribution in Jordan* (Boulder, Westview Press, 1990), pp. 125–40.

Nabli, M. K. and Nugent, J. B., 'The New Institutional Economics and Its Application to Development', *World Development*, 17 (1989) 1333–47.

Nafziger, E. W., 'Africa Capitalism, State Power, and Economic Development', *Journal of Modern African Studies*, 28 (1990) 141–50.

Nankani, H. B., 'Lessons of Privatization in Developing Countries', *Finance & Development*, 27 (1990) 43–5.

Nellis, J. R., *Public Enterprises in Sub-Saharan Africa*, World Bank Discussion Paper no. 1 (Washington, DC: World Bank, 1986).

Niskanen, W. A., *Bureaucracy and Representative Government* (Chicago: Aldine, 1971).

——, *Bureaucracy: Servant or Master?* Hobart Paperback 5 London: IEA, 1973).

Nixson, F. I., 'Industrialization and Structural Change in Developing Countries', *Journal of International Development*, 2 (1990) 310–33.

North, D. C., 'Institutions and Economic Growth: An Historical Introduction', *World Development*, 17 (1989) 1319–32.

——, *Institutions, Institutional Change and Economic Performance* (Cambridge: Cambridge University Press, 1991).

Nugent, J., 'Between State, Markets and Households: A Neoinstitutional Analysis of Local Organizations and Institutions', *World Development*, 21 (1993) 623–32.

Nunnenkump, P., 'State Enterprises in Developing Countries', *Intereconomics*, 21, (1986) 186–93.

Olson, M., *The Logic of Collective Action* (Cambridge: Harvard University Press, 1965).

——, *The Rise and Decline of Nations: Economic Growth, Stagflation and Social Rigidities* (New Haven and London: Yale University Press, 1982).

Ott, A. F., 'Privatization in Egypt: Reassessing the Role and Size of the Public Sector', in Ott, A. F. and Hartley, K. (eds), *Privatization and Economic Efficiency: A Comparative Analysis of Developed and Developing Countries* (Aldershot: Edward Elgar, 1991), pp. 184–222.

Owen, R., *State, Power and Politics in the Making of the Middle East* (London and New York: Routledge, 1992).

Page, J. M., 'The East Asian Miracle: An Introduction', *World Development*, 22 (1994) 615–25.

Park, Y. C., 'Evaluating the Performance of Korea's Government-Invested Enterprises', *Finance & Development*, 24 (1987) 25–7.

Pereira, L. C., 'Economic Reforms and Cycles of State Intervention', *World Development*, 21 (1993) 1337–53.

Perera, M. H., *Privatization as a Strategy for Economic Development*, PhD thesis (Alabama: Auburn University, 1991).

Perkins, D. H., 'There Are At Least Three Models of East Asian Development', *World Development*, 22 (1994) 655–61.

# References

Pfeffermann, G. P. and Madarassy, A., *Trends in Private Investment in Developing Countries 1993: Statistics for 1970–1991*, The IFC Discussion Paper no. 16 (Washington, DC: World Bank, 1992).

Polanyi, K., *The Great Transformation*, 2nd edn (Beacon Hill, Boston: Beacon Press, 1957).

Pool, D., 'The Links between Economic and Political Liberalization', in Niblock, T. and Murphy, E. (eds), *Economic and Political Liberalization in the Middle East* (London and New York: British Academic Press, 1993), pp. 40–54.

Posner, R. A., 'The Social Costs of Monopoly and Regulation', in Buchanan, J. M., Tollison, R. D. and Tullock, G. (eds), *Toward a Theory of the Rent-Seeking Society* (College Stations: Texas A&M University Press, 1980), Ch. 5.

Potts, D., 'Nationalisation and Denationalisation of Estate Agriculture in Tanzania 1967–90', in Cook, P. and Kirkpatrick, C. (eds), *Privatisation Policy and Performance, International Perspectives* (New York, London: Prentice-Hall/Harvester Wheatsheaf, 1995), pp. 178–97.

Pourgerami, A., 'The Political Economy of Development: A Cross-national Causality Test of Development-democracy-growth Hypothesis', *Public Choice*, 58 (1988) 123–41.

Powell, V., *Improving Public Enterprise: Performance Concepts and Techniques* (Geneva: International Labour Organization, 1987).

Pradhan, B. K., Ratha, D. K., and Sarma, A., 'Complementarity between Public and Private Investment in India', *Journal of Development Economics*, 33 (1990) 101–16.

Pradhan, S. and Swaroop, V., 'Public Spending and Adjustment', *Finance & Development*, 30 (1993) 28–31.

Prager, J., 'Is Privatization a Panacea for LDCs? Market Failure Versus Public Sector Failure', *The Journal of Developing Areas*, 126 (1992) 301–22.

Prebish, R., 'Commercial Policy in the Underdeveloped Countries', *American Economic Review*, 49 (1959) 251–73.

*Privatisation International Ltd*, 'Privatisation Yearbook' (London: Privatisation International Ltd, various issues).

Radzicki, M., 'Institutional Dynamics: An Extension of the Institutional Approach to Socioeconomic Analysis', *Journal of Economic Issues*, 22 (1988) 633–65.

Ram, R., 'Government Size and Economic Growth: A New Framework and Some Evidence from Cross-Section and Time-Series Data', *American Economic Review*, 76 (1986) 191–203.

Ramamurti, R., 'Why are Developing Countries Privatizing?', *Journal of International Business Studies*, 23 (1992) 225–49.

Ramanadham, V. V., 'Privatisation: The UK Experience and Developing Countries', in Ramanadham, V. V. (ed.), *Privatisation in Developing Countries* (London and New York: Routledge, 1989), pp. 3–61.

Ramirez, M. D., 'Stabilization and Adjustment in Latin America: A Neostructuralist Perspective', *Journal of Economic Issues*, xxvii (1993) 1015–39.

Reddy, Y., 'Privatisation in India', in Ramanadham, V. V. (ed.), *Privatisation in Developing Countries* (London and New York: Routledge, 1989), pp. 178–91.

Rees, R., 'The Theory of Principal and Agent: Part 1', *Bulletin of Economic Research*, 37 (1985a) 3–26.

——, 'The Theory of Principal and Agent: Part 2', *Bulletin of Economic Research*, 37 (1985b) 75–95.

——, 'Is There an Economic Case for Privatization?', *Public Money*, 6 (1986) 19–26.

——, 'Inefficiency, Public Enterprises and Privatisation', *European Economic Review*, 32 (1988) 422–31.

——, *Public Enterprise Economics*, 2nd edn (Oxford: Philip Allan Publishers, 1989).

Reid, M., 'Institutional Preconditions of Privatization in Market-based Political Economies: Implications for Jordan', *Public Administration and Development*, 14 (1994) 65–77.

Reilly, B. J. and Zangeneh, H., 'The Value-based Islamic Economic System and Other Optimal Economic Systems: A Critical Comparative Analysis', *International Journal of Social Economics*, 17 (1990) 21–35.

Reuter, 'Jordan sells 54 per cent in top hotel' (20 February 1995) (from Reuter Information Services).

——, 'Jordan: Jordan Parliament Passes Telecommunications Law' (24 December 1995) (from Reuter Information Services).

Riddel, R., *Regional Development Policy* (New York: St Martin's Press, 1985).

Robertson, A. F., *People and the State* (Cambridge: Cambridge University Press, 1984).

Robins, P., *Jordan to 1990: Coping with Change*, Special Report no. 1074 (London and New York: EIU, December 1986).

——, 'Jordan's Election: A New Era', *Middle East Report*, 20 (1990) 55–7.

Rodrick, D., 'Policy Uncertainty and Private Investment in Developing Countries', *Journal of Development Economics*, 36 (1991) 229–42.

Romer, P. M., 'Increasing Returns and Long-Run Growth', *Journal of Political Economy*, 94 (1986) 1002–37.

Rondinelli, D. A. and Nellis, J. R., 'Assessing Decentralization Policies in Developing Countries: The Case for Cautious Optimism', *Development Policy Review*, 4 (1986) 3–23.

Rondinelli, D. A., McCullough, J. S., and Johnson, R. W., 'Analysing Decentralization Policies in Developing Countries: A Political-Economy Framework', *Development and Change*, 20 (1989) 57–87.

Ross, S. A., 'The Economic Theory of Agency: The Principal's Problem', *American Economic Review*, 63 (1973) 134–9.

Rostow, W. W., *The Stages of Economic Growth* (Cambridge: Cambridge University Press, 1960).

Ruangrong, P., *Privatization of State-Owned Electric Utility in Thailand: Expected Effects on Economic Efficiency*, PhD thesis (Pennsylvania: University of Pennsylvania, 1992).

Sader, F., *Privatization and Foreign Investment in the Developing World 1988–92*, International Economic Department (Washington, DC: World Bank, 1993).

Sadik, F. and Al-Khasawneh, M., *Idarat At-tanmiah Ar-refiah fi Al-urdun* (The Administration of Rural Development in Jordan) (Amman, Royal Scientific Society, 1990).

Sah, R. K., 'Fallibility in Human Organizations and Political Systems', *Journal of Economic Perspectives*, 5 (1991) 67–88.

Said, A. A., 'The Paradox of Development in the Middle East', *Futures*, 21 (1989) 619–27.

Samuels, W. J. and Mercuro, N., 'A Critique of Rent-Seeking Theory', in Colander, D. (ed.), *Neoclassical Political Economy: The Analysis of Rent-Seeking and DUP Activities* (Cambridge: Massachusetts, Balling Publishing Company, 1984), Ch. 4.

Sappington, D. E., 'Incentives in Principal–Agent Relationships', *Journal of Economic Perspectives*, 5 (1991) 45–66.

Sappington, D. and Stiglitz, J., 'Privatization, Information and Incentives', *Journal of Policy Analysis and Management*, 6 (1987) 567–82.

Satloff, R., 'Jordan's Great Gamble: Economic Crisis and Political Reform', in Barkey, H. J. (ed.), *The Politics of Economic Reform in the Middle East* (New York: St Martin's Press, 1992), pp. 129–52.

Shackleton, J. R., 'Privatising the Third World', *Banca Nazional Del Lavoro*, 159 (1986) 429–39.

Schmitz, H. and Hewitt, T., 'Learning to Raise Infants: A Case Study in Industrial Policy', in Colclough, C. and Manor, J. (eds), *States or Markets? Neo-Liberalism and Development Policy Debate* (Oxford: Clarendon Press, 1991), pp. 173–96.

Schumacher, U. and Hutchinson, C., 'Privatization in Developing Countries: The Case of Jamaica', in Ott, A. F. and Hartley, K. (eds), *Privatization and Economic Efficiency: A Comparative Analysis of Developed and Developing Countries* (Aldershot: Edward Elgar, 1991), pp. 223–53.

Scitovsky, T., 'Two Concepts of External Economies', *Journal of Political Economy*, 62 (1954) 143–51.

——, 'The Benefits of Asymmetric Markets', *Journal of Economic Perspectives*, 4 (1990) 135–48.

Scully, G. W., 'The Size of the State, Economic Growth and the Efficient Utilization of National Resources', *Public Choice*, 63 (1989) 149–64.

Sen, A., 'The Concept of Development', in Chenery, H. B. and Srinivasan, T. N. (eds), *Handbook of Development Economics*, Vol. 1 (Amsterdam: Elsevier Science Publishers, 1988), pp. 9–26.

——, 'Food and Freedom', *World Development,* 17 (1989) 769–81.

——, 'Development as Capability Expansion', in Griffin, K. and Knight, J. (eds), *Human Development and the International Development Strategy for the 1990s* (London: Macmillan in association with the United Nations, 1990), pp. 41–58.

Serven, L., 'Debt Crisis, Adjustment Policies and Capital Formation in Developing Countries: Where Do We Stand?', *World Development,* 21 (1993) 127–40.

Shamaileh, A. Y., *Impact of Government Egalitarian Policies on Income Inequality and Poverty in Jordan,* PhD thesis, (New York: The State University of New York, 1990).

Shapiro, C. and Willig, R. D., 'Economic Rationales for the Scope of Privatization', in Suleiman, E. N. and Waterbury, J. (eds), *The Political Economy of Public Sector Reform and Privatization* (Oxford: Westview Press, 1990), pp. 55–87.

Shapiro, H. and Taylor, L., 'The State and Industrial Strategy', *World Development,* 18 (1990) 861–78.

Sha'sha, Z. J., 'The Role of the Private Sector in Jordan's Economy', in Wilson, R. (ed.), *Politics and the Economy in Jordan* (London and New York: Routledge, 1991), pp. 79–89.

Shirly, M. M., *The Reform of State-Owned Enterprises: Lessons from World Bank Lending* (Washington, DC: World Bank, 1990).

Shirly, M. M. and Nellis, J., *Public Enterprise Reform: The Lessons of Experience* (Washington, DC: World Bank, 1991).

Short, R. P., 'The Role of Public Enterprises: An International Statistical Comparison', in Floyed, R. H., Gray, C. S. and Short, R. P., *Public Enterprises in Mixed Economies: Some Macroeconomic Aspects* (Washington, DC: International Monetary Fund, 1984), pp. 110–82.

Simon, H. A., 'Organizations and Markets', *Journal of Economic Perspectives,* 5 (1991) 25–44.

Singer, H. W., 'The Distribution of Gains Between Investing and Borrowing Countries', *American Economic Review,* 40 (1950) 473–85.

Sinha, R., 'Economic Reform in Developing Counntries: Some Conceptual Issues', *World Development,* 23 (1995) 557–75.

Slater, D., 'Territorial Power and the Peripheral State: The Issue of Decentralization', *Development and Change,* 20 (1989) 501–31.

Smith, B. C., *Decentralization: The Territorial Dimension of the State* (London: George Allen & Unwin, 1985).

*Spore,* 'Winners and Losers in the Privatization Game', No. 41 (October 1992), pp. 1–4.

Srinivasan, T. N., 'Neoclassical Political Economy, the State and Economic Development', *Asian Development Review,* 3 (1985) 38–58.

Starr, P., 'The Limits of Privatization', in Gayle, D. J. and Goodrich, J. N. (eds), *Privatization and Deregulation in Global Perspective* (London: Pinter Publishers, 1990), pp. 109–25.

Steidlmeier, P., 'The Business Community and the Poor: Rethinking Business Strategies and Social Policy', *American Journal of Economics and Sociology*, 52 (1993) 209–21.

Stephen, L., 'Culture as a Source: Four Cases of Self-Managed Indigenous Craft Production in Latin America', *Economic Development and Cultural Change*, 40 (1991) 101–30.

Stigler, G. J., 'The Xistence of X-Efficiency', *American Economic Review*, 66 (1976) 213–16.

Stiglitz, J. E., 'Credit Markets and Control of Capital', *Journal of Money, Credit, and Banking Lecture*, xvii (1985) 133–51.

——, 'Markets, Market Failures, and Development', *American Economic Review*, 79 (1989) 197–203.

——, 'Comment on "Toward A Counter-Counterrevolution in Development Theory" By Krugman', Annual Conference on Development Economics 1992, *Supplement to the World Bank Economic Review and the World Bank Research Observer* (1993) 39–49.

Stohr, W. B., 'Development from Below: The Bottom-Up and Periphery-Inward Development Paradigm', in Stohr, W. B., and Taylor, D. R. (eds), *Development from Above or Below?: The Dialectics of Regional Planning in Developing Countries* (Chichester: Wiley, 1981), pp. 39–72.

Stohr, W. B. and Taylor, D. R. (eds), *Development from Above or Below?: The Dialectics of Regional Planning in Developing Countries* (Chichester: Wiley, 1981).

Stohr, W. B., *Global Challenge and Local Response: Initiatives for Economic Regeneration in Contemporary Europe* (London and New York: Mansell, The United Nations University, 1990).

Street, J. H. and James, D. D., 'Institutionalism, Structuralism, and Dependency', *Journal of Economic Issues*, xvi (1982) 673–89.

Streeten, P., 'The Judo Trick or "Crowding In"', in Sharma, S. (ed.), *Development Policy* (New York: St Martin's Press, 1992), pp. 96–111.

——, 'Markets and States: Against Minimalism', *World Development*, 21 (1993) 1281–98.

Strong, N. and Waterson, M., 'Principals and Agents and Information', in Clarke, R. and McGuinness, T. (eds), *The Economics of the Firm* (Oxford: Basil Blackwell, 1987), pp. 18–41.

Suleiman, E. and Waterbury, J. (eds), *The Political Economy of Public Sector Reform and Privatization* (Oxford: Westview Press, 1990).

Susser, A., 'Jordan', in Ayalon, A. (ed.), *Middle East Contemporary Survey, vol. xiv, 1990* (Boulder: Westview Press, 1992), pp. 457–499.

——, 'Jordan', in Ayalon, A. (ed.), *Middle East Contemporary Survey vol. xv, 1991* (Boulder: Westview Press, 1993), pp. 482–519.

Swanson, D. and Wolde-Semait, T., *Africa's Public Enterprise Sector and Evidence of Reform*, World Bank Technical Papers, ISSN 0253-7494 (Washington, DC: World Bank, 1989).

Tandon, P., *Welfare Consequences of Selling Public Enterprises: Case Studies from Mexico* (Washington, DC: World Bank Conference on the welfare consequences of selling public enterprises, June 11–12 1992).

Taylor, D. R. and Mackenzie, F. (eds), *Development from Within: Survival in Rural Africa* (London and New York: Routledge, 1992).

Taylor, D. R., 'Development from Within and Survival in Rural Africa: A synthesis of theory and practice', in Taylor, D. R. and Mackenzie, F. (eds), *Development from Within: Survival in Rural Africa* (London and New York: Routledge, 1992), pp. 214–58.

Taylor, L., 'Economic Openness; Problems to the Century's End', in Banuri, T. (ed.), *Economic Liberalization: No Panacea; The Experiences of Latin America and Asia* (Oxford: Clarendon Press, 1991), Ch. 4.

——, 'The Rocky Road to Reform: Trade, Industrial, Financial, and Agricultural Strategies', *World Development*, 21 (1993) 577–90.

*The Economist*, 'The Selling of Russia', 337 (18 November 1995), p. 136.

——, 'A Beastly Bureaucratic Burden', 337 (2 December 1995), p. 120.

——, 'A Survey of Latin American Finance', 337 (9 December 1995).

——, 'Jordan: Charging a Head of his People', 337 (16 December 1995), p. 68.

*The Middle East Report*, 'King Hussein Takes the Helm' (February 1992), pp. 5–8.

Tilman, R., 'New Light on John Dewey, Clarence Ayres, and the Development of Evolutionary Economics', *Journal of Economic Issues*, 24 (1990) 963–79.

Tollison, R. D., 'Rent Seeking: A Survey', *Kyklos*, 35 (1982) 575–602.

Toye, J., *Dilemmas of Development* (Oxford: Basil Blackwell, 1987).

Trebat, T. J., *Brazil's State-Owned Enterprises; A Case of the State as Entrepreneur* (Cambridge: Cambridge University Press, 1983).

UNDP, *Human Development Report* (New York and Oxford: Oxford University Press for the UNDP, 1990, 1991, 1992, 1993, 1994, 1995).

Uphoff, N., 'Fitting Projects to People', in Cernea, M. (ed.), *Putting People First: Sociological Variables in Rural Development* (New York: published for the World Bank, Oxford University Press, 1991).

——, 'Grassroots Organizations and the NGOs in Rural Development: Opportunities with Diminishing States and Expanding Markets', *World Development*, 21 (1993) 607–22.

Vernon, R., 'Introduction: The Promise and the Challenge', in Vernon, R. (ed.), *The Promise of Privatization: A Challenge for U.S. Policy* (New York: Council on Foreign Relations, 1988), pp. 1–22.

Vickers, J. and Yarrow, G., *Privatization: An Economic Analysis* (Cambridge: MIT Press, 1988).

——, 'Economic Perspectives on Privatization', *Journal of Economic Perspectives*, 5 (1991) 111–32.

Vining, A. R. and Weimer, D. L., 'Government Supply and Government Production Failure: A Framework Based on Contestability', *Journal of Public Policy*, 10 (1990) 1–22.

Wade, R., *Governing the Market: Economic Theory and the Role of Government in East Asian Industrialization* (Princeton, New Jersey: Princeton University Press, 1990).

Waterbury, J., 'The Political Context of Public Sector Reform and Privatization in Egypt, India, Mexico, and Turkey', in Suleiman, E. N. and Waterbury, J. (eds), *The Political Economy of Public Sector Reform and Privatization* (Oxford: Westview Press, 1990), pp. 293–318.

——, 'The Heart of the Matter? Public Enterprises and the Adjustment Process', in Haggard, S. and Kaufman, R. R. (eds), *The Politics of Economic Adjustment: International Constraints, Distributive Conflicts, and the State* (Princeton: Princeton University Press, 1992), pp. 182–217.

Weiss, J., 'Mexico: Comparative Performance of State and Private Industrial Corporations', in Cook, P. and Kirkpatrick, C. (eds), *Privatisation Policy and Performance, International Perspectives* (New York, London: Prentice-Hall/Harvester Wheatsheaf, 1995), pp. 213–24.

Weissman, S. R., 'Structural Adjustment in Africa: Insights from the Experiences of Ghana and Senegal', *World Development*, 18 (1990) 1621–34.

Westphal, L. E., 'Industrial Policy in an Export-Propelled Economy: Lessons from South Korea's Experience', *Journal of Economic Perspectives*, 14 (1990) 41–59.

Whittington, J., 'Oasis in the Jobs Desert', *The Times Higher Education Supplement*, 11 December 1992, p. 10.

Wilber, C. K. and Harrison, R. S., 'The Methodological Basis of Institutional Economics: Pattern Model, Story Telling and Holism', *Journal of Economic Issues*, xii (1978) 61–89.

Williamson, O. E., 'Organization Form, Residual Claimants, and Corporate Control', *Journal of Law & Economics*, xxvi (1983) 351–66.

——, *The Economic Institutions of Capitalism* (New York: Free Press, 1985).

World Bank, *Decentralization in Developing Countries: A Review of Recent Experience* (Washington, DC: World Bank, 1984).

——, *World Development Report* (Oxford and New York: Oxford University Press for the World Bank, 1987–95).

——, *World Tables* (Washington, DC: Johns Hopkins University Press for the World Bank, 1987, 1990, 1991, 1992).

——, *World Debt Tables* (Washington, DC: Johns Hopkins University Press for the World Bank, 1990–95).

——, *The East Asian Miracle: Economic Growth and Public Policy*, Policy Research Report (Washington, DC: World Bank, 1993).

——, *Bureaucrats in Business: The Economics and Politics of Government Ownership*, Policy Research Report (Washington, DC: Oxford University Press, 1995).

Yaffey, Michael, 'Privatisation Policy: The Lessons of Nationalisation in East Africa', in Cook, P. and Kirkpatrick, C. (eds), *Privatisation Policy and Performance: International Perspectives* (New York, London: Prentice-Hall/Harvester Wheatsheaf, 1995), pp. 198–212.

Yoder, R. A., Brokholder, P. L. and Friesen, B. D., 'Privatization and Development: The Empirical Evidence', *Journal of Developing Areas*, 25 (1991) 425–34.

# Index

Aboul Kheir, K.  148, 180
Abu Kharmeh, S.  181, 183, 198
Adam, C.  1, 47
Adelman, Irma  26, 29
Aeromexico  89
Africa  19, 38, 40–5, 79–80, 86–7, 101, 109
agency costs and problems  56–7, 59–60, 63, 120
agricultural-demand-led industrialization (ADLI)  29–30
Agricultural Credit Corporation  162
Al-Ahmed, A. K.  185–6, 200, 218
Al-Khasawneth, M.  185, 187, 191, 200, 218
Al-Quaryoty, M. Q.  143, 151, 159
Alchain, Armen  53–4
Alia Gateway hotel  166
allocative efficiency, welfare economics orientation  36–8, 48, 74
Amman Financial Market (AFM)  172–5
Anani, J.  142, 151, 160
appropriate technology  6, 92–3, 119–21, 218
Arab Food and Medical Appliances  142
*Arab News*  160, 165–6
Arab Potash Company (APC)  142, 158, 172
Arab–Israeli conflict  180
Argentina  44, 50, 70, 90, 98
Asia  38, 40–1, 43–4, 86
asymmetric information  56–7, 59–60, 170

Balassa, Bela  21, 74
Bangladesh  89–90, 98, 193
Bank Act (1844)  15

Banuri, T.  29, 32–3, 44, 101–2, 120, 201
Bardhan, Pranab  17, 27–8, 112
Barnes, T. J.  104, 201
Bhagwati, J. N.  20, 32
Bishop, M.  54, 58
bottom-up approach  93, 112, 183, 216
bounded rationality  52, 57, 63, 224
Boycko, M.  2, 61
Brand, L. A.  140, 159
Brazil  45–6, 50, 66, 70, 97, 116, 121, 193
Britain, 55, 59, 96–7, 150, 192
British Caledonian Airways  163
British Steel  59
Buchanan, James  20–2, 137
budgetary deficit, public enterprises and  83–5, 91, 101, 220
'bureaucracies'  62, 101
*Bureaucrats in Business: The Economics and Politics of Government Ownership*  71

Candoy-Sekse, Rebecca  162, 169
capability  94–5, 99, 116, 221
capital intensity ratio (CIR)  40, 223
capital markets  7–8, 61, 63, 97
Cardosa, Eliana  79, 103
Caribbean  66, 70
Central Bank of Jordan  144, 148
Chambers, R.  106, 108
'change from within'  100–1
Chile  50, 66, 70, 75, 106, 116, 191
CHILGNER (electrical company, Chile)  88
China  44–5, 74
choice  6, 22, 33, 92, 95–6, 98–9, 221
'Cities and Villages Development Bank'  194–5

Civelek, M. A. 173–4
Civil Employees Consumption Corporation 140
commanding heights of the economy, SOEs and 39, 140, 159
Compañia de Teléfonos de Chile 88
corruption 101, 132, 137, 160, 213
cost–benefit analysis, private versus public ownership 62
Côte d'Ivoire 66, 80
'Counter-ideology of Reversals' 108
crowding-in 80, 123, 211, 217
crowding-out 7, 77–9, 84, 90, 109, 114, 173
Crown Prince Hassan 182, 197, 199, 202

De Soto, Hernando 55, 137
decentralization 4, 6, 92, 101–3, 118
  participation and 8–9, 102–4, 124, 179, 182
  in practice 185–7
  privatization and 6, 94
decentralization and participation 102–4
  design of 6–7, 183–5
  objectives of 180–3
  shift from 207–10
decentralized development paradigms: bottom-up and periphery-inward 106–8; from within 109–12; strategy of reversal 108–9
decision-makers 7, 9, 34, 128, 138, 176, 199, 208
democracy 7, 101, 103, 179, 203, 220
deregulation policies 35, 94, 167
Dessouki, A. E. 148, 180
developing countries 7, 14, 22
  capital intensity ratio in SOEs 40, 223
  decentralization 115
  decision-makers 7, 14
  econometric study on investment 79
  effect of uncertainty 78
  evidence on privatization 65–72, 91
  financial autonomy ratios 116–18
  foreign direct investment 87, 123
  informal sector 121–2, 216–19
  'interest groups' 101–2, 171
  ISI and 119
  lack of capital markets 61
  over-extended public sector 80
  poverty in 115, *see also* Jordan
  privatization in 3, 5–6, 33, 35–6
development 4, 6, 8, 16, 93–4, 104–5
  alternative approaches to rural 113
  from above 105
  from below 106–8
  income-centred approach 92, 94–5
  neoclassical counter-revolution in 13, 17
  privatization and 85–6, 91–2
  role of the State 13–14, 28
'developmentalism' ideology 35
devolution 92, 103, 105, 113, 121
'directly unproductive, profit-seeking activities' (DUP) 20–1, 29, 33, 137
'distributional coalitions' 19
'distributional justice' 22

East Asian countries 14, 21, 25–6, 34, 70, 80, 131, 212
Eastern Europe 70, 98, 119
*The East Asian Miracle: Economic Growth and Public Policy* 26
economic efficiency
  devolution to local level 113
  neoclassical theory and 50, 223–4
  privatization and 3, 87, 92
  profit and 7, 62
  requirements for 29, 80
  total factor productivity (TFP) change 45

# Index

economies of scale  31, 36–7, 77, 111, 151, 217
economies of scope, natural monopolies  37
*Economist, The* (1995)  54, 84, 87, 206
education  37, 48–9, 95, 113
efficiency, privatization and  72–7, 208, 217
Egypt  45, 83–4
empowerment  8–9, 93, 103, 111, 114–15, 118, 124, 183, 207–8
ENERSIS  88
'exit' option  8, 99–100, 202, 211, 218
externalities  28, 30–1, 33, 37, 40, 46, 220

financial autonomy ratio (FAR), 116, 193, 226
fiscal decentralization  103, 117
Fisher, W. B.  159–61, 163
foreign direct investment (FDI)  87, 123
former Soviet Union  44, 93, 119
free market policies  18, 22, 26, 28, 30, 32–3, 110, 136, 179, 219
Free Zones Corporation  140
'free-rider problem'  18–19, 23, 37
functional decentralization  3, 102, 104, 202–3, 222
   difference between territorial and 112–15

Galal, Ahmed  2, 84, 88
Gerschenkron, Alexander  15, 41, 70
'get/getting the price right'  15, 17–18, 26–8, 78, 109, 199, 202, 217
'getting the basics right'  26–7
Ghana  45, 114, 193
Gini coefficient measurement  197, 226
Goulet, D.  110, 123, 214
'government failure'  3, 18–19, 21, 24, 27, 29–30, 32–3
government size, economic growth and  80–3

governorates (Jordan)  183, 195, 208
grassroots organizations (GROs)  105, 112–13, 124, 206
Great Depression (1930s)  40
Griffin, K.  102, 111
growth, human development and  33, 93–6
*Guardian* (1989)  160, 201
Gulf states  127, 145, 173
Gulf War  146, 158, 160, 164, 175

Hanke, Steve H.  54, 96, 173
Harrod–Domar formula  14
health spending  37, 48–9, 95, 113, 209
Hirschman, A. O.  16, 33, 99–100, 120, 180, 202
Honey, R.  181, 183, 198
Human Development Index (HDI)  72, 94, 208
Human Development Reports  94, 114, 116, 187, 192, 194, 209

'identification method'  60
IMF  3, 8, 19, 86–7, 114–15, 133, 148, 150, 177, 201, 208
import substitution industrialization (ISI)  16, 18, 40, 44, 119
income-centred approach, development and  92, 94–5
India  28, 43–4, 44, 47, 73, 78, 83–4, 97, 101
industrialization  15, 33, 39, 40–1
inertia costs  52
informal sector  121–3, 211, 216–19, 217
information, asymmetrical  23, 27–8, 36, 51, 56–7, 60–1, 63, 170
infrastructure, government investment and  27, 37–8, 79, 83, 120, 139
Ingham, B.  93–4, 111, 118
institutional role, dissatisfaction and  199–203

# Index

Intercontinental Jordan hotel   161, 166–7
International Finance Corporation (IFC)   78
Iraq   72–3, 174
Irbid Electricity Company   143
Israel   127, 167, 174, 177

Jamaica   46, 66, 98
James, D. D.   16, 107, 121
James, J.   26, 55
Japan   43, 106
Jensen, M. C.   50, 57
Jones, L. P.   47, 88, 212–13
Jordan   4–7, 126
  bureaucratic reforms   215–16
  corruption   132, 137, 160
  decision-makers   7, 128, 138, 176, 199, 208
  economy   131–2, 136–7
  education and health   134–6, 191, 209
  five-year development plan (1993–97)   178, 180, 207–8, 211
  future prospects   176–8
  human development   128, 195, 208–9
  legal decentralization   218–19
  National Charter (1991)   203–5, 211
  obstacles to privatization: inefficient capital market   8, 172–5; lack of regulatory capacity   170–1; non-economic factors   8, 175–8; process of valuation   168–9; restructuring and rehabilitation   169
  Parliamentary government   204
  participation in production   139–40, 143
  poverty   127, 131–2, 134, 175, 196, 208, 216
  privatization   127–9, 211; objectives of   4, 6, 222; plan (1986)   8, 176; progress to date 161–8; regional planning units (1986–90) 184; small farmers and 196–9
  riots (1989)   201–3
  role of the state: government ownership   138–40; government regulations 136–8; government spending 129–36
  semi-rentier economy   128, 209
  state cement industry (1951)   139
  structural adjustment plan   133, 201, 203, 207–8; supporting the informal sector   216–19; taxation   132–3, 139; workforce   130, 134, 138, 140, 175
Jordan Cement Factories company   142, 159
Jordan Development Conference (1986)   143
Jordan Electric Company   151
Jordan Electricity Authority (JEA)   4–5, 7, 128, 141, 143, 151–4, 166; financial performance 154–6
Jordan Glass Industry Company (JGIC)   142, 159
Jordan Hotel and Tourism Company   166
Jordan Investment Corporation (JIC)   157, 164, 177
Jordan Marriot   167
Jordan Pension Fund   157, 162
Jordan Petroleum Refinery   166
Jordan Phosphate Mines Company (JPMC)   158–9
Jordan Ports Corporation   160, 165
Jordan Social Security Corporation   166
Jordan Telecommunication Corporation (TCC)   128, 148–9, 162, 164–5, 169–3, 178
Jordan Water Authority   141, 160
Jordanian Company for Marketing and Processing Agricultural Products   162

# Index

Jordan's Fertilizer Industries Company (JFIC)  159

Kelang Container Terminal  88
Kenya  80, 191
Khalaf, R.  141–3, 151, 159–60, 162
Khan, M. S.  78, 81–2
Khasawneh, M.  134, 146, 208
Kikeri, Sunita  45, 94–5, 97
King Hussain  163, 178, 203, 206, 216
Korea  27, 43
Krueger, A. O.  20, 27
Krugman, P.  30, 32

*laissez-faire* policies  18–19, 40, 139
Lal, D.  29, 132
Latin America  26, 38–40, 43–4, 47, 49–50, 66, 70–1, 79–80, 86–7, 101, 116, 121
learning by doing  120
Leibenstein, H.  52, 54
less developed countries (LDCs)
   'appropriate technology'  93, 119
   economic growth  81–2
   factors determining private investment  77
   globalization and  93
   interest groups and  19, 171
   linkage effects and  16
   over-extended public sector  85
   poverty  120
   problems of information, coordination and externalities  28, 97
   public enterprises  83–4
   public and private enterprises in  73
   structural adjustment loans (SALs)  94
liberalization  25, 35, 167
linkages  6, 16, 18, 30, 92, 104, 120–1, 123, 127, 183, 217
Lipton, D.  56, 118, 197
lobbying  19, 22
Lockhead Tristar jets  163

M-form structure, private organization and  54
Madarassy, A.  78, 80
Malawi  84, 191
Malaysia  47, 75, 88, 129
Malaysian Airlines  88
Marglin, S. A.  99, 118
market failure  21, 24, 29, 36–8, 40, 48
market structure and institutions, privatization and  7, 27, 35, 63, 75, 77
Marsh, D.  96–7
'Master-key project'  119, 217
Mauritius  80, 84
measuring decentralization and participation
   estimated ratios  190–1; methodology  191
   expenditure decentralized ratios  191–2
   indicators  187–8
   ratios (1980–84)  188–90
   revenue decentralization ratios  192–3
Meckling, W. H.  50, 57
*MEED*  166–7, 170, 178
mercantile economy  137–8
Mexicana Airline  89
Mexico  28, 38, 50, 70, 76–7, 83–4, 89, 97
Middle East and North Africa Economic Summit (1995)  177
Miller, B.  104, 113
Millward, R.  54, 73–4
Ministry of Planning (Jordan)  127, 136, 139, 150, 172, 181–3, 198, 207
monitoring  46, 59–60
monopoly rent, private monopolists and  48
multi-national corporations (MNCs)  87
Murphy, K. M.  30–1

natural monopoly, public sector and  48
Nellis, J. R.  2, 42, 45, 93, 115

neo-classical counter-revolution 17, 21, 24, 29, 31
Neo-classical Political Economy (NPE) 3, 13, 18, 20, 31, 50–1
neo-Liberal economic theory 108, 132
New Institutional Economics (NIE) 3, 13, 17–18, 24, 27, 33
Nigeria 66, 73, 116
no-industrialization trap 30–1, 42
non-governmental organizations (NGOs) 101, 214
North, D. C. 23–4, 29, 171, 197–8
Nugent, J. 118, 198, 200

oil prices 129, 144, 181
opportunism 23, 51, 55, 63, 120, 214
opportunity costs 15, 62, 132
organizations, 'selective incentives' and 19, 223
over-extended public sector 7, 17, 79–80, 85

Pakistan 47, 97, 118
'Palestinian' question 127, 145, 173–4, 180
Pareto efficiency 36–8, 48, 137
participation 4, 6–8, 92, 100–2, 123–4, 179, 182, 214, 220
 decentralization and 98, 102–4, 110–11, 120
participation and development, allocation of projects at local level 194–6
'peer pressure' 60
'people capitalism' 96–7
'people-centred' development 110, 112–13, 124
Petra Bank scandal 163, 172
Phosphate Mines Company 158
Poland 45, 98
Poor Law (1834) 15
POSCO (South Korea) 73
Post Office (Britain) 59
poverty reduction 3, 32, 92–3, 95, 103, 115
'power of belief' 99, 199

Prager, J. 2, 58
Principal–Agent theory 56–62, 63, 119, 170, 212, 224
private investment, factors determining 77–80
private ownership, incentive systems 55
privatization 1–3, 7, 35, 92, 96
 choice and participation 96–9
 competition in the market place 77
 dangers 47
 decentralization and 102, 104, 111, 115, 225
 democracy, participation and 8, 203–7
 in developing countries 5–6, 35–6, 55, 62, 64, 65–72
 development and 85–6, 91
 distribution of gains and losses and 88–90
 economics of 36
 exit or voice 100–2
 impact on employment 89–90, 119
 implementation phase 72, 101
 industrialized countries and 68
 market structure and institutions 7, 63
 opposition in developing countries 105–6
 and the poor 93, 103, 123
 reaction to financial crisis 7–8
 reasons behind 86–7
 scope of actual limited in poor countries 71–2
 sectoral adjustment loans (SECALS) 94
 seven sins of implementation 101
 technical efficiency and 38, 121
 technological choice and informal sector 119–23
 territorial decentralization: space factor 104–5; structure of government 105–6
 theoretical ideal of 4

# Index

X-efficiency and  52
profit maximization in the marketplace  42, 44, 48–9, 58, 101, 217
property rights
  economic theory  33, 53, 63, 171; risk-bearing  54–5; transferability of ownership  54–6, 59, 76
  inefficient  7, 23–4
  state and  13, 171
  X-efficiency and  52, 55
public enterprises
  agency costs and inefficiency  59–61
  budgetary deficit and  83–5
  developing countries and  62
  LDCs impact on public budget  84
public goods and externalities, market failure and  36–7, 40
public management, goals of  58
public resources, selective activities and  83
public sector, natural monopoly and  48
public sector growth
  origins  38; balanced regional development  43; commanding heights of the economy  39–40; employment generation  42–3; ideological and political factors  39; industrialization and modernization  40–1; lack of local private enterpreneurs  41–2; nationalization  38–9
Public Transport Corporation (PTC) Jordan  128, 141, 149, 159, 162, 169
public utilities  38, 40

Ramamunti, R.  86–7
Ramanadham, V. V.  1, 98, 106
rationality assumption  21, 23, 110, 225

Rees, R.  2, 37, 39, 60
regional development, SOEs  43–4
Reinhart, C. M.  81–2
rent-seeking  19–20, 22, 32, 33, 99, 138
repeal of the Corn Law (1846)  15
reward schemes  58–9, 61
Robins, P.  151, 203
*The Role of the Private Sector in Development*  143
Romer, P. M.  31, 42
Rondinelli, D. A.  93, 103, 114–15
Rostow, W. W.  14–15
Royal Jordanian Airlines (RJ)  128, 141, 149, 160, 162–3, 168–9
Royal Jordanian corporation  164

Sachs, J.  26, 56
Sadik, F.  185, 187, 190–1, 200, 218
SAIL (India)  73
Sappington, D. E.  60–1
Satloff, R.  201–2
Shackleton, J. R.  47, 81
Scitovsky, T.  16, 18, 51
sectoral adjustment loans (SECALS), privatization and  94
'selective incentives', organizations and  19, 223
'self-reliance'  16, 120
Senegal  80, 84, 109
Shapiro, C.  58, 61
share-owning  59, 97–8
Sheppard, E.  104, 201
Shleifer, A.  2, 30, 61
signalling device, capital market as  61, 213
signals, decentralized market agents and  25
Simon, H. A.  61–2
Slater, D.  101, 118, 201
Smith, Adam  32
social justice  181–2
'social objective'  22
social opportunity cost  46, 48–9
'social safety nets'  96
'social welfare function'  22

SOEs  2, 4, 6, 16–17
  agency costs  60
  expansion of  35, 39
  foreign lenders and aid agencies  42
  goals in developing countries  43–4
  'overuse' of  86
  performance of  44–50
  privatizing (1980s)  13
  problems in  7, 91, 98
  reform of  115, 220
  social benefits and  96
SOEs in Jordan  128, 140–1, 177, 208
  economic performance: financial 154–6; general 150–4; general financial 156–61
  reasons for privatization 143–4; attracting foreign investment 149–50; debt crisis 147–8, 176; economic recession 144–6; growing budgetary deficit 146–7; imitation factor 150, 176
  reforming  211–15
  role on the sectoral level: equity sharing 142; mixed sectors 142–3; pure domination 141–2
  six reasons for inefficiency of  160–1
South Cement Company (Jordan)  159
South Korea  28, 73–4, 90, 98, 116, 121, 129, 193
Soviet model of development, influence of  17, 39
'spatial reversal' factor  199, 203
Sports Toto  88
Sri Lanka  73, 83, 97–8
Srinvasan, T. N.  20–1
state
  active with strategic capacity  25–33
  allocative role  62
  interventionist with unlimited capacity  14–17
  minimalist with limited capacity 7, 17–18, 222; interest groups and collective action theory 18–20, 171; international trade theory of rent-seeking activities 20–1, 23; public choice theory 21–2, 28, 33; transaction cost theory and institutional change 23–5
  role in development  13–15, 28
state expansion, theory of public economics and  35
state intervention, 'directive' versus 'promotional'  26
state-owned enterprises see SOEs
statism  18
Stiglitz, G. J.  28, 60–1
Stohr, W. B.  106–7, 120
Street, J. H.  16, 107, 121
Streeten, P.  32, 122
structural adjustment loans (SALs), LDCs and  87, 94
structural adjustment programme  49, 114, 133, 201, 207–8
sub-Saharan Africa  42, 66–8, 70–1, 79, 87, 94, 97, 109, 116, 121, 123
Suleiman, E.  97, 106
Susser, A.  137, 204
sustainable development  3, 93, 109, 113–14, 124, 221
Swanson, D.  43, 45

Taiwan  28, 43, 218
Taylor, D. R.  106, 110–11, 120
Taylor, L.  29, 121
Technical Centre for Agriculture and Rural Cooperation (CTA)  109
technical efficiency, allocative efficiency and  38, 72–3
technological capabilities  27, 29
technology, control and inside innovation  83, 104, 120–1
TELEMEX  89
territorial decentralization  6, 92, 102, 104, 108, 181, 198
  appropriate technology and  120

# Index

difference between function and 112–15
 informal sector and 121–2
 privatization and 104–6
Thailand 74, 84
theory of X-efficiency, the firm and 50–2, 119
Third World countries 40, 85, 87, 220–1
Thompson, D. 54, 58
'threat effect' 48
top-down approach 8, 110–11, 180, 195, 210, 219
total factor productivity (TFP) 45, 74, 224
training 83, 214
transaction costs 50–1, 119, 132, 168
 dimensions of 23, 223
 divestiture and 64
 efficient property rights and 24, 33
 structure of organization 63
transactions, factors inherent in 51
'trickle-down' effect 3, 95
Turkey 45, 83–4
Turkish cement industry 75
Tyer Maker (Intirub) 98
type of ownership, economic performance 74–7

U-form structure, private organization and 54
uncertainty 23, 36, 51, 78
UNDP (1993) 48–9, 94, 96, 100, 114, 118, 136, 191, 195, 197, 209
United States 74, 84, 142, 150, 198
United States Agency for International Development (USAID) 181

Uphoff, N. 113, 118, 120, 199
*Urban Functions in Rural Development Strategy* 181, 226
utility-maximizing individuals 21, 23–4, 223

vertical integration 18
vested interests, privatization and 88
Vickers, J. 58–9, 61
Vining, A. R. 61, 74
Vishny, R. W. 2, 30, 61
voice 6, 8, 92, 99–101, 202, 211, 218

Wade, R. 25–6
Walters, Stephen J. K. 54, 96, 173
Waterbury, J. 47, 83–4, 97, 106
*Welfare Consequences of Selling Public Enterprises* (1992) 89
welfare economics 21, 36
Westphal, L. E. 27, 131
Williamson, O. E. 51, 54
Willig, R. D. 58, 61
Wire and Wireless Communication Establishment (WWCE) 162
Wolde-Semait, T. 43, 45
World Bank 3, 8, 16, 19, 26–7, 32, 49, 60–1, 65, 71, 83, 86, 87, 92, 94, 95–7, 103, 114–15, 119, 132, 134, 148, 150, 181, 201, 209
World Bank Conference 89
*World Development Report (WDR)* 61, 83, 94–5, 103

X-efficiency 51–3, 55, 63, 172
X-inefficiency 51–2

Yarrow, G. 58–9, 61

Zimbabwe 116, 191, 193